2

The Other Side of the Wall

Unbreakable

Kathleen St.Ours

Watercolors19

Dedication

I compassionately dedicate my memoir to survivors of sexual assault. May you be blessed with a safe place to find your voice and let it be heard. Releasing your truth can be the beginning of your healing journey. Please never give up, even in the dark days. Follow your path one footprint at a time. You are beautiful and deserve to be happy. I walk with you always.

Acknowledgements

To my dear friend Patti. From the very beginning you gave me the support and confidence that I could write this book. As you read each chapter back to me out loud, it was like I heard the story for the first time. Each revision at your kitchen table was an experience I will never forget. Your patience and love were ever present. Thank you for all of that and for always seeing the beauty on the other side of the wall.

To my son Tim. Thank you simply for being you, the true light in my life. I am here to tell my story because of my love for you.

To my husband Mike for loving all parts of me even when it was complicated and uncomfortable. Your love never wavers. Thank you for all of that and for my favorite sentence you have shared with me many times. You said, "The best thing I ever did in my life was helping you feel safe." I am very lucky and beyond grateful to have found you to walk through life with.

To my parents. Thank you for the light on the safe side of the wall. Your unconditional love reminded me daily that there was hope and to never give up. You held me up when I thought all was lost. You are where I learned true love. I know you are watching from above as I tell my truth in this book. I love you both more than I can describe.

My dear Sarah. I know the Universe was working overtime when she brought us together in friendship. Our relationship has had such an impact in my life. Thank you for introducing me to a daily yoga practice even when I was sure that was not for me. That daily visit to my yoga mat helped me recognize I had a body to be valued. I appreciate the time, effort and patience it took to transform my chapters written in different fonts and colors into what now looks like a book. Thank you also for co editing my memoir. Thank you for believing my story could be told.

To Sexual Assault Crisis Services (SACS). Thank you for showing me that there are people in the world that make it their lives work to listen and support survivors of sexual assault. Your listening is one of the greatest gifts of all.

To my beloved therapists. John, Virginia, and Marci. Without the countless hours of helping put Humpty Dumpty back together again, I don't know where I would be. Thank you for always being there for me no matter what. Marci, you have been my lifeline the longest and I do believe you are,"My Marci." Thank you for believing me always. Thank you for holding space for all parts of me. I am forever grateful.

To my Meditation group. Thank you for keeping safe all parts of me. You make having a voice easy. Whether in a sacred room or on Zoom, somehow the space we hold together is a beautiful exhale.

To Elena. Thank you for your generosity of spirit. Right from the first time we met, you listened to me, gave me a blessing with your hug and a gift. Thank you for teaching me my yoga practice remotely every morning. Yoga has changed my life and so have you. You played a big part in me believing I was good enough, smart enough and real enough to bring this book to life in a world beyond my own. Thank you mostly for your friendship. Namaste.

About the cover

The artist in me has created some version of this watercolor painting possibly fifty times since I was a child. Finally, I decided to paint one depiction of The Other Side of the Wall that I didn't feel the need to hide away in the back of a closet. Deep inside of me was a dark picture of the wall I had to cross over to follow the lure of my perpetrator. Walls such as these have been a trigger most of my life until I finally found my voice and spoke my truth. As with all my paintings I found some level of comfort and safety in the repetitive motions of the process, from the first stroke to the last. In this painting there are a few stone walls to navigate both figuratively and literally, which is exactly where the title of my memoir originated. At one time, each stone represented the obstacle of silence which kept me powerless to seek out safety. Now, as in this painting, I see new growth surrounding my personal blockades and envision the individual stones supporting each other with their strength. Through my eyes, this scene is set in early fall, the very moment an extremely brave part of me chose to walk away from the trauma in my very young life. In that moment I could finally see clearly that the safe side of the wall was always there...

Table of Contents

Foreword

The decision to finally attempt to write this book came on a lazy Saturday afternoon, in the fall of 2015. My husband Mike and I had gone to a late lunch and returned home to relax. The windows were wide open. I breathed in the wonderful New England fall air I had been waiting for. Mike was reading on his iPad. I was laying on the couch with our sheltie, curled up on my chest. He was very glad we were home again and so was I. These safe, quiet afternoons in our home are so comforting to me.

After a while I saw Mike walking slowly from his chair over to me and my dog on the couch. He had this cautious look on his face. It was that loving, protective look I have come to know over the last 19 years. Mike knows me so well. He knows all of me and has always welcomed "the good, the bad and the ugly" to use my words. I so love him for that.

He got to the couch and very slowly handed me his iPad. He said, "I think you might like to see this. It could be triggering but I know you would want to see it anyway." I then knew it would be about sexual assault. I appreciated his care to warn me. And yes, I wanted to see what he was sharing with me. I learned to trust Mike totally years before and accepted what he was handing me.

Feeling that familiar flutter in my stomach, I saw that this was a music video. I put my earbuds in so I could hear the music more clearly. It felt more private hearing it that way. The song was sung by Lady Gaga. The title was "Til It Happens To You." When I read that, the feeling in my stomach changed into a hot flush throughout my body. I touched the little red arrow on the YouTube music video.

From the first note and the first visual of a young woman walking in her socks down the darkened hall of her college dorm, I was swept into a familiar place deep in my soul. A place that only I truly know. This place I have now revisited in therapy for many years. My story was different from the survivors in this video, but the feelings struck like lightening into my heart. I wept for them. I wept for me. Lady Gaga's voice was so powerful. I knew as she sang, that THIS had happened to her. Because of her honesty, my personal floodgates burst open…

The swirl of emotions rose: the feeling of disbelief that this was happening to me, the wonder of what is happening to me, the panic of get me away from here, the inability to run, the feeling of "no way out", the pain in my little body, the feeling that this is the worst day of my life, the disgusting shame, the need to hide, the feeling of can I tell my mommy and daddy, the feelings of deep, dark silence I carried for over 30 years, the fear of telling, knowing no one would ever believe this happened to me, how would I ever clean my body, the feeling of being garbage, how can I hide something this awful, the feeling of what "awfulness" feels like, worthlessness, deep sadness, the feeling of how do I make these feelings go away, how can I turn what happened to me into just a bad dream that did not happen, that huge alone feeling that resurfaces so often.

Then I felt hopeful as the song and video came nearer to the end. I felt the care and love that I received in healing after I did the very hard job of telling. I felt the freedom that came with the eruption of telling. I felt the scary feeling of going from victim to survivor. The tears were now pouring as I felt the hope that I can be me, that I can say no, that some will listen. That I was believed and loved, that my perpetrators lied over and over again, and that I am good. I was reminded that I have a voice, and it can be really loud when I let it out.

So I thank you Lady Gaga and Dianne Warren for creating this piece of music and sharing it with all of us. YouTube says this video is 5 minutes and 25 seconds long. In that short amount of time I felt that huge emotional flood and more.This marked the moment that I believed it was possible to take on the challenge of writing this book. It would take all the strength I have gained over my healing years to open up and use my newly found voice in a creative way. I would step out of my safe box and share what happened to me. My prayer is that by sharing my truth, I might help even just one person heal from their worst nightmare. This book is many things to me. Most of them are very difficult, to say the least. This book is about finding myself again and discovering the goodness in myself I sometimes forget. It is about observing the incredible journey it took to get to this place where I am now.

I am 65 years old. I am a mother of a 31 year old son who I am blessed with and he is the reason I am here today. I am a woman, a wife, a daughter, a sister, a friend, a nurse, a dog lover, a painter and so much more. I am Kathy. I am the sum of many parts of myself, and I am a survivor of repetitive childhood sexual assault. This began when I was 6 and ended when shortly after my 13th birthday. Being a survivor of childhood sexual assault, I will never call it sexual "abuse", as many do. The word "abuse" does not define what happened to me. I was raped/sexually assaulted over and over again.

I write this book with love and great compassion for survivors of sexual assault. I pray that in some small way this book can help you safely find your voice in what ever way you can. I also write this book for those people that have loved you through this trauma. I, in a small way, want to stand by your side. Lady Gaga's voice reminded me that I am not alone. I hope that I too, can help you feel less alone.

Dissociation

I received my first pair of rosary beads when I made my First Holy Communion. This had been a very special day in my little girl Catholic life. Feeling like a bride, I wore white from head to toe. It was a beautiful, pure white dress with little puffy sleeves, a lacy white veil complete with a tiara on my head, ruffled white ankle socks, and shiny white patent leather shoes;

Perfect…

Before I walked down the aisle of the church that day, I had made my first confession and cleansed my six-year-old soul behind the curtain. Walking out of that sacred space, I remember feeling ready to receive the body of Christ. Afterwards there was a big family celebration with cake and gifts. I thought this was even better than a birthday party! As I look back at the few pictures marking that day from the early sixties, I can see the innocent joy in my crooked smile and bright blue eyes. My hands were folded in that familiar prayer position. The backdrop was a lovely spring day in my childhood yard, complete with flowers and a matching white fence separating our yard from the kind, old couple next door. I called them my aunt and uncle even though we were not related. I've searched every inch of these photographs for evidence of the perfect day before my neighbor a couple doors down became my perpetrator. I've examined the pictures more closely to see if in the background he was watching me, waiting for school get out for the summer, so he could tear this perfect day from me. I wondered how many days passed between my perfect day and the day Daryl put his evil plan into motion.

I am grateful that my parents took pictures that day so I have proof of that perfect moment in time. I still belong to the same church and pass by it every day. In May every year there is this one Saturday afternoon that I run by the church and wonder why the parking lot is so full. Then I see them; the perfect, innocent, pure, little children moving slowly up the same front steps of the church that I had once walked, having their best day, just like me. This vision tugs hard at my grown-up heart. I want to run closer to see each little face with proud, renewed smiles. However, not being dressed for this special occasion, I run only as far as the boundary of the side walk. From that distance, I pray for each little six-year-old. I pray that they, in their patent leather shoes, hold tight to this moment. I pray that their next memory after this celebration of new life is something light, like putting on their ballet slippers in preparation to use their precious bodies to dance… the way it should have been for me.

I still have the rosary beads I received that day. When I hold them in the case they came in, I am transported to many places. Holding them in my hands I can identify, without looking, each bead as I roll them between my fingers to pray. I carried those beads everywhere as a child. They were my first pair, given to me by my mother on my special day. These beads were so sparkly in the sunlight, I thought they resembled diamonds. Before that first day in Daryl's garage, I prayed simple little girl wishes; a special doll for my birthday, to get a gold star on my homework, or to help me find my skate key I was forever losing. I would kneel beside my bed, head bowed, and pray; knowing that this pious position surely was the best chance of my prayers making it to heaven.

After Daryl, my prayers changed forever. They became urgent cries for help, pleadings for an immediate rescue. I could practically see the bolt of lightening striking my assailant's heart, stopping him in his tracks. God could do that, I thought. Or maybe the answer would be watching the green garage from the safety of my bedroom window, burn to the ground with my perpetrator stuck behind that locked door. In one enormous burst of flames, it would be over. I would never have to tell what happened to me and all my shame would magically disappear. I could just forget what was done to my body and feel clean once again.

During my healing process as an adult, I began to understand that the blaze of fire I had envisioned seemed like the perfect instant answer to my prayer when I was six. That young part of me thought surely God would act without hesitation if He was a really powerful God. I could not imagine what the hold up had been. I remember the feeling of abandonment, when not as much as a puff of smoke appeared to scare Daryl away. In my darkest moments, I believed that surely the Divine had lost my address. Maybe He really could not see through that one smokey window of the dilapidated green garage where the raping began. Maybe the Blessed Mother did not want to dirty her blue dress on the oily floor inside that evil place.The crazy thing was that I could totally understand that reasoning...

But then one day, when I may have reached a breaking point, I was granted relief with the creative ability to dissociate from the unimaginable. With seemingly no effort, I could escape two hours of horror by splitting in pieces. Maybe this was my crack of lightening …

I am not writing this part to the book to define dissociation and its wide continuum. I have read more books than I could fit into my house on this controversial subject. They were hidden under couches, in the back corners of closets, and in locked trunks. Other than my therapists, I was obviously keeping this life-saving gift a secret. Among those thousands of pages, I read about my experience and actually felt a sense of relief. It was very hard to swallow the fact that even during the healing phase of my life, I had many voices in my head. I recognized some and wondered who the heck the others were. I found myself in unusual places without any memory of how I got there. My son was always astounded by my super power to totally not hear things that might be scary or ugly. Did it bother me that some would think of me as clinically crazy? Maybe. Did I understand all the technical terms, or care? Not really. What I can speak to as I am writing this book, is what it feels like to be an Us, and how my prayers were answered.

Even though dissociation is incredibly confusing and scary, it gave me respite and strength to get away from the torture that had come to take over part of my life. I could not physically break away from this evil, but I learned to escape it in my head. Any way out was a good way out. In the very beginning of my little girl story, I had to just endure the assaults. I had not yet learned how to secretly get away from my perpetrator. I don't really remember the first time our mind games were successful, but I presume that when my innocent soul could not tolerate what was happening any longer, something simply had to give. It was those times when my lungs ceased to function and suffocation enveloped me. I felt abandoned by everyone except this evil rapist and the disgusting air surrounding him; this toxic air feeling too dirty for me to breathe. I believe it was then that I was given this creative gift to save myself. Was it by the grace of God that I found a way to step outside myself and to turn into someone else, who gave Little Kathy a moment to inhale and free herself from such pain, shame, or terror? Or is every human brain made with the power to get away when there is no running allowed? In real time did the little girl in me care who was responsible for the slightest reprieve? No, she was too busy slipping away from a place where there was no possible exit. The feeling or change that happened inside may just be indescribable, and I apologize for that. What I do know is that this foggy feeling that overcame me helped me slide into a quiet space until my new unexpected internal friends came to help me get through whatever this overwhelming invasion was. This six-year-old girl somehow got released from enduring the unimaginable. Just like that. A snap of a finger, a puff of smoke, a wave of a wand, a simple breath in and out, or maybe saying that special prayer just the right way... and she was released from her Hell, even if for just a few minutes. Mercifully, from out of nowhere the Calvary arrived, one soldier at a time. And that became the newly created power within her to find safety from the torturous war zone called Daryl.

Some may think this extreme dissociation, is not a thing, or even that it is total bullshit. It is very hard to explain or describe in a way that makes it real for those who have not experienced it. How can a person having different people in one body be true? Sadly I can't give you the answer you may be looking for, but I can tell you my story which includes my inner parts and how we survived. I love them for selflessly stepping in and taking this innocent child's place, my place.

The first section of this book shares how all of us inside survived this seemingly endless trauma together. I do my best to explain how my inside creative team walked, crawled, and fought through six years of hell, and lived. All of us have names. We told our Truth in therapy and began to heal. We did not all heal in unison. Sometimes healing was a real internal battle and possibly more painful than the actual trauma itself.

So I would like to thank my Blessed Mother and God for hearing my voice even when it was a mere whisper. I would like to believe that my inner team was the gift that empowered me to be able to protect myself through dissociation. I am grateful for a therapist that helped me recognize that I was not abandoned, and that, in fact, my prayers were answered. I accepted the creativity bestowed upon me to form this internal family of parts, who appeared to live in separate rooms. For the longest time they did not know each other, which made for some undeniable chaos. This was a mountain of un-containable energy to be lassoed and corralled. Another unnerving aspect of Dissociative Identity Disorder is something called losing time. I felt like chunks of time were missing from my life. Those were times that I absolutely felt like I was going crazy. But as I look back, that was probably the beauty of the process while the terror reined. I would not be here today, if not for their beautiful separate-ness and their eventual desire to work together to stay in one piece.

I was never alone. There was Little Kathy, Emma, Lilly, Rachel, Rose, Candy, Andria, Black Flower, Invisible, Ellen, Marie, Caryl, Kevni, Scarecrow, Prince, Iris, Lady, Daryl Part, Big Kathy, and me, Kathleen.

Part One:
My Truth in Real Time

The Lure

My therapists have suggested that I stay away from watching certain TV shows like "Law and Order: SVU" and "Criminal Minds" due to my trauma history, but I find that I am obsessed with watching them. I have also read the book, and then watched the movie "The Lovely Bones" more times than I can count. You might think I would run in the opposite direction from all of this, but the pull of these stories was inescapable. The magnet was the need to see the bad guys get what they deserved in the end. I wanted to see the perpetrator go to jail forever or die a slow and painful death. That anger in me has always been and still remains a difficult part of me to address. These fictional stories were a private outlet for me. I usually reacted to the words and visuals with many tears, but the stories still seemed to teach me something. I did get some satisfaction in the end, even though many times I wanted to rewrite the closing scenes.

I think I took ten breaths while watching the first 30 minutes of the movie "The Lovely Bones". Every step Susie took as she walked through the lure of her perpetrator just stopped my heart. I could barely breathe, repeatedly wanting to shout "STOP!!" at the top of my lungs, begging her not to listen to the monster's lies. I can't help but hop from Susie's story to Little Kathy's journey through Daryl's lure.

It is easy as an adult to see a child should not have fallen for that lure. I spent a long time blaming the child in me for not being more cautious. Could she not tell this was a trick? What I know now is that 6 year old Little Kathy could not see what was about to happen to her. She never knew anything bad like that could ever happen, especially not to her. All she really knew was the safety of her family and friends. She knew nothing of such evil. She saw the opportunity to be cool and hang out with the "big kids"… Today, I no longer think "Why did you go with them?" "Don't you know when someone tells you not to tell your parents, that you should promptly tell them?" "Why didn't you ask your mom if it was ok to be in this play?" "Why did you go into that garage?" After years of therapy I have learned to simply listen to this little girl, and to forgive myself.

And so Little Kathy will tell this story because it is hers to tell.

…so Debra came to knock on my door. she asked me to come outside. wow this is cool. she is one of the big kids. she never knocked on my door before. we did sometimes talk to our nice next door neighbor together. I called him uncle Don. he always liked me. we both sat on his lap before. someone even took a picture of the three of us a couple weeks ago. that was a fun day. maybe she liked me. that would be so cool if i could be in their group. they got to play the music loud at their house. i don't think their mom and dad were home when they did that. maybe i should get my little radio. we could listen to music while we played. but i don't think she wants to play. she says she wants to talk to me about something. we go sit on the little wall next to the driveway. i like to sit on this wall. i can see everybody from here. i can watch the cars go by. i can hear my mom if she calls. i can see if my best friend, Amy is home. i can wave her over. i don't even have to go to her door. i didn't really like her mom. she yells a lot. i don't think she likes me either.

anyway, Debra whispers she has a big secret to tell me. she makes me promise not to tell anyone. no, not even Amy. not my brother and especially not my mom and dad.

wow this is a big secret... she must think i am a good secret keeper. i can do that. so i swear i won't tell anybody. "cross my heart and hope to die," i tell her.

Debra says "we are having a play in the neighborhood. the big kids are setting it up, but you can come and try out for it in our garage. i think you would be good in it and i bet you get in. my brother is gonna run it. wanna come?"

wanna come?! holy cow! i want to jump up and down and scream. they picked me. i say "yes, but i have to ask my mother."

she reminds me that it is a secret.

oh ya... hmmmm, well i would just be going a couple houses over, and how long could the tryouts be?... my parents will be so proud to see me in a real play.

Debra says they are gonna charge everyone 10 cents to come and see it. they will have soda, lemonade, and popcorn.

this will be so much fun. i really wish i could tell Amy so we could go together. i am nervous already. i better answer now or they might change their minds. "yes, i will tryout."

Debra puts her arm around my shoulder and gives me a squeeze. she says, "great! come on over Monday morning at 10 o'clock. just knock on the garage door. i'll be there to let you in, and remember don't tell anybody. this is gonna be a big surprise for everybody."

again i cross my heart in sworn silence. Debra steps over the wall to go back home.

it's Sunday night. it was a great day. i love Sundays and never want them to end. but this Sunday i wanna take my bath early, get in my PJ's, jump in my bed and sleep fast so it will be Monday. Tryout Monday. but i cant sleep. i keep wondering what they will want me to do. i can sing a song from school or church, but i don't think i have a very nice voice. oh well, they invited me, they must think i can do something good. and if i don't make it to be in the play i could maybe just help out and sell popcorn. it will just be so cool to be with them.. go to sleep, please go to sleep. i shut my eyes tight and pull my tiny tears doll under my arm. she is my favorite. i got her for Christmas from Santa. he must have gotten my letter. she was first on my list. i just love her. i take my pretty diamond rosary beads i got for my first holy communion and start to say my prayers ...

i open my eyes, the sun is out. oh boy! it is Monday! tryout day!!! i quickly search the bed for my beads. they always get lost in the sheets while i sleep. i never want to lose them. maybe i will bring them with me today for good luck. i'll just keep them in my pocket. i better find some shorts to wear that have pockets. i don't want anyone to see my rosary beads. they might not think it's cool to carry them around. my secret. what time is it? i have to be out the door by five minutes to ten. don't want to be late. so i run around finding a pair of shorts with pockets and a cute shirt to wear with my new sneakers. i think that will be ok. it is kinda hot out today. mom offers me cinnamon toast and a glass of cold, cold, milk for breakfast. my favorite. ok i better hurry up. oops i did not think of where i was gonna say i am going this morning... i would say i am gonna start my day by walking down the street facing the traffic, of course, to the drugstore. i like to look at magazines and comic books. after that i would say maybe Amy would want to play outside in her back yard. i had never fibbed before so my mom said ok. i don't like how fibbing feels.

since i had said i was going to the drug store i didn't take the short cut over the wall, through two yards to get to the garage. i walked down the driveway instead, went left down the street like i was going to drugstore, looking both ways, just checking that no one sees me. then i walk up the driveway to their garage. nobody is around. gee, did i get the time wrong? maybe they already picked somebody else. maybe this was a big joke... so i just knock on the side door anyway. the door has curtains. we don't have a garage. didn't know garages have side doors with windows. i really just thought cars go in garages.

yes! Debra opens the door. she smiles and waves me in. it seems awful dark in here. how are they gonna see the tryout? and then this light comes on above me. it's just a plain lightbulb on the ceiling. i don't think garages are too nice. Debra closes the door. this is a big secret tryout... Debra goes over to the table and pours me a glass of soda. i don't like soda. i wish it was lemonade. but it was nice of her to give it to me, so i say thank you. i wanted to be polite. i see Daryl standing over by this table with shelves behind it. there were a lot of tools over there. maybe they fix things in here too, like my daddy does in the cellar at my house. i don't really know Debra's brother but i am glad he thinks i would be good in the play. he has a t-shirt on and i see pictures on his arms. did he draw those pictures with magic markers or crayons? i couldn't really see what the pictures were. he is a big kid even though he is skinny. he didn't look like he took a bath last night. and i don't like the smell in this place. oh well, how long could this take? he is holding a big wood stick. i see this other big kid. i never saw him before either. he has pictures on his arms too... and he is holding a camera. hmmm, maybe they are gonna take pictures of the winner. i will smile big. i hope i don't have to put pictures on my arms. i think my mom would make me wash them off as soon as i got home. and she might wonder where they came from. and i would have to fib again. i will tell them i can't have pictures on my arms. hope that is ok.

there is this long curtain in the corner. it is not over a window though. what is that for? and then Daryl tells me what that is for. he doesn't say hello or anything.

he says. "GO BEHIND THAT CURTAIN WITH DEBRA AND TAKE YOUR CLOTHES OFF."

i think maybe there is a costume behind the curtain and i will have to change into it for the tryout. maybe i will be wearing it to do my part in the play. i don't want to change in front of Debra though.

"DEB, BRING HER BEHIND THE CURTAIN!"

all of a sudden i don't feel so good. Daryl's voice did not sound like this was going to be fun. it sounds like he is mad at me and his sister. my hands and legs start shaking a little and maybe i shouldn't have eaten my cinnamon toast. i think i might throw up. so i tell them i don't feel so good and i think i have to go home. i wouldn't be very good in this play anyway. Debra doesn't listen to me. she takes my hand and starts to lead me to the curtain. i whisper to her, "no, i don't want to go behind there. i want to go home." i feel tears starting to come out. they will think i am a baby, but who cares. i don't want to be in this stupid play anymore. i see the other guy go over to the door. he slides that old chair over to the door and tucks it under the door handle. i saw my mom do that once when she wanted to be sure we were safe. i don't feel safe now. i just feel locked in. i have to get out of here but Debra keeps pulling me closer to that curtain. now i can't help it, i start to really cry and Daryl takes two giant steps forward and pokes me with that big stick right in the middle of my chest.

"GET BEHIND THE CURTAIN AND TAKE THOSE DAMN CLOTHES OFF!!!"

ouch, that hurts, but i say nothing. my mouth is so dry, i don't think any words would come out anyway. Debra pulls me hard enough to get behind the curtain. there is no costume behind the curtain. the curtain closed in front of us. right away i can't breathe so good. my chest tries hard to get some air but there is no air back here. so i try harder. i feel dizzy like i might fall down. i have to get out of here now!!!! Debra does not let go of my arm.

then she says. "Kathy, there is no way out of this. you have to listen to him or he will hurt you. just do what i do, and you will be ok."

ok? i am not ok. she helps me take off my shirt. i cover my chest with my arms. girls aren't supposed to take their shirts off unless you are in your bedroom changing. mom says we have to be private. she also said boys and girls have private parts. if i take these shorts off in front of them they will see my private parts. that is bad. Debra tells me to take off my shorts and underpants. i do what she says. she's right, there is no way out... oh i just want to go home. i should have asked permission to come here. why did i disobey?... then she started to take off her shirt and pants. i look down at the floor. i feel embarrassed. i was trying to let her have privacy. privacy is good, but i peek, and she looks different than me. i don't have hair on me and she does. i don't think i like that. i thought just animals had fur. i don't know anything. i look down away from her again. the next thing she asks me to do, i know i cannot. my legs won't even move from where my feet were standing. my legs are too wobbly.

so she says, "just come with me and do what he says and then you can go home."

i really do want to go home, so i follow her. she is still holding my hand. so there we stand in front of these two big kids and they are boys. this is so yuck. i try to swallow the puke that sits in my throat. and i wish i could stop these tears. i cannot. i start to cry. Daryl takes two big steps forward and pokes that stick in my chest again. he did it harder this time. he thinks that will make me shut up. i just want to cry harder, but he wins. i stop crying. i am really scared.

"DEB, NOW SHOW HER WHAT WE DO HERE AND HURRY UP. THIS IS TAKING TOO LONG!!"

she turns to me and starts to touch me. she puts her arm around my shoulders like she did when we were sitting on the wall. "please take me back to the wall", i whisper in my head. i thought you liked me...next she started to touch me in all the places i know were wrong and she put my hand on her parts that were private. i try to take two giant steps backward and can't... i just want to be in my back yard playing Simon Says. there i could take those steps, and it was a fun game... why would anybody do these things, this is not nice and i feel like i need to go take a bath again. i feel so sick and dizzy, like i am falling asleep. but i am wide awake. i close my eyes as i touch her grown up body. i make believe this is a dream, a real bad one.

"OPEN YOUR FUCKING EYES GIRL!!"

his voice jerks me back into the room. my eyes pop wide open. i may never close them again. he yells so loud and says very bad words. he scares me bad. why is he so mad?...

while this yucky touching is going on, that other guys takes his painted arms, picks up that camera and flashes three pictures of me and Debra doing bad things. i can never tell anybody about this. i guess they were right. this will be a big secret. my mom said i could always tell her anything ... i can't hold back anymore and i throw up on the floor. a little puke got on my bare feet.

all i hear is "YOU LITTLE BITCH, CLEAN THAT UP NOW!"

Debra hurries to get a rag to help clean up my mess. i think she may be scared of him too. why would her brother be so mean to her too... no one yells in our house. i know i will try never to cry or throw up here again... but i am never coming back. ever...

"NOW GO GET DRESSED AND HURRY UP!" no problem. i cannot wait to have my clothes back on. i pull up my shorts and feel my rosary beads in my pocket. they did not bring me good luck. i should have prayed. i was so scared, i forgot. oh my, did God see this? i just want to go hide in my closet. at least no one else saw this. they would think i was a really bad girl. i feel so dirty.

i come out from behind the curtain and Daryl is standing right there with the three pictures in his hands. holds them right in front of my face. i still have my blue glasses on so i can see these dirty pictures. my heart feels heavy like it may just fall out of my chest. i would never do anything like those pictures. but i see my face and my glasses in those pictures. i thought this was a secret. why did they take pictures of a big secret?... but then daryl answers my silent question.

"YOU TELL ANYBODY ABOUT ANY OF THIS AND I WILL SHOW THESE PICTURES TO ALL YOUR LITTLE FRIENDS AND THEN MAIL THEM TO YOU PARENTS AND SEE WHAT THEY THINK OF THEIR LITTLE SWEET GIRL. THEY WILL KNOW YOU LIED TO COME HERE AND DISOBEYED ALL THEIR STUPID RULES. THEY WILL KNOW WHAT YOU ARE REALLY LIKE. SO YOU KEEP YOUR MOUTH FUCKING SHUT AND BE BACK HERE NEXT MONDAY TEN O'CLOCK. DO NOT PEE BEFORE YOU COME AND GET HERE ON TIME. AND SEE THOSE KNIVES ON THE SHELF. THEY ARE NOT THERE FOR DECORATION. THEY ARE VERY SHARP. NOW GO!!!!!"

i was given permission to leave and i can't move. i am stuck to this floor. he lifts that stick to poke me again and my feet pull from their spot. Debra fumbles with the chair at the door but it opens and out i run. i am so glad i have my new sneakers. i could run faster in them. i run right across the street through the other yards to go sit by the stream. i must hide for a while. when i get there i take off my shoes to make sure all the puke was off my feet. i washed my face and arms and legs with the cool water. i wish i had soap and a washcloth. i wish i had some of my mom's nice smelling perfume. i must smell yucky, just like the garage. i sit on a rock until my legs stop shaking. i am so tired.

i slowly walk back to my house. when i get to the driveway, i stop and sit on the wall for a bit. i just can't go inside yet. i have to find my smile first. then my dad pulls up into the driveway in our car. he always comes home to have lunch with us. we sit in the living room with TV trays and watch, "Love of Life" as we eat. i am not too hungry today but i am glad to see my dad. i want to run and hug him and tell him my awfulness but i don't dare. i hear Daryl's words in my head even though I am a couple houses away from him. walking into the kitchen i smell cheese dreams cooking. i love them but really just want to go nap under the covers in my room. i have to look like i had just gone to the drug store and then played with amy. usually i can't wait for lunch time. everything must look like the last couple hours did not happen. i force the cheese dream down with a smile. secret kept. i am safe. i don't feel safe.

Little Kathy's Beads

Almost every Monday Little Kathy brought her rosary beads with her to the garage. This always made her feel safer, even though they did not seem to change things once she got there. She thought the beads were her secret and maybe they were, until they were not.....

i know what day it is. i know where i have to go. i know the lies i will tell today. i don't like me very much. i used to be a good girl that just played in the backyard and listened to my radio. i kept my room clean because i knew it made my mom happy. i liked to keep things clean. but nothing feels clean anymore, even after i make my room look real pretty. my mom helps me clean the bedroom floor and wash the sheets and blankets. We open the windows and everything smells real nice. i put all my clothes in my drawers and shoes under my bed. it was kinda fun doing this with my mom. she knows how to make things real clean. i just always feel dirty no matter how many showers or bubble baths i take. i scrub my skin so hard it gets all red and hurts a little bit too. but if i thought i could be clean again, i would take a little more pain. i love the smell of ivory soap and my mom's perfume. but it smells better on her. sometimes all i can smell is Daryl on my skin. yuck, i hate that smell. that smell is mean and smells like dirty sweat. it's a smell i never knew was a real smell. now, that is all i can smell on me sometimes. how do i let him keep doing this to me? i keep going back to that garage and let him put more of that smell on me. i let him touch me. i let him put his hands where i know they should not be. i listen to his bad words my dad would tell me to walk away from. i should not be near people that talk like that. we don't talk like that. but i stay there and my ears hear all that trash mouth talk. why don't i just run away? if i ran away he could not touch me anymore, but then i would have no where to live and i would miss my family so much. i want to tell my mom and dad. boy if they knew, they would call the police and Daryl would go straight to jail...but telling scares me. Daryl promised that he would kill my family way before the police could catch him. if my dad found out, he would be so mad. my dad would probably take the baseball bat from Jeffrey's room and beat his head in. Jeffrey is my little brother. my dad is a nice man, but he would want to beat Daryl up. then what if my dad had to go to jail? oh what a mess this is. i guess i just have to go back and do what Daryl says for my whole life. i hope i don't live very long.

i keep thinking my body will just break one of these Mondays. i don't feel like i deserve to live too many more years. if you want to know what i really think, i think he will just kill me one day and bury me in the ugly, scary cemetery he talks about. i imagine there will be ghosts there.

no one will ever find me. his secret will be buried. my parents will just think i ran away. they will think i don't love them. that will be so terrible. i do love them. i want to be good. i don't want to lie anymore. i don't want to do things i know are wrong. Daryl will not let me stop. maybe i should pray to die before i walk over that wall another time. well, that time would be right now. do i do what daryl said about killing myself? he taught me how i could kill myself. he said if i ever decide to tell, i should kill myself before he does. daryl said it will hurt more if he does it. today i will think about this plan a little longer. i will just walk over there, on time, and take what i deserve. i feel so bad inside... so i walk out the kitchen door, kiss my mom goodbye, tell my lie, and off i go. oops i forgot something. i need my rosary beads. i really can't go there without them. i keep hoping the prayers i say with them will come true. so i open the kitchen door and zoom to my bedroom, search my bed, and find the beads. they are in their shiny little case. i will keep them in the case today. i slip the pretty case into my right pocket. out the door one more time. maybe today could be my last Monday.

it is sunny and hot again this week. i hope Daryl puts that dirty old fan on. i won't ask though. if i ever ask him anything he says no. maybe i could go to the pool after. i think there is a one o'clock session for kids. Daryl will be done with me by then. i'll think about that while i am in the garage. it is fun to think about swimming in that big pool with all the other kids. everybody is happy there. my dad taught me how to swim and i can make it all the way across the pool without stopping. the best part is how cool and clean the water is. it has chlorine in the water. that has to clean even better than ivory soap. the cuts on my legs are almost gone now. i could wear my bathing suit and not worry that someone will see them.

why does this walk over the wall to Daryl never get easier? other than the first time, when i was happy to go to the garage, the walk feels like i am carrying a ton of rocks on my back. i want to walk tall so no one suspects anything bad is going on, but my back and shoulders just want to slump over. each footstep takes more air out of me. i wish i would just stop breathing...

when i get there, the garage door is open. maybe he wants to let some fresh air in that awful place. i know once i get inside that the door will close shut and it will smell like always. he did shut the door as i walked in but i see that fan is on. well i got my wish... maybe that will give me extra air today. the fan makes this loud ticking sound. something must be stuck in it. stuck, just like me... i see the pee bucket on the floor. i walk a few more heavy steps over to it and pee. i don't even try to get out of it anymore. and i really have to go bad this morning. i am disgusting.

i wait for my orders and then follow them. as i am taking off my clothes, i hear something fall onto the dirty floor. it wasn't a loud sound but i look down and feel this hot flush on my face. i see this shiny little case on the floor. my rosary bead case catches the light with it's glitter. oh Blessed Mother, what have i done? your beads should never touch this filth, and now they are on the floor of this sinful place. they are no longer in the safety of my pocket. i never should have brought them here. maybe Daryl won't see them, and i can put them back in my pocket. i will scrub them later. maybe i could bring them in the chlorine water. as i am looking down i see his boot step right on them.... oh my God, i am so sorry. I am sorry. i am so sorry...

"SO WHAT DO WE HAVE HERE? DID YOU BRING ME A PRESENT?"

silently, i plead with him not to open the case. please do not touch my rosary beads. my priest blessed them with holy water. please do not put your evil smell on my beads. please don't break them. don't take them from me. i received them when i made my first holy communion. i bring them to church with me. at confession on Saturdays, i say my penance with them. i can not sleep without them in my hand. oh my God, what will he do with them? "hail Mary full of grace"... i pray faster than ever before. please hear my prayers... he stoops down and swipes them up. i can't even bear to look up. i don't have to look far because he is so in my face. his smile looks mean. Daryl opens the shiny case and pulls out my beads and laughs at what he has found.

in my bravest voice i say, "can i please have them back?"

this only makes him laugh harder. i keep my head down, eyes squinted tight. i won't let myself think of what he will do to this thing that is so special to me. i'm so sorry...

"THIS IS WHAT I THINK OF THESE STUPID BEADS. YOU REALLY THINK A FEW HAIL MARY'S CAN HELP YOU NOW?"

how does he know anything about Hail Mary's? he should not even say the words. then i hear a small splash and my beads hitting the inside of the bucket which holds my dirty pee. i feel my heart fall to the ground. maybe today is the day i die. i feel the tears starting a puddle in my eyes. i pray, don't let them fall, but my heart is breaking worse than ever. i can't let him see what this is doing to my insides. i will be punished for sure. right now i feel like i deserve a punishment.

he lifts me onto the table, ties my arms and legs to it. he has not done that in a few weeks. why today? i promise i won't move. he knows that. i don't want any more cuts on my legs, that fighting him would earn me. i am scared, but all i can think about is my precious beads in that dirty bucket. he comes over to me and he is holding the beads. thank God, they are not sitting in my pee anymore. maybe he will put them in my hand. i did ask if i could have them back... if i have them in my hand, what he is about to do to me would be easier. he is still laughing and his buddy is standing there doing the same, holding his camera.

all i heard was, "HERE, YOU CAN HAVE THEM BACK."

i feel a quick second of happy, until he pushes the beads inside my girl part. a big flash goes off, but not in my eyes. did that guy just take a picture of my girl part? please don't let the beads be seen in this most unholy picture. maybe my face did not get in the picture. but i know it is there. and so does God, i think... it hurts my body, but mostly it hurts deep inside my chest. there is surely no heart left in my chest. it is empty.

"NOW GO BRING YOUR LITTLE DIRTY BEADS HOME TO YOUR MOMMY AND TELL HER WHERE THEY HAVE BEEN!!"

i don't want to go home ever again. i am too sinful. i feel dead inside. i know now, i will go straight to hell if i should die. i will never ever tell anyone what just happened to me. i am so disgusting.

he unties my arms and legs. is it time to go home already? i guess he figured that was enough fun for one day. i must take the beads out of my body. i don't know if i can do this. my cry is so loud inside. can this cry be heard in the garage? can tears fall inside my face? i have to get out of here without crying. i couldn't take another punishment. so somehow i climb off the table and walk slowly to my clothes. gently, i pull the beads out. there is a little blood on them. this is too much. please let me die. i bend over and put them in their case. it is not so shiny anymore. i need to get to the stream and wash them. that thought gives me a little power to get my clothes on.

after i am dressed and about to walk out the door, daryl stops me and pushes that ugly picture in my face. my eyes are wide open, even though i want to close them tight. the picture is worse than i could ever imagine. i can actually see the cross hanging outside of my girl part. i feel dizzy, like i might faint and my head hurts so bad. how will i get out of here... i hear this loud, angry voice that kinda sounds like me...but i never yell...

"you are a son of a bitch!! how could you do that to her? leave her alone! pick on somebody your own size!"

Daryl looked shocked at the words coming out of my mouth and then yelled back "WHAT DO YOU MEAN, HOW COULD I DO THAT TO HER? WHO THE FUCK ARE YOU?"

silently, I say, "my name is Rachel", but that is none of his business. he is really pissing me off. she doesn't deserve this crap and i go right over and kick the pee bucket across the garage.

all i hear is, "BIG MISTAKE. VERY BIG MISTAKE!!!!"

sometimes i just can't hold it in anymore, and blow up. i hate what he does to Little Kathy. she is just little, and can't fight him like me. he yanks my hair and drags me like a rag doll to the back wall of the garage. he holds my wrists up against the wall. his camera buddy comes to take over hold-ing me there. i bet they are surprised how strong i am. my fists are tight and ready to punch his face out. then i see Daryl holding his gun. i have seen it before. i saw him shoot at something once from our house. I wonder if he knew I saw him that day. i don't like to think about that though... he walks over to me. he is pointing the gun right at my head. would he really shoot a real person? i think yes. but wouldn't someone hear that big bang sound? then i feel that round circle at the tip of the gun on my head, right next to my ear. oh boy, i should not have kicked that pee bucket. i was just so mad. i wanted to kill him and now he is gonna kill me. maybe it's best. Sorry Little Kathy. i feel my legs shaking. i never shake. i am not afraid of anything.

i hear him say "LIGHTS OUT"!!! and he fires once. no big bang, only a click. i am not dead.

"THERE IS ONE BULLET IN THIS GUN AND IT HAS YOUR NAME ON IT." click again, and again. i am still alive, but i am feeling pee run down my leg. my fists fall open and i just disappear into nowhere...

i wake up, and i am laying on the floor in the back of the garage. who put me over here? uh oh, i peed a little on my pants. please don't let him notice. i get up on all fours and pull myself from the ground. i remember what he did with my beads. i check for them in my pocket and they are there. i know that i will never bring them here again. but how can i come here without them? maybe i could hide them in my sock...

as i am crossing the road to go to the stream to clean off, i wish a car would just strike me dead. i don't look both ways, i just walk. no cars today.

i have cried so many tears sitting on this rock while i try to wash the stink from my body. today, i feel numb. i don't think i feel anything. all i can see is that horrible picture in my eyes. can i wash this picture from my eyes? i could try, but i don't think it will work. i reach down to get my beads. i pull the beads from the case and drown them in the water. i rub the ivory soap i brought from home all over both the case and the beads. i walk right in the water. i know it will be impossible to clean them because my sins are just too big. every time i hold them i will know where they have been. even if they smell like soap, it won't matter. can i even pray my prayers again? i am sure no one will ever hear me now. i feel all by myself. my beads used to help me feel close to the Blessed Mother. she always made me feel safe, but now i feel so far away from her. i don't think i deserve her time anymore. i am not the same girl i was when i got her special beads. i am so sorry... i want to lay down at the bottom of the stream and never come up again.

The Price of Silence

Because I never addressed the effects of my lifelong silence until I finally revealed snippets of my truth at age 38, I only saw the price of my silence from an adult's point of view. Only since I started to write this book, did I then see that I have been paying for my silence since I was 6. It has become very clear to me now just how much was taken from my life, keeping this very dark secret.

Many times in therapy I have said, "Why didn't I tell? Everything would have been different if only I told." Those judgmental thoughts have run through my mind and were woven throughout my journals like threads in a tapestry.

I have beat myself up many times, doubting my decision to stay quiet. I believe, as an adult, that justice could have prevailed, and my perpetrator might have been forced to stop his evil acts. As a mom, I have imagined that if my son had ever been abused, I would have not slept until that bastard was put down forever. I know my parents would have done the same for me if I had revealed what was happening to me. But that is me, a 65 year old woman thinking back and questioning the decision made by a defenseless, frightened child. I needed to open myself to see the decision to remain silent through Little Kathy's beautiful blue eyes. Truly, it looked much different to her.

Many times when I share my story with others, I am asked the same questions concerning why I stayed silent. When I hear, "Why didn't you tell?" I feel myself become very defensive and want to protect the little girl inside who made an impossible choice. I think to myself, this didn't happen to you, it happened to me when I was six. It is that moment when I recognize that my voice inside gets really loud and strong. I feel my chest puff up like a lioness protecting her cubs from the predators of the world. I envision myself taking a step forward in protection and support of my internal child's decision. I become a mother of a little girl, that has finally heard her daughter's scared, shaky, little words, tell her worst secret. Breathless and shocked, I become that broken hearted mom, gently wiping those shamed filled tears, falling from her daughter's eyes. I want to keep her safe from those that ask, "Why didn't you tell your mom the first time he hurt you?" or even worse, "Are you sure that happened? Why would he do that?"

I have searched my soul endlessly for the reasons why I stayed silent. I have asked these same questions of myself over and over. But finally, while writing this book, I have come to the place of knowing, that I needed to ask them. There was a huge price We paid for this silence. I know that now. I finally realize it must be the kids inside who shed light on the price of our silence because they were the ones who were there… My deep reflection into this part of my truth brings me to a place of compassion for all parts of myself.

Little Kathy's Promise

...to me, not telling a secret feels kinda like a lie. i always tell my mom everything i do. i love telling her all the fun things i do at school every day. she is always so interested in how my day went. i love sitting in the kitchen, still holding my lunch box, blurting out the whole story, all at once so i don't forget a thing. i even tell her some bad stuff, like when i get a bad grade on an arithmetic test. my mom always listens, and asks lots of questions. i love talking to my mom. she is kinda like a girlfriend, sorta. but she is still my mom. i never used to lie to my mom, until something so bad happened that i couldn't tell her.

when all the bad stuff started in Daryl's garage, it was so hard to not tell. I knew my mom and dad would not want me to be there. they would have been real mad that Daryl did those kind of things to me. i knew they were bad, dirty things. good little girls don't do stuff like that. having my rosary beads in my pocket when i went to that yucky place would not have made them any less mad at me. I didn't want to do what Daryl said, but because i didn't tell, i had to keep going back. every time i went back something worser would happen.

way in the beginning when i couldn't keep as quiet as i was supposed to, i got in big trouble. Daryl put his face right up against mine. i don't like looking at his face, but if i dared to close my eyes, i would break his rule, and get in more trouble. then he started talking to me in his library voice, but mean and loud sounding. i don't know how you can be quiet and yell all at the same time, but Daryl knows how. what he says, when he talks like that is usually not very nice. that is when he scares me the most. it makes me wonder what horrible thing he is thinking to do next. i never know that answer till he tricks me with some new bad thing.

the "no noise" rule is one of his hardest rules cuz when he says, no noise, he means no noise, at all. no words, no sounds, no whimpering, definitely no crying. God forbid if a tear falls, there better not be any sniffling noises mixed in. it is very hard not to make any noises when something hurts, or i want to scream no, or stop that, or let me go home now. sometimes it just pops out, even though i know what happens if he hears my little sounds.

i really, really didn't mean to, but one time i just blurted out, "I'm gonna tell my daddy, and your gonna get in trouble!!" terrified by what was about to happen, i shut my mouth with my hand. how did that slip out? i didn't mean it. maybe i didn't really say it out loud... i knew i would never tell, because i had been punished so many times already, even without telling. but, there they were... my words, all over the garage floor, and i bet everybody heard me, because Daryl, Debra, and the guy with the camera were all looking at me. i think maybe they were as surprised as i was by my mistake. they looked real mad. i just broke two rules. i said words when i wasn't supposed to, and i said i was gonna tell, right out loud. i could hear my voice saying, i'm sorry, i'm sorry, i'm sorry, over and over again. my legs were already shaking, even before i apologized. what i now was thinking was, please don't hurt me, please don't hurt me, i'll be good... i was waiting to be slapped, or poked with his big stick, but that didn't happen. he slowly walked over to me.

he put his face right up to my right ear. his stinky cigarette breath makes my face scrunch up, because it smells so bad. i try not to scrunch because that probably isn't nice. then he said, "OH, YOU ARE GONNA TELL ARE YOU? HOW ABOUT I TELL THEM FOR YOU. WHEN YOU LEAVE HERE I AM GONNA GO PUT A PILE OF THOSE SEX PICTURES OF YOU IN A BIG ENVELOPE, AND MAIL THEM SPECIAL DELIVERY, TO YOUR PRECIOUS MOM AND DAD. LET'S SEE WHAT THEY DO WITH THAT. WHAT WILL THEY THINK ABOUT THEIR GOOD LITTLE CATHOLIC GIRL AFTER LAYING THEIR EYES ON THOSE? YOU BEST WAIT FOR THAT MAIL MAN EVERYDAY. IT WILL BE THE BIG MANILLA ENVELOPE. YOU WONT BE ABLE TO MISS IT. YOU WANNA PICK OUT THE BEST PICTURES TO SEND?" he kept going on and on in my ear. i felt his spit while he yelled in that quiet voice. i didn't hear his words anymore. i was already panicking, trying to think of a way to beat my mom to the mailbox. oh God please, my mom and dad can never see those yucky, ugly pictures. i was so dirty and bad in those pictures. they made me sick to even think of them. as he screamed in that scary, quiet voice, i felt the garage spin. i begged my legs not to give up. i think i went deaf. i could see his mouth moving, but my ears somehow got turned off.

this secret just gets bigger and bigger. it takes all the space in my head. it makes my head hurt, and my eyes burn from crying under my pillow. why does this keep happening? why won't he stop? i wish i could make him stop. could my dad make him stop? Daryl says once he sees these pictures, he won't want me anymore. i won't be his same sweet, little girl anymore. i believe what Daryl tells me. he always keeps his promises and his promises scare me. he says he will cut me up in little pieces if i tell. he says he will surprise us in the nighttime and burn down our house. he says he will hurt my little brother, so i can't tell. i just can't. how much worse could Mondays get? there is no way out of this. i have to do what he says. so, i have to make a good plan to keep those pictures away from my parents, unless i run straight into their bedroom right now, and just tell everything...

i get up really early the next morning, and say i am going over to my friend's house to play today. my real plan is to sit in this corner against the house covered by this big bush. it's a great hiding place for hide and seek. no one ever finds me there. that bush is a little prickly but it doesn't matter. from this spot, i will have a view of the mailman climbing our front steps to deliver the mail. if i sit there, the mailbox will be right over my head. i can look up, and see if he tries to put any manilla colored envelopes in the box. i think manilla envelopes are the kind our report cards come in. i wish i was just waiting for my report card. this kinda feels like a report card with all F's, only worse.

no one can see me in this spot. this fat bush hides me. i can see anyone coming up our sidewalk. oh yuck, what if Daryl sneaks over, and delivers the pictures himself? what if he finds me trying to get the pictures? he would probably laugh at me. he and the camera guy would love knowing how scared i was of all this. he always wins.

i don't like sitting here though. i know my shorts are getting dirty and i am afraid some spiders or snakes might crawl on me. i couldn't bring my transistor radio with me to pass the time because the music would definitely give me away. to let nice breezes into the house, my mom just uses the screen door in the summer, so i need to be as quiet as a mouse. yikes mice. please don't let any mice find my spot.

the mailman usually comes around lunch time, but today i am not taking any chances. i am here very early. i did bring a little leftover popcorn with me in case i got hungry. i hope he comes before lunch. while i am sitting here, those pictures keep flashing past my eyes. i feel sick wondering what my parents would think of me if they got to them first. well, that cannot happen. i will get them. i am not moving until i can get them in my hands and tear them all up. i want to rip them into the tiniest pieces ever. pixie dust size would be best, so that it all can just blow away in the wind. please mister mailman just get here. i am tired from thinking about all this. i didn't sleep too much last night.

finally between the branches, i can see the mail truck drive onto the street. oh no, i think i am gonna throw up. what if my mom is watching for the mailman too? i have to be fast and very quiet. if i stand on the top step, real high on my tippy toes, i can reach the mailbox now.

i know the mailman is making his way to our house, and my legs start shaking. that is not good. i need strong legs to keep this dirty mail from reaching my house. calm down! calm down! Hail Mary full of grace the Lord is with thee... praying as fast as i can.

oh my, he's coming up the driveway. i can see his arms full of everybody's mail for this side of the street. which ones are for us? anything that looks like a report card? i can barely look. i can't breathe. my hands are kinda covering my eyes, but i can still see through two of my fingers. i see that color. i hate manilla. please let that be for the lady next door. as i look up i can see the mailman sorting through each envelope, trying to see which ones are for us. i can't let him see me, so i don't move a muscle, and no crying!! ok, as soon as he closes the mailbox, and gets down to the bottom of the driveway, i will come out of hiding, just tiptoe up the steps, and see what horrible thing is in the box. but before i could do that, i see the screen door open, and out my mom's hand comes to open the box. she takes out the letters one by one. white, white, blue, white, and one small little package. no manilla envelope today. but what is in that package? gosh, this is awful. my mom closes the door, and i puke in the dirt. over for today... then i remember i have to do this every day until Monday again. maybe this punishment could be over by then. i will never, ever, ever, say i am gonna tell again. ever!!

how long can it take to open those few letters? i wait the length of at least three rosaries, before i crawl out of this spot. my dad will be coming up the driveway for lunch soon. i dust myself off, and try to just be normal. i find my smile and bounce in the back door. "hi mom, what's for lunch? any good mail?" my mom said, "no, just more bills honey." and i let out all the air i was holding onto. letting the yellow kitchen wall hold me up, i asked, "i think i will have my lunch later mom. i wanna color for a while, then i'll eat, ok?"

for the next six days, i repeated this waiting game behind the bush. once i knew exactly what time the mailman showed up, i didn't have to sit in the dirt so long waiting for him. i could set my wristwatch by this mailman. there he was, the same time every day. this was good because then i didn't have to spend so much time worrying while i waited. i would rather be playing somewhere. but most of all, it was less time i had to think about those gross pictures. the mailman came, and either me or my mom got the mail first. if my mom got it, i tried to sneak a peak at what she was opening. no manilla envelope meant i was safe for another day. but the scariest part came when i did actually get to the mailbox first. i held my breath, closed my eyes, and slowly lifted the top of the mailbox. opened one eye and then the other. all white envelopes. thank you God.

maybe Daryl was just trying to scare me, and he didn't really mean he was gonna send those pictures. i wonder if he knows i am sitting here everyday waiting for the mail. he probably would get a good laugh out of that. he knows how scared i am that my parents might see what their little girl is really all about...

i wake up extra early on Monday morning. i keep thinking, maybe he will say the picture threat would be over. i pray that this past week was punishment enough for that stupid threatening sentence i accidentally said out loud. i had promised to never tell over and over again before i left there last Monday. it is really too hard to watch for the mail everyday and besides what would i do during school in the fall? i am not gonna think about that now. it makes me feel a little sick. i am just not that smart. he is smarter than me.

ten o'clock. i knock on the garage door. it opens right away. i guess they are waiting for me. i walk in, do the same thing i do every time. i go straight to the pee bucket, pee, and go over to the table to drink my soda. i am like a little girl robot. my arms and legs are moving in the right direc- tions. i do all my jobs. my head doesn't want to do my jobs, so my legs and arms do them for me. it's like someone just turned on a little button in my back that makes me move around the garage. maybe that's how my "Chatty Kathy" doll feels when i pull her string. the magic string makes her talk. maybe she doesn't really want to talk, and i still make her. i think when i get home today i won't ask her to talk. i will let her rest. i think she is tired.

while i am doing my embarrassing jobs, i notice there is something different in the garage. it is kind of dark in here today, because they have the windows covered. up against the back wall i can see this big green wooden box. it looks like that box the city puts all the dirt in, for throwing on sidewalks in the winter. what does he have one of those for? the old chair is moved over by the table today. i don't like anything new in the garage. Daryl always has a reason for doing new stuff. just wondering if he has a new trick today makes me take two little steps backward. i want to back out that door. camera guy is already standing there by the door blocking my exit. he must be a robot too, because unless he is taking pictures, he stands like a guard in front of my only escape.

Daryl finally says, "GET THOSE ROPES AND SIT IN THAT CHAIR." my eyes see my body looking like the "Tin Man". he kinda looks like a robot. i clunk over to the shelves and get the ropes. i get four because he usually wants four, and I clunk back to the chair. i like being the Tin Man. he is bigger than Daryl, and he doesn't have any skin, only tin. when Daryl starts to pull on my ankles, tying them to the chair, i look down, and see little girl knees. my Tin Man has left me. bye bye Tin Man...

the rest happens so fast, i don't know which way to turn. all four of my robot limbs are tied so tight that my skin stretches. now i really know my Tin Man is gone forever. Daryl seems real mad. he stands right in front of me like a statue. if i just look straight ahead, i can only see his pants and thankfully not his face. he unzips his fly. why is he doing that? i am not laying down on the table. i am tied in the chair so tightly my fingers and toes feel tingly, but not tight enough to hold down my terrified, shaking arms and legs. he is too close to my face. i want to scream, "back up!" but i know better. he is blocking my part of the air in this shrinking room. next he takes his boy part out from behind the zipper, and forces it into my mouth. my head jerks back, and is stopped by camera guy who is now behind me. i am stuck in hell, and i can't get out. my voice inside screams NO! NO! NO! NO! NO! i don't move a muscle. what do i do now? i don't know. silently, i beg, "Debra help me please." nobody moves. as he starts to push himself at me, and in me, he blurts out, "THIS WILL TEACH YOU NOT TO TELL ANYONE. TRY AND TALK NOW YOU LITTLE BITCH!!! SEE IF ANYONE CAN HEAR YOU NOW!!!" i am positive i am gonna die, i can't breathe, and my stomach really hurts. i gag about five times. i hear him making those yucky sounds, then he laughs at me, and steps back. Debra brings me a towel and some water. she says, "clean your mouth" and walks away. no, my mouth will never be clean. a water hose on full blast could not clean my mouth. how can i ever eat with my dirty mouth again...

oh my God. oh my God. i think to myself, please somebody hand me that knife over there. i want to die right now. i can never leave this room. the sunshine can never see my filthy skin again. how do i go home after this?

camera guy starts to untie my arms and legs. when my legs are free, i slide my chair back with my untied feet. i thought maybe, camera guy was gonna hurt me now. i don't want anybody to touch me. i don't want to be in my skin anymore. i try to find my Tin Man in my head somewhere. he is really gone. and i am left here, with my filthy girl skin.

i take the towel and water from Debra, and try to swish out my mouth, and then spit my yuck into the pee bucket. with the spit comes vomit from my stomach. i am lucky none gets on the floor. who cares, the garage floor is so dirty. the last time i puked on this floor, i got in a lot of trouble. in the background i hear Daryl laughing. i want to yell, "stop!" i hate that sound. i always hear that laugh even when i am back in my house. why is making me sick so funny? i rinse my mouth with the last little bit of water and wipe my mouth. is it time to go home yet? i really want to go down to the stream and wash, and rest. i am so tired. my legs feel like they have never walked before. please it must be twelve o'clock by now. i look over at the smokey looking alarm clock in the corner, but the clock says it is not even eleven. how can that be? i feel like i have been here forever.

Daryl has stopped laughing. he walks over to me, grabs my arm, and drags me to that wooden green box. what is in there? i am afraid when he opens the top, something bad will pop out, like a scary jack-in-the-box. i just want to go home.

i learned my lesson for today. i will never tell anybody about Daryl, or this horrible place. see, i know this rule... i hear a little sound coming from the box. what is that sound? i am scared of everything. here comes that hot feeling inside. the feeling that says something bad is about to happen. what i see in the box, i could never have imagined. way in the corner of the box, this little thing is flopping around like it is trying to get up. i just barely hear a tweet sound. no, no, no, it can not be a bird. i am gonna faint. i whip my head around. i gotta get out of here. birds scare me. even before Daryl, i have always been scared of birds. their scary wings sneak into my nightmares all the time. anything that can fly in your face, scares me. is this the sparrow i found behind that bush last week, when i was waiting for the mailman? did Daryl put him there? i thought maybe that bird had smashed into our picture window that is right above my hiding place. oh my, Daryl must have put him there. how does he know so much about me? how come he knows everything that scares me? i will never get away from him... i think, please close that box. before i know it, my scared feeling makes my hands slam that box shut. i was afraid the bird would get out, and fly around the garage. too much! too much! Daryl grabs my arm tighter, and flings open the top again. he puts both his hands on my waist. i think, damn you! don't touch me anymore. i can't believe he is lowering me into the box with this bird. i close my eyes. maybe this is not really happening. maybe this part is just a dream and I am really home. please little bird, stay on your side of the box. my body seems to have a mind of its own. my back slides right up the corner of the box trying to escape without notice. my back must want to get away from the bird too. ouch! my back gets a sliver trying to get out. how will i get a sliver out of my back? my hands won't reach...

my head feels Daryl's hands pushing me down into the box again, like i am the jack-in-the-box. my eyes see that knife being handed to me. i wanted that knife just a few minutes ago... was that only a few minutes ago? i feel like i am having a dream. nothing feels real. my ears faintly hear Daryl's voice. "YOU HAVE TWO FUCKING CHOICES. YOU CAN TAKE THE KNIFE AND FINISH OFF THAT HALF DEAD BIRD, AND SAVE YOUR SORRY ASS, OR CUT YOURSELF LIKE I SHOWED YOU, AS A PROMISE TO KEEP YOUR FUCKING MOUTH SHUT. YOU BETTER CHOOSE THE RIGHT ANSWER OR THERE WILL BE MORE PUNISHMENTS FOR YOU LITTLE GIRL!!

the box is slammed shut. me, the bird, and the knife, sitting on the floor of the box. Daryl doesn't know there is one more choice in my head... i want to just cut both my wrists, or stab me somewhere, to make myself die. that is what i really want to do, but then that damn bird started tweeting again. i was terrified of this little biddy bird and pushed harder into my corner of the box. i wish i could fly away like you, little bird. there is a hole in the box. you could fit through, but one of your wings looks broke. oh God, what do i do? what does Daryl want me to do?... the bird hops closer. oh please, little bird don't get too close, i might do something mean. please don't hurt me. i don't want his wing to get better. please don't fly now little bird. no, i cannot kill a bird. this bird did not want to come to this garage either. he wants to be outside. maybe his mama can find him, help him get stronger and fly away... i wish i was a bird. i would sneak out of that little hole, and fly away from Daryl, and never come back. i would never tell, cuz i would only know how to tweet. i could say no words. so i would be safe... so my hand picks up the knife. i pull my shorts up a little bit higher, and pick that perfect spot to cut. i choose the place i think Daryl will want. my thigh knows the knife is coming, and it just goes to sleep. i cut Daryl's symbol of evil into my skin, not too deep, just enough to see it. only a little blood. just like he showed me. with that cut, i make my promise to never tell a living soul what Daryl is doing to me. i tap lightly on the top of the box. i am thinking, i made my choice. i cut my promise into my leg for Daryl to see. i hope i did it good enough. i am never good enough. the box is not opening. i tap louder and say, "i am all done." still the top is closed. i start to panic. i really can't breathe now. BANG! BANG! BANG! i pound on the box wall. "i am all done, i made my choice." slowly the box opens, my eyes squint from the light, and then a big flash comes into my hurting eyes. camera guy doing his job. Daryl says, "I SEE YOU MADE THE RIGHT CHOICE. LET ME SEE YOUR LEG." i show him. "GOOD JOB, AND THAT PICTURE IS PROOF OF YOUR PROMISE TO NEVER TELL. DON'T FUCKING BREAK IT. YOU WON'T LIKE THE NEXT PUNISHMENT. OH, AND I SEE YOU KILLED THAT USELESS, PATHETIC, BIRD TOO. LOOK, IT IS DEAD. NO MORE SCARY TWEETING." i did not kill the bird. i cut my leg, not him. i look down, and see the little bird. he is not flopping anymore. maybe he is just sleeping. sleep little bird... then when my eyes can see a little better, i see blood around his tiny head. i didn't do that. did i do that? who did that?... oh God, i should have slit my throat until i laid quiet and still forever. i chose to hurt me, not a bird. no good choices in the garage...

the next thing i know, i am down at the stream scrubbing my disgusting, evil skin and mouth. i take off my clothes, and step right into the water. i don't care who sees. everything is so dirty and bad. my hands, my mouth, my thigh, my face. i wish i could scrub behind my eyes. i want to forget this day ever happened, and my eyes cannot make what they saw go away. closing my eyes only makes it worse. i squiggle all around in the water, trying to shake off my skin. i hate my skin. i wish i was a snake. i want to shed my skin.

my eyes pop wide open, as i look down at my thigh. i see the evil promise sign, still bleeding a little. this symbol cut into my body will be my reminder to NEVER tell. lesson learned, forever.

Kidnapping, Rose Goes for a Ride

it's Monday again. will Mondays ever just be another day? will Daryl ever forget about me? this summer has been so long and awful. i want to tell my dad what he is doing to me. i want to say i'm sorry i didn't tell before. i am so embarrassed and ashamed. i am gonna try to go to confession on Saturday.

how do i even tell this in confession? the priest might get mad at me for being so bad. every Saturday i walk to my church with the promise to tell the truth in the confessional. i know i will be alone in the confessional. the priest can't see me. that sliding window and curtain will hide me and i could duck down real low. he might recognize my voice though. on Sundays after church, i help the priest and some nice ladies open the church envelopes. our priest likes me, i think. when he talks to me, he always smiles. if i tell this secret he might not like me anymore. that is bad. i practice my yucky speech in my head when i walk to church... i think God already might know everything already. He has seen me in that dirty garage. i pray for it to stop in the garage, but it never does... God must not hear me or i am just way too bad to be forgiven. Daryl says i am a very bad girl and i must never breathe a word of this. he says if i tell anyone that he will hurt me worse next Monday. he says he will do this to my little brother. he says he will burn our house down. he says he will mail those disgusting pictures to my parents. he says he will shoot my mom and dad with his gun that he keeps in the garage. Daryl is so angry and mean to me. i believe every word he says...

i still want to be forgiven, so i walk into the church on Saturday, even though i am scared. i start my penance early, because i know he will give me one hundred prayers when he hears my secret sins. there is someone in the confessional already. i can see the light above the confessional curtain, and that means i have to wait. whew, a couple more minutes. this could be my chance to run out. instead, i kneel down in one of the pews and try to go over my speech. uh oh, the light changes and some nice lady comes out. i am sure she did not have to tell anything this awful. i feel a little sick to my stomach. but i have to do this, today. i want to feel clean inside my chest. Daryl has been making a bruise in the middle of my chest with his dirty stick. that's where i think my soul lives. my soul is probably all black and blue. it hurts terrible inside. i walk slowly, hands folded on my way to the confessional... as i get closer my feet don't want to move anymore. i see the green curtain and i feel faint. i cannot go behind the curtain. i had been behind that curtain plenty of times before, but today all i can see is Daryl's curtain in the garage. i feel a little dizzy. it is awful hot in my church today. i have to go behind the curtain if i want to feel clean. i want my sins wiped away. i am really, really sorry... Father Joe may not even believe me and think i am telling fibs. then i will get more prayers to say. i finally get the courage to sneak behind the curtain. no one tells me i have to take my clothes off like in the garage. that's good. am i safe here? will Father tell my parents? i don't think he can. in catechism they said confession is private between me, God and the priest. when the curtain closes behind me i can't breathe. i want to run back out. my heart is pounding so hard, i am sure Father can hear it. i have to do this really fast and get out of here. there is no air here today. so i start to say my confession prayer. "bless me Father, for i have sinned..." i get thru that part. we practiced it in Sunday school over and over again. i knew that by heart. then i quickly got to that part where i have to say, "my sins are..." all i hear myself say is, "i disobeyed my mother two times. i lied once to my dad. i argued with my little brother." and then, "I am very sorry for these sins..." done. i think, "please father give me my penance, so i can get out from behind this curtain." i silently promise to pray double. he blesses me, asks me to always tell the truth, and to sin no more. he tells me to say ten Our Father's and ten Hail Mary's. i bow my head and say, "thank you Father." i get up off my knees and try to run out from behind the curtain, but my legs are shaking so hard I can barely walk. i ask God to please get me to the altar so i can do my penance for the lies i just made up in the confessional. i couldn't tell my big mortal sins. i kneel and pray, defeated again. my promise to Daryl won. i run from the church searching for some air to breathe. i don't even know where to go. i feel so alone. i belong nowhere. i am lost. maybe i will be braver next Saturday.

my walk home from church usually takes ten minutes. today i walk very slow. i am so tired and ashamed of myself. i will never be clean again. i am sure God is hearing all my lies. i hope he knows why i couldn't tell the priest. i am too afraid. just two more days and i have to go back to sin again... i am doing nothing right. i hate Daryl. i never hated anybody before. my dad says i shouldn't hate anybody. i think if he knew what Daryl was doing, he would hate him too.

the two days after confession go by too fast. again it is Monday morning and i do all the same rituals of not peeing at home and getting to the garage at ten; not a moment later. i walk over the wall in a fog. i feel empty inside. i feel like i am only sending my body to the garage. i want to stay behind, and yet i watch my feet take one step and then another. i really wish this was simply play practice i was going to. boy, was that a big fat, lying trick. i feel so stupid. who would believe such a stupid story? as i am walking, i rehearse the rules i must follow when i get there. knock on the door, wait for it to open, walk in the door, take off my clothes, put them behind the curtain, pee in the bucket, take a drink of the soda, go get the ropes, hand them to Daryl and whoever else shows up. the last couple times there were different guys i didn't know. they all have pictures on their arms. they are mean pictures. everyone always has black on. black t-shirts makes them look meaner. i like blue.

as i cross into Daryl's driveway i see a van. i never saw that before. it doesn't have to many windows. i wish they would park the van in the garage so there was no room for me in there, then i could go home and skip a Monday. not today… the garage door opens before i get a chance to knock. i am scared. will i be punished for not knocking? am i late? i am prepared to be punished. i put my head down waiting…

Daryl steps out carrying his big stick and the soda. i don't like soda. we don't drink it at home and it makes me feel sleepy. i drink it only because he makes me. Daryl says we are going for a ride to get some ice cream instead of garage time today. could my prayers have been answered? really? ice cream? he got in the van first, then me and then this other guy behind me. i thought, i want a chocolate cone. yum, my favorite. then i saw the ropes in Daryl's back pocket. no, he can't tie my hands. how will i eat my ice cream? i don't think i want to go for a ride. i'd rather stay in the garage. i know what goes on there. i don't like this van. it is dark in here. it stinks like beer, cigarettes and dirty feet. yuck, i wanna get out. i turn around quick to run and the door slams shut before i can reach it. Daryl jerks me onto the floor. he takes my blue glasses off. oh no don't take them. i need them to see better. "give them back please." he says nothing. before i know it he pulls my purple shirt up over my head. the shirt stays over my face. i feel him tie a belt around my waist and i think he is tying a rope around that belt. i want to puke again, but i hold my lips tight. the puke will go all over me inside this upside down shirt. how will i clean my shirt to go home later?

i don't think we are going to Friendly's for that ice cream. that was sad enough, but where is he taking me? i feel the van go down backwards out of the driveway. i start shaking. i can't make it stop. i can't see anything but purple. i like purple, but i want to see where we are going. why does Daryl have my eyes covered? he always wants my eyes open. he always makes me watch. i want my glasses. how will i get home? what if they leave me somewhere and i can't find my way back? i want to go back to the garage. even that awful place is better than this. i feel like a dog. this leash around my belly feels tight. i will never get away being tied like this. i can't breathe under this shirt. i just want to sleep...

...Rose whispers, "go to sleep Little Kathy. i like purple more than you. you are so tired. i will go for this ride." Little Kathy sleeps....

i will be very quiet. i heard all Daryl's rules once before. he scared me so much i never wanted to come back, but today Little Kathy is so tired and scared. i want to come help her. where are we going? i cover up my chest and belly with my arms. i wish they would pull the purple shirt down to cover me up. i promise i will close my eyes. so i ask, "can i pull this shirt back down? i won't open my eyes." he pulls tight on the rope. my leash. "SHUT THE FUCK UP! I WILL TELL YOU WHAT TO DO! NOT ANOTHER WORD!" ok, ok, no more words. i can do that. i will not move a muscle, and no sounds. i'll go over the rules again... no crying, no talking, no puking, no moving. and no breathing. that is my rule. breathing makes me cry too easy. just a little breath every now and that should be enough.

the van makes a big right turn, and I slide sideways a little. the road feels so bumpy. i don't like bumpy roads. it kinda hurts sitting on the floor of this old van. there is no rug, just a metal floor. and then we stop moving. could we be back home? oh i hope so, but my street is not a bumpy one. is he gonna let me out? i hope he lets me fix this shirt, but i won't ask again. i hear a big door open. i wish i could take a really big deep breath. it won't matter because this shirt doesn't let much air in. i can hear some other voices outside. sounds like all boys. big boys. they are laughing and saying words that i would never say. i don't think i like it here. maybe i should just stay in this smelly van. i feel a pull on my waist. "GET OUT OF THE VAN AND FOLLOW ME!" how can i follow you when i can't see you? i guess i make believe i am a dog. i will follow the way the leash goes. i am glad i have sneakers on my feet. i feel sticks and little rocks under my feet. we start to walk up a hill. bushes are scraping my legs. Daryl is pulling too hard. i can't go as fast as he does. i can feel the sun, but i can't see it or any light through this shirt. it's hard to breathe under here, walking up this hill. i am tired, but he keeps pulling me. i hope the pricker bushes don't make my legs bleed. what will Little Kathy's mom say? i will try to be careful. will i ever get back to her house? it is nice there. i was there once on a Monday morning when Little Kathy did not want to go to the garage. when is this hike gonna be over? i don't think Little Kathy is suppose to be gone this long...

finally, i think the ground is flat. i can smell smoke. this smoke smells funny, not like a fireplace. yuck, i don't like it. i start to cry under my shirt. no sound though, only little tears. he can't see them. ouch! the belt tightens and up I go, i don't feel the ground under my sneakers anymore. i don't like this. my feet start running in the air. there is no ground. then as my feet hit the ground, somebody pulls off my shirt from my head and i hear boys laughing like this is a funny joke. all i can see is the sun above me, but not around me. where am i? oh no, I think i am in a hole. i just see dirt around me. this hole is so small. i can barely move around. my eyes hurt when i try to look up at the sun. let me out of here. did i say that out loud? do i dare talk? do i beg them to pull me out of here? "SHUT UP OR I WILL BURY YOU RIGHT THERE!!!!" i feel some dirt fall on my hair. i will be quiet. i will be real quiet. i feel Little Kathy starting to shake inside. "no, Little Kathy you stay there, you don't want to come here." then, i hear a little voice. this voice sounds far away, and the voice is crying... "no little voice, don't cry. it will just get worse if you do." i think there is another little kid here, but not with me. that makes me want to cry again. maybe this boy doesn't know the rules yet. the voice sounds like a little boy. i just stand in this hole looking up. it is too small to sit down, and I don't want to get my shorts all dirty anyway. do these shorts have pockets? did Little Kathy put her pretty beads in there? i reach down. no. no pockets. no beads. i wish she wore pockets today... the sun hurts my eyes. i can barely open them. maybe, i will just die here. maybe, that would be better. the sun feels warm. i wonder will anybody out there save me. please, someone come pull me out. i don't try to climb out. i will be good. i will do anything you ask. i promise i won't make a sound. i won't tell. i won't cry. i won't move. i will just do what you say. please, please get me out of here. my head is gonna pop with all my secret words. my eyes are all squinty, but i see two arms coming down inside my hole. the arms block the sun. thank you! thank you! thank you! i don't even care that these arms have mean pictures on them. then i see the face at the end of the arms. it's Daryl's face. Daryl is gonna save me? does that mean he is not mad at me anymore? could he hear me begging to get out of the hole? once my feet are on the grass again, he starts to put my shirt back on. i want to say thank you, but my words might get me in trouble. i don't say a single word and i am glad i didn't. it feels so good to tuck my shirt into my shorts. Finally, i feel covered. then he did something i never thought would happen. he yanks my purple shirt out of my shorts and back up over my head again. i hear laughing. someone lifts me up onto a hard surface. it feels like it's made of rock. this table is hot. oh no! oh! oh! i feel hands all over me... oh please put me back in the hole... and then i feel nothing. my body feels no hands touching it. all i know is that the sky is blue and the trees are blocking the sun from hurting my eyes... nothing.

the next thing i see are my legs climbing out of the van. my shirt is on the way it is supposed to be. no belt or rope to be found. i am so tired. it is time for me to leave. sorry Little Kathy...

...where did all this dirt come from? my belly hurts. i feel sticky and just awful. Daryl says, "GO HOME AND MAKE IT QUICK!" i run down the driveway, cross the street, sneak through the back yards to my hiding place by the stream. i am so glad i hid a wash cloth and soap between the rocks. i scrub my legs and arms. the water feels so nice and cool. my legs have tiny scratches on them. where did i get those? i put my legs right in the cool water. that feels nice. what day is it? did i miss Monday? nope, i remember that van in Daryl's driveway. i don't want to think about that anyway. this water feels cool. i love the sound of the moving water. i better be careful not to get my shorts wet though. mommy doesn't like me to come down to the stream. she says the big kids hang out here. i better go home now. daddy will be coming home for lunch. i hope i didn't miss lunch time.

Rose's Worst Days

This part of our story is the most difficult to tell. What happened to Rose was unspeakable. God love her, I don't know how she survived these dreadful days. I honor her for helping Little Kathy get away from this piece of our story. I will hold this sweet girl close as she tells her truth. It does surprise me that she is able share this at all. Her everlasting fear of telling is almost too strong to finally break free and reveal some of our darkest secrets. Thankfully she had the Rachel and Candy parts of us to step in when she nearly gave up. I stand next to her with love, strength and forgiveness, which I sense she still needs. Her name is so appropriate. In my eyes she is as beautiful as a perfect rose. She did not think she was perfect. But I do.

i confess, i do a lot of sleeping walking. Little Kathy does too. i wonder if everybody does... i think everybody probably has nightmares, but do they walk around when they are sleeping? are we the only ones? this silliness started after Daryl began to hurt us. sometimes i think i was trying to tell Daryl's secret without really telling. i don't know what i say in my sleep, but i can remember some of my bad dreams. when i sleepwalk i end up saying some things out loud that i am not supposed to say. the words just pop out when i am not listening. the nightmares are so scary. sometimes there is no one else in the nightmares at all. i just get this really awful feeling inside, like there is no way to escape. when i do wake up, i breathe like i just ran around the block. i huff and puff and can't catch my breath.

sometimes Little Kathy has the same dreams as me. when she wakes up she says her favorite prayer. she says it real fast, like it was one big long word. "hailMaryfullof-grace..." and she says it over and over and over. i admit sometimes i thought she would never stop. when her Hail Mary's stopped working, i started to say the ABC's real fast, just like her, to see if that would work. sometimes it did, and sometimes nothing really made the dream go away. we just woke up and felt awful. i remember one time i told Little Kathy's parents i was being eaten by a whale and couldn't get out of his belly. i never liked that whale dream at all. it was dark in that belly and i was all by myself. i couldn't squeeze out between his big teeth, no matter how hard i tried.

really, the only bad thing about sleepwalking is everyone wants to just lead you right back to your bed to go back to sleep, to have more bad dreams. Little Kathy's parents just wanted her to get a good night's sleep, so they would wake us up, say everything was gonna be ok, and tuck us back in. i did kinda like that part. we didn't always sleepwalk, but secretly, i wish we did. maybe, if it happened all the time, they would have thought something was really wrong. but, then our secret might have been told and we would all be in a lot of trouble. this feels all mixed up.

one night, when Little Kathy was about eleven or twelve, she walked down the stairs sound asleep. i always wondered how she didn't fall down those stairs. anyway, she went into her parent's room, sat on the edge of the bed. she shook her dad to wake them both up. she told them she was pregnant... really, it was me that was pregnant, and it was not a dream. it was real.

she knew all about the "birds and the bees" and yucky periods. Little Kathy was younger than a lot of girls when she got her period. She got it for her tenth birthday. the worst birthday present ever! her mom had told her all the things she needed to know about sex. the way her mom told the story, it sounded like a good thing. i never saw it that way. she didn't know the way Daryl's story went. his story did not have the word "love" in it. the other thing she said was only big people were supposed to do that kind of thing. so many things don't make sense...

one thing about being a girl is that your period is private. i never told anybody i had my period. some girls even called their period their "friend". yuck, not my "friend". this period thing just got me in trouble with Daryl. i knew it was supposed to be normal to bleed there once a month, but it still felt scary to me. i knew i shouldn't talk about that kind of thing because not all kids knew this stuff yet. it was not a secret, but private i guess. that's ok. i never got to play with Little Kathy's friends anyway. i really just got to go know Daryl. he is not our friend. i didn't ever want to tell him i had my period. that's the crazy thing, i never had to tell him it was my time of the month. he always found out. i could never make my period stop, just because it was Monday. i couldn't hide this from him. i could never cover that ugly part of the body from him or the camera guy. Yuck, I don't like talking about this. i even felt worse than usual on Mondays when this would happen. they made fun of me. i used to think they would leave me alone on those days, but i was wrong. i was so embarrassed. they made me take off those special pads, that are suppose to be sanitary. there was nothing sanitary or private with Daryl. i wished I could just disappear at that time of the month, but i stayed for Little Kathy. she can't always do Mondays without shaking or crying, and getting punished. she needed me.

Daryl knows everything. it seems like he has a crystal ball that tells him all our secrets, even period secrets. everything he sees in that crystal ball, he uses to hurt me. i know i can hide nothing from him. i guess thats why I don't like looking at his eyes. i know they are green cuz i looked once. that was enough for one peak. everything that scared me lived in his mean eyes. his green made me wonder what is he gonna do next and how did he think the next mean trick up? i don't want to think about that. i am too tired trying to figure him out. i gave up wondering about that a long time ago. i just listen to his voice and do what he says.

i got real scared one day when Little Kathy's mom told us, once a girl gets a period, she could then have a baby. when she explained how you get a baby in there it was no longer that stork story they used to tell. getting a baby sounded a lot like what Daryl was already doing to me. i wondered if that was how Little Kathy got born?... but her dad would never do that to her mom. they love each other. i am sure Daryl did not love me. did Daryl love me? no yuck. he did not. i feel very confused.

the last couple years of Mondays that Daryl was the boss of me were the worst. he always drove me to the outside place, which i was used to, but he always had new tricks and games every time. i think he did that just to scare me even more than the week before. does he have a special mean book that teaches him all this?... he was really like the boogeyman. maybe he was the boogeyman... he definitely was my boogeyman. nobody knew that though. just me.

when Little Kathy was twelve, and school let out, i didn't know it would be the last summer i had to go back to see Daryl. on the last drive home from school that year, everyone on the bus was singing that song "no more pencils, no more books, no more teachers' dirty looks...". they were all smiling and laughing. the kids were so excited summer was finally here. Marie, (she went to school for us) was smiling big. inside i was not. school was a safe place and there would be no school for a couple months. Marie would rest and my Hell would begin. i wish i was happy like the kids on the bus. Marie helped us hide Daryl's secret because she really knew nothing about it. i wish i was Marie. she got the fun job. she always had a big smile. she hopped off the bus and ran home to a big hug from Little Kathy's mom. i want to walk slow and go the other way. could i just run away? Daryl always said there was no place to hide. he would always find me no matter how hard i tried to escape the awful summer weeks full of Mondays. i wished this could be the year i told. every year i tried to come up with a plan to tell and not get caught. but that was just another dream.

i remember thinking that first Monday that after school let out, thank God i had my period a couple of weeks ago. one wish granted...

i wish just one day, that van would run out of gas or break down, so we couldn't go to the outside place. he would never drive me there on his motorcycle. on the motorcycle he couldn't get me and his big stick there at the same time. but the biggest problem with that is, everybody would see me drive off sitting behind him and he would get in trouble. you can't keep many secrets on the bike. daryl is the king of secrets.

so up the hill we climb. i don't want to go. i can't take another summer of this. i walk pretty slow. he doesn't pull my shirt up over my face. he must be sure i will never tell anybody about this place. so i wonder why he still puts that belt and rope around my waist... does he really think i would risk trying to get away? he should know he did his job well. nope, i will never tell. i won't try to run either. he is faster than me, and how would i find my way home. besides all that, there is this very scary, old cemetery across the street from the hill we have to climb. a lot of the gravestones are broken. it looks spooky to me even in the daylight. being as bad as i am, i am sure some ghost will get me down there. so i am just stuck climbing and i know it.

as soon as we get up the hill, Daryl orders me to take off my cloths and get up on that stone altar first thing.

that is not always the order. Sometimes, he would tie me to the wooden benches that sits around the altar. then it would be my turn to get up on the altar. but today it was the altar. oh please no. i don't want to climb up there. i can do that by myself now cause i grew a few inches. i feel really mad all of a sudden. i try to stuff down that angry feeling. only Daryl gets to be angry, and then i hear these bad words come out of my mouth. i feel dizzy and funny inside. maybe it is that soda he made me drink in the garage...

"nope! i am not getting up on that fucking altar!!! go ahead! try to make me. you can not push us around like that"... i can sorta hear this strange voice and then i don't...

"just take me home! you don't know who you are talking to. i don't answer to anybody!" am i really trying to run back down the hill?

Daryl screams, "KATHY STOP!! GET THE FUCK UP THERE!! WHAT DO YOU THINK YOU ARE DOING?!!!

hahaha you can't make me. just try and catch me. who does he think he is, ordering me around? i am not doing anything he says. he can't keep doing this shit anymore. i will fight him with my fists. i will grab that stupid stick everyone is so afraid of and hit him right between the eyes. those eyes don't scare me. i have been waiting for this moment a long time.

so Daryl look out!! and just see if you can catch me. i am faster than the others.

"KATHY JUST SHUT THE HELL UP!!! DO WHAT I SAY! YOU KNOW THERE IS NO WAY OFF THIS HILL!!" ya, watch me! off i go into the woods and down the hill. i take that stupid belt off my waist. you can't put a leash on me, like a dog. i am not a dog. i am not even Kathy or Rose. i am Rachel, and don't you forget it. did i say that out loud? no. just keep running. i can get us back home. faster, faster... i can see the clearing at the bottom of the hill. for a big kid, Daryl is pretty slow. i can barely breathe and my heart is popping out of my chest, but i can keep running. my legs are getting scratched by the pricker bushes, and i don't care. finally, i can see the road. ok, i think i go left down the bumpy road. i won't look at that cemetery. maybe i will go right. then i see them. there is a big group of guys getting off their motorcycles. those bikes are big. they all have high handle bars. their arms must hurt to hold on. the guys are mean looking. they are drinking from big bottles. they all have those pictures on their arms. i know the pictures are called tattoos. i heard someone talking about that once. we hate tattoos. they are on all the arms that have hurt every one of us. i should get a tattoo. maybe i would look tougher. maybe they would be afraid of me.

i make it to the road. i hear laughing from the biker guys and see them pointing at me. i feel breathless and embarrassed so I bend over. then i saw what they were laughing at. i have no clothes on...

i tried to hide my body, but got interrupted by the sound of footsteps moving fast toward me. part of me is still mad, but now i feel like i might be sick. i feel this red hot feeling starting from my belly and moving fast to my face. i don't even think to cover myself any longer. i try to figure out a way to get around the motorcycle guys. sadly i recognize some of them and i know they will not let me pass. they are drinking beers and other stuff out of big bottles. they are smoking cigarettes and are dressed partially in black, with no shirts on. frozen in place, i feel that belt being wrapped around my waist again. he ties a rope to it just like he does to Rose. a few yards away is that cemetery. Daryl pulls me to the ground. i feel those pine needles on my back. i know it is Daryl without even looking. i can smell his smell. all i could hear was laughing. i do not hear anyone barking orders, but i know they are coming. he walks over to the van that is parked along the side of the road at the bottom of the hill, and brings out his knife. in the snap of his finger, one of the motorcycles revs up. the ground under me seems to shake with that loud sound. i lift my head to move out of the way, and feel Daryl yank on my hair to pull me back to the ground. that bike turns around in a circle and all this dust gets in my face. Daryl says we are gonna play a little game. he says this game is called, "chicken." i never heard of this game before. he recites the rules. they are simple. the "chicken game" rules are just like his. "KEEP YOUR EYES OPEN. DON'T MOVE OR MAKE A SOUND!" the motorcycle gets louder, the ground shakes harder. i know now i am not gonna like this game and i probably won't win. so i will just follow the rules. my angry feeling is getting smaller and smaller. "THIS WILL TEACH YOU TO RUN OFF!!" all at once i see a dusty tire come straight at my head, and i am sure he will run me over. i roll over to get away and the belt tightens. Daryl shows me his sharp knife. the bike backs up pretty far. i feel myself exhale my held breath and think, game over, i lose, right? wrong. the loud motorcycle sound hurts my ears like there is no other sound in the world. there is no way out. i am sure i will die. i can see in the corner of my eye a huge motorcycle zooming right at me. it stops hard and skids right next to my face. i feel the big heat from the bike on my skin and it smells of burnt rubber. i can almost taste that awful smell. now i know why the game is called "chicken." i was frozen like a statue. frozen solid in heat of summer. i could feel wet between my shaking legs and right then i know that pee is running down my leg, like a baby... yuck, i have never done that before. only Little Kathy has pee accidents like that. please don't let him see that. maybe the pine needles will soak it up. all i hear is laughing. i feel Daryl's stick in my ribs. i still don't move. he reminds me not to ever run away again. he reminds me to never talk back or get pissed off at him again. he says if i do, that tire will crush my head next time. i feel like i may cry, something i have never done before. i will not cry in front of him. my chest and throat hurt as i try to choke back these stupid, little girl tears. i know then that i am so out of here. screw this. sorry Rose, gotta go...

oh God, didn't i already climb this hill once today? my legs feel scratched. they are shaking more than usual. i have all these pine needles in my hair. how did they get there? doesn't matter i guess. i just go where this leash pulls me. how is this any different than any other Monday. i feel so little climbing up this hill. Daryl is not saying a word. he is not laughing at me and not one sound is coming out of his mouth. i wonder what he's thinking. his silence scares me. as soon as i see the altar, he just picks me up and puts me on it, and tells me to lay down. i hate this place. he has already laid that blanket on the stone altar top. i know what that is for. i wait for what is to come. i won't fight. it will hurt less, and i think he really likes a little fight. i will not give him that. just get it over with. he lays his knife next to my head...

he starts to do what he likes to do most. there is that Daryl smell again. something i will never forget. this familiar smell brings terror to what is left of my soul. the girl body part of me begins to hurt bad. he is more forceful than i ever remember. he must be real mad today. i keep my eyes open. following the rules can be good sometimes. being in the outside place laying on my back, i get to feel the sunshine on my face and look at all those pretty clouds. what pictures will i see up there today? my girl parts start to hurt less when i go to the sky. the sun feels warm, dry and clean. the clouds are puffy and so soft. we like to draw clouds. clouds can be any shape at all. no rules with clouds. i think i would even like to be one of those soft clouds. he could never catch me if i was a cloud. sometimes they even look like cotton candy. just before night time, the clouds are really the prettiest. pink, orange, white, and blue. what a pretty painting that would be. Little Kathy has colored pencils. she could make such a nice picture. much prettier than those ugly pictures on Daryl's arms. nope don't think about his arms... i will just stay here in the sky, forever.

a big flash comes in front of my eyes. Could that be the sun? nope, it is another disgusting picture me. my heart crashes back down from the sky to this filthy altar. my insides fill up with shame and my whole body feels ripped apart. i want to beg for those ugly pictures. Camera guy always takes pictures of my sinful body. i wonder if the pictures show that big hole in the middle of my chest. i think that hole just let my soul fly away. poof! gone, never to be found again. instead of a girl, i bet i look like saggy dirty skin with no parts inside. that is what he got a picture of. that and Daryl; the Satan in my life. is that what Satan looks like? Daryl? that skinny man with ugly arms, a big Adam's apple, and no eyes?

the only good thing about the picture taking is that then i can go home. they got what they needed, and i can get dressed again. not today... Daryl gets up and grabs the camera from his buddy's hands. i think to myself, thank you Daryl, you are gonna throw the camera to the ground and break it. pictures could get you in trouble... did he ever think of that? but he did not break it and the instant pictures already popped out of the camera. he tells the camera guy it is his turn. turn for what? oh please no... please Daryl don't let him do this. i will be good. i will do anything you say. please, i don't know him. he scares me. please save me from him. this can not be happening. i feel no sunshine, i see no clouds, and i feel no warmth from the sun. i only feel my body part of me and nothing else. why can i not get away? i know i will die today, right here in this sinful place...

somehow i manage to get to the stream by our house to wash this filth off. i have never been gone so long on Monday. surely i missed lunch. i am gonna have to think of a really good story on why i'm late. where can i say i was? but first, i have to wash extra good. my legs are sticky and gross. i use a lot of soap especially at my girl parts. my legs won't stop shaking. my body hurts more than other Mondays. nothing feels normal. i feel dizzying and i have the worst headache ever. my eyes scratch like some dirt got in them. it just seems so bright outside today. i wish i had my sunglasses. that would make them feel better. if i could see better maybe i could remember what happened today. i feel like i lost a big chunk of today. i probably didn't miss anything fun anyway. i just want to climb in my bed.

at the end of the summer my belly felt funny like maybe i was getting my period. i tried to remember when i had it the last time. for sure it was gonna be due on a Monday before school started again. i took my calendar off the wall to check it out. my secret for remembering was putting a little blue dot on the day i got it and then counted 28 days until the next time. i didn't see any blue dots since May. that seemed strange. maybe i just forgot to mark it down. thank God, summer was almost over. trying to picture the changing colors of the leaves, that every year saves me. i wondered if i could make it to my favorite season without seeing Daryl again. i closed my eyes tight for a couple seconds to make my wish come true. i search for a strong prayer, but i am too tired to say one. this is summer number six of Daryl's terror. how could i have let this happen? I am so happy there are only a couple more weeks and school would start again. i could find safety there on Mondays once again. i have to go to school and he knows it.

Can i just skip it this one Monday? i really don't feel so good. i'd like to just disappear, but Little Kathy just wants to sleep this morning. that is not an option, so i came to get her to the garage door by 10am. Little Kathy always looks so comfy holding her baby doll while she sleeps. it's weird though, that is the same baby doll she cut with knife last week. one other time she even burned the baby doll's hair. afterwards, she cried real hard and washed the baby doll with ivory soap, wrapped her all up in a warm blanket, and rocked her back to sleep... this morning she threw up when she was in the bathroom brushing her teeth. after eating her breakfast, she ran back into the bathroom to do it again. she must be nervous, and who wouldn't be? yuck i hate to throw up. we can't do that at the outside place. we will get in trouble. i just want this day to pass quickly without any extra trouble...

regardless of my wishful prayers, Daryl drags me once again up the hill. how do you think a girl gets used to something like this? except for his tricks that really scare me, he does a lot of the same things... they are awful things, but we usually can think about other things, hold our breath and be done. holding our breath is a good trick. if you hold your breath, it stops the tears from falling down. when i take a big deep breath and then let it out, down those tears come, immediately followed by a punishment or another trick. the tricks are the worst things. i do feel a little dizzy when i hold my breath, but dizzy is better than a trick. i get an A+ at holding my breath...

lately, i feel like there is nothing to hurt inside me anyway. i feel tired, maybe like a rag doll. he just jerks me around all the time. i go numb and take whatever he does. sometimes, i think i am like the scarecrow in my favorite movie, "The Wizard of Oz." the scarecrow has a lot of parts that can get ripped apart. this sweet scarecrow believes he has no heart, so he is always looking for one. i always liked him. even though he was made only of straw, it seemed like he had a heart tucked in there. he just didn't know it. having a heart hurts sometimes though. he got burned by the wicked witch once, and then those mean monkeys ripped his parts off and threw them all over the place. i feel like him a lot. Daryl is my wicked witch, and his friends are the mean monkeys. sounds silly i suppose, but i have a lot of time to think when i don't want to be at the outside place. on this Monday i had to get on the altar first again. he gets on top of me and does what he does. holding my breath, i look up and there is no pretty sky to watch today, just grey clouds. everything feels sticky and gross on my skin. he gets down and starts yelling at me and the other guys come gather around me. i hear them laughing that mean laugh, like this is some kind of a joke. that makes me scared. he starts yelling things i don't really understand. but what i do hear in my right ear makes me want to vomit. i hate my right ear.

they start calling me a little hoar. i know that is a really bad girl who does these things because she wants to. i don't want to. they are wrong. i am not a hoar. then i clearly just hear Daryl's voice. he told me we have made a baby. he said, "YOU STUPID BITCH, HAVEN'T YOU NOTICED THAT YOUR PERIOD HAS NOT COME SINCE THE BEGINNING OF THIS SUMMER.? YOU ARE GONNA HAVE MY BABY!"... is he right? is that possible? i have missed my period a couple times. could the calendar be right? i didn't see any blue dots... i was so happy not to have it. but this can not be true. i am to little. oh, i feel so dirty. i don't like seeing blood there. sometimes when i was little, after Monday mornings, there was some blood. that was because they hurt me inside. i knew it was because my body was little and his was big. nobody should do that to a little girl. oh God, this cannot be true. what would i do? how would i hide such a thing. when Little Kathy's mom had her little brother, her belly got really big and she had to wear special shirts and pants so they would fit. i cannot have a baby. he must just be tricking me again. if i got pregnant how would i explain who the boy was that made this happen? would i have to tell what happened? Daryl would not allow that. oh my God, what do i do? i can't breathe, because i cannot breathe. i no longer hear any of his words, because i have too many of my own in my head. this is too much. i start feeling like our nightmares feel. i hate this feeling. i know there is no way out of this anymore. i cannot wake up from this nightmare. if this is just a nightmare, wake up now dammit! i just want to disappear, never to be seen again. missing forever.

again, i hear him abuse my right ear. he's telling me to lay down flat again. i realize i had curled myself up in a little ball. he hadn't tied me in any particular way today other than the belt around my waist. i don't want to open my arms and legs. i want to be gone. some smart part of me relaxes my body and does what he says. punishment on top of what he is saying would be more than i could take. i try to focus on the grey clouds and then i feel this sharp pain inside me. what is he doing? i see the stick in his hand. he is pushing it inside me. it hurts. my belly hurts. i hurt. everything hurts. i can't seem to get away from this pain. i feel wet down there. Daryl's laughing, and a motorcycle from down the hill is the only sound i hear. i hate both those sounds... next thing i know, in the middle of this craziness, he pulls on the belt signaling me to sit up and get off the altar. thank God. can i get off this hill. i want to be anywhere but here. how can i go home after this? maybe i won't. maybe i will cut myself really hard, and not stop. i won't do it here. i don't want to die in this awful place. maybe down by the stream where I can wash first. i like it there. i get clean there. i wish i was clean. can i ever be clean again?

i get off the altar and i see the pee bucket. he never brought that bucket here before. how did i miss that? he says to sit on it and pee. so i do. but i try to pee and everything burns and hurts. i don't pee, but i feel something coming out. it feels warm but i still hurt everywhere. he pushes me off the bucket. i fall onto the ground in the dirt. the bucket falls over, and then i see it. a lot of blood pours into the dirt. did that all come out of me. i feel really dizzy. my head lies in the dirt. i must be dying.... "WAKE UP. PROBLEM FIXED. YOU DON'T THINK I WAS GONNA LET YOUR HOAR BODY BREAK THE SECRET. THERE IS NO BABY ANYMORE. SO STOP YOUR DRAMA! NO ONE WILL EVER KNOW WHAT HAPPENED. NOW GO GET DRESSED! TIME TO GO!"

i can't move. i don't even feel like i am alive. i can see my body, but it cannot move. i look to my right and see all the blood on the pine needles. next, my body moves towards the blood and i am gonna faint again...

"Rose honey, you sleep. i will help you do what is right. it's me, Candy. i will bury this baby. "

on my hands and knees, i gather all the blood. it has dirt in it and i can't keep it separate. i move slowly out of respect, and pray Little Kathy's prayer, over and over again. it is what is right. poor Rose, and this innocent little baby?... i feel so confused. Daryl is not just mean. he is evil. i wish i could take this baby to a real cemetery, with no ghosts. i know i don't have much time. Daryl won't allow that. he is over there smoking. i hate that smell... just keep moving. he won't notice for a few minutes, and so what if he does. i am burying her. i will name her Sara. Rose will like that. God bless both of them. i look for a nice place to bury her. a special place that someday i can once again find her. i will think of a holy place to bring her someday. not this filthy piece of Hell. Picking up a rock, i start to dig. i almost manage to get every blood part into the tiny grave, when I feels boot stamp on this special place i prepared. squish. "WHAT THE FUCK ARE YOU DOING?! GET DRESSED I SAID. IT'S LATE. DON'T YOU WANT TO GET BACK TO YOUR LITTLE WHITE HOUSE? MOVE! YOU ARE SO PATHETIC. MOVE!!" i try to cover my hands and lay the rock down as a marker. Looking around i try to take a picture in my head which tree i am under. on hands and knees i try to lift my body. with all my might, i stumble over to Rose's clothes. before i start to dress, Daryl hands me this wet cloth to wash my legs. he has never done that for the others. maybe he is a little scared there is too much blood on me to clean. he doesn't know we have a place to clean that has good soap. i wash. i feel tears fall. don't care. i get dressed.

After Candy gets Rose to the stream, she leaves her to her soap and water. Rose did not kill herself that day even though the pull to do that was so strong. She knew, however, she would end her life soon. The guilt she felt about what had just happened was the final straw. She felt there was nothing left to save. Daryl had taken everything from her. She was not aware of how Candy helped her try to honor and bury the baby that she knew had been forced upon her, and then taken away. Somehow though, she must have heard Candy, and remembered her baby's name. Sara...

The Anger Part of Me

before Daryl, i never knew much about being angry. in my house i didn't see my parents get angry very often. they didn't yell at me or my brothers very much. i was usually pretty good and followed the rules in our house. i did what my parents said. we never got spankings like other kids that i remember. oh, i think that is not absolutely true. my parents have told a story many times about me getting a spanking in the back yard once....

they said when i was about two years old my mom had gotten me all dressed up to go to see my Nana. it must have been a Sunday because they said the dress was a church dress. it was white with pretty pink roses and puffy sleeves. Nana was going to love it. my mom said we were leaving soon and not to get this dress dirty. well, i thought i would go out anyway and ended up in the sandbox doing what i liked to do best. i still love playing in the sandbox. My parents said i liked to make pies and cakes mixing sand and water. i guess i didn't have my listening ears on that day and started playing make-believe baking. probably, two year olds just do what they want sometimes, right? anyway, i must have made a real fancy mud pie, because as the story goes, i decorated the pie with the little pink roses that crawled on the back wall. my dad spotted me back there in the sandbox. that was a place where a girl could really get a dress pretty dirty. my dad kept calling me into the house. they were ready to go to Nana's. i guess i wasn't quite finished with this pie and didn't come when they called. i think sometimes a two year old can be a little stubborn too. if it was me now, i would have definitely come when i heard my dad's voice and would definitely not have gotten that dress dirty. anyway, my dad yelled out a warning to listen right now, but this little 2 year old definitely did not listen. she was threatened with a spanking, she had never received before and never received since. still she did not listen. the story says that my dad did go out to the sandbox, took my hand pulling me out of the box, pulled my pants down, and spanked me twice on the fanny. he sent me into the house and my mom cleaned me up. i think there must have been words like, "shame on you Kathleen Marie! next time, you come when i call, and never disobey me like that again. you hear me?" yes daddy, i won't do that ever again... and that was the end of it. that was the only spanking i ever got in my childhood home. the thing about that was, even after being scolded and punished, by having to go to our room, there was always a hug and an i love you that followed during that day, or at least before bed. i always knew they loved me. the few angry moments were never mean and didn't last long. mostly i loved being wherever my parents were.

sometimes my parents disagreed about money or not having enough of it, but no one ever said bad words when they talked loud. i could always tell they were on the same team. my mom had her jobs and my dad had his, and they were many. they worked very hard to keep us fed, happy and safe...

anyway i never thought much about being angry in our house, and we were always taught, "if you don't have something nice to say about someone, don't say anything at all." i like that rule. people can feel bad if you talk bad about them. i know that is why i didn't much like going over to Amy's house. her mom and dad did not have those rules. they yelled at her a lot. poor Amy.

oh, and me and my brother Jeffrey argued over TV shows. we had to take turns picking a show. that made me mad, but my mom would be the decision maker on that one. discussion over. so by the time i was six i guess i saw a little bit of what angry looked like and maybe what it sounded like too.

angry looked much different on the other side of that wall. Daryl must have practiced angry a lot before he met me, and so Daryl somehow became my angry teacher.

i thought once, that being angry was a feeling you had if somebody made you mad. you know like if someone called you a bad name or maybe how you felt if someone took a toy away from you when you were trying to play with it, or how i felt if my brother changed the channel on the TV when i was trying to watch Dick Van Dyke.

in my house my parents didn't like us to yell at each other. if we did yell at each other we might get sent to our rooms. i think that might have made me mad too. my parents taught me that i was supposed to talk nice to my brother. so when you feel angry, what do you do?... is angry an action word?...being angry is hard to understand. and i always wondered, is it ok to be angry?

after i started going to Daryl's garage, understanding the word angry got even harder to figure out. angry was not the same on both sides of the wall. Daryl's garage is where i learned to hate and fear whatever angry is.

Little Kathy was never good at the angry thing. in the garage she learned that if she got scared or angry and actually used her voice saying "NO!!" really loud, she was silenced. if she tried to get away from whatever Daryl wanted her to do, angry became very big and scary. it was much bigger than her. she always felt very little when Daryl would get mean and wore that angry face. he would hurt her with a yank of her hair, a slap to her face or worse... much worse. she was a fast learner in the garage. soon after all that started she did a couple smart things. first she learned to be very quiet. stuffing that bad angry feeling deep inside was the only safe thing to do. The bad thing about stuffing those big feelings inside is, it made her throw up sometimes. she learned how to hold her breath for a really long time. it helped her keep the angry in that hidden place. she also learned that looking into Daryl's eyes was just too scary. she made believe he had no eyes, and just never saw them anymore. his eyes seemed liked they had lasers that could dig into her head... so poof!!! no eyes. from that day she only saw him up to his nose and nothing further. she became like a balloon and could hold her anger in just like the air captured a balloon. i think even balloons can only hold so much air and then they pop...

this is where i came in. my name is Rachel. i am a little bigger than Little Kathy. she doesn't really know much about me. but, i know about her. it pisses me off that she could not say NO when she felt like it. i don't care what anybody thinks about me being angry. i got strong fists and i know how to use them. i am not afraid to say ugly words. a slap doesn't stop me. he can pull my hair. he can even cut me, because i don't feel it.

mostly, i don't want Little Kathy to be so afraid of everything. i especially don't want her to keep getting hurt because then her angry pops out by accident. i won't let her explode. when she starts to feel like that balloon can't hold any more air, i take over for her. when she gets dizzy from holding herself so tight, i let her rest, because i am stronger than her. she can keep her silence and i get to have my words. sometimes i even spit in his face. granted he then tapes my mouth, but i don't just lay there and take it. i fight and that really pisses him off. i like pissing him off. i don't feel pain the way Little Kathy does.

when i am with Daryl, i admit he looks more like "angry" than i do. when i think of "angry", i see a huge ugly room that is dark and smelly, filled with mean monsters. these monsters speak with loud voices that almost make you deaf. there is no way out of this big room. you are stuck there and you always get punished in the angry room. sometimes you feel like you could die from being angry.

even though being angry is what i do best, it is hard to use my words when i try to describe "angry." i do like to draw pictures though, and i think i can color angry better than speak it. the colors i picture are black, red, and sometimes orange. the pictures sometimes look like the pictures on Daryl's arms. i can draw those pictures real good. when i draw them, my crayons get all worn down to the nub and sometimes break. the paper even rips when i am real mad. my fingers turn the color of the crayons from pressing so hard. my pictures really do look like "angry".

i didn't go to Little Kathy's house too much unless it was to be in her bedroom when she was alone. sometimes if Little Kathy or Marie started getting bad headaches or the panicky feelings started, i would take over. i knew all i had to do was cut my arm or leg with something sharp so everyone could relax. the cuts let a little air out of the balloon. i hid the cuts so they might not see them. scaring them was not my job. we all just wanted to feel better. the cutting helped. is cutting what "angry " looks like? i don't really know the answer to that one.

one time i went back to the house with Little Kathy. she was feeling awful from the garage, and i decided we should draw our angry feeling. we needed something real hard to draw on. this angry would rip any paper we might use. her mom was in the kitchen, so i laid under their coffee table, got my two angry crayons and i drew pictures of Daryl hurting Little Kathy. i drew a picture of his stupid stick. i really wanted to break that stick. i bet i could break it easy if i could just get it away from him... anyway i heard Little Kathy's mom say, "Kathleen, what do you think you are doing? you don't color under the table. you have plenty of coloring books. now go get them and don't ever do that again!" of course that was definitely my cue to go... poof! bye bye! but i always came back.

Kevni - My Knight
in Shining Armor

No, it is not a typo. Kevni is his name. It has taken me a long time to get to his part of our story. I was not sure we would even write this chapter. In therapy it took great bravery to be able to say what it is about him that was so essential to us making it out alive. We will always pause breathlessly when thinking of Kevni.

What I need to say up front about Kevni is that he is that part of me that stutters and struggles to read. His inside out spelling will be probably the most noticeable thing you will see about him.

I sit and breathe slowly and deep before I hand my keyboard over to him. His story is heartbreaking. I owe him so much. Knowing Kevni, he will share very little. He is not very talkative and his story is one nobody likes to hear. But we stand with you Kevni as you did for us…

"i cuodl hrea Dalyr benig mane to rsoe. rale mane. he tlles hre to od soemtihng so bda i thnki she gonna thorw up. she cires luod.

dotn do taht rsoe. do wtha he syas. Seh is fghitign to mcuh. i wnta to srceam utb he mihgt ues taht bgi gnu he gto…

Ochu. he tiwtsde my lge so hrad. Dalry ylleing in my era luod. he syas to trun ovre on the rcok atlar. i htea hmi. i htea hmi!!! thsi hurst . thsi rcok srcapes my skni bda. all tiwstde up. my rtghit cheke is pushde ftla on teh rcko. i cnta mvoe. dotn elt lieltlt kthays feca gte srcathces. hre mom catn' see thme. whta dose he wnta?

O Gdo no!! NO!!… it hruts stpo!… no wya otu…i fele vomti dripinpg out of het corner of my muoth. thye are on my back, puhsign ovre adn ovre… hwo cna thye do thsi? owwwhhhhhhh!!!!…

i opne my letf eye. my rihgt eye is smshaed clsode on thta rock. i dotn' rellay watn to see aynwya.. but thsi boyd hutrs me adn i wnta to get away berofe thye thorw me ni the fier leik the littel rabtti. dotn' thkin abtou thta. oh loko i can see Dalry's big stcki. it si lenaing on the bencesh wheer thye wacth thsi yuykc stffu. he thknis he si so improtatn wtih that stick. he sasy it has suerp powsre....

i gbra thta stcki rale fats. it doesn't bunr my hadns leik I thghout. my hadsn are free to swnig it ta him hrad. he catn' hutr me. my naem is kevni ton rseo. i ndee soem cloeths. i see mister tni ma'ns siut. thta will fti prefcet. you cna bnag on it hrad and nothing can touch my skin. juts try Darly!! no one gest insedi my amror. so od yoru maen thisgn. uyo cat'n hurrt me or roes aynmoer. stttaaand backkkk!!! i try to piont the stcki to hsi ulgy fcae. shhhe is my frrrriednl! is ti ninghte tmie alradey? whattt happppenned?? its dakr. my eyse cannnt sssseeee. i think is't roes's shitr on my faec. i can semll that girly perfmue on the blnidfold. ut oh i thnik i pooopde a little. cna i go now? thne I smlel teh poop ni my faec. hwo wlli i clene poor rsoes faec? i hoep her body dotn hutr like mnie. by by rseo. soryr, so soryr. i cna cemo back ainga soem tiem. i haave a shieyn suit. i wnot lte hmi hutr yuo."

I apologize for how difficult it may have been to read these jumbled words, but I cannot edit them. They are Kevni's precious words, the words of Rose's Knight in Shining Armor. He did his very best to endure the unthinkable. Just a young boy that thought only of protecting Rose in that moment and many more unbearable ones. Even with the perceived power of Daryl's stick and his strong inner Tin Man, he never really felt brave. When all was said and done, and he stepped back to the hidden safety deep inside us, he felt shame, embarrassment, and a deep dark silence.

Kevni is very thin, with dark eyes that would never meet yours. His hair is never combed and his clothes don't change much. His clothes are not clean. He is bothered by a very unsettled stomach. He cannot keep his food inside and frequently had diarrhea after eating. He almost never speaks, but sometimes he will come out when I am under great stress. I know this because, even in the present, sometimes I find that my shoulders slump and I lose my ability to spell. Thankfully Kevni found his way to feel safe with our current therapist. Her name is Marci, and he loves her as much as I do. Those are the times we get to hear his barely audible voice. We all listen very carefully to our most protective Knight... Maybe one day he will see himself as we do.

I painted a picture of him once that lives in a very visible spot in my home... Rose and I are in the forefront of the painting. We are sitting in a field, enveloped by wild flowers and pricker bushes. We are looking up to where Kevni is leaning against an old tree with a few dead leaves still left on the branches. He has his back to us as he flies Rose's kite. Symbolically, he is letting his favorite sister of the heart be free to soar into the sky that set her free from the horrors of that time in her life. This was painted to show how protective and giving Kevni was to Rose on her worst days. When I put paint to paper here, I remember trying to express a great love and respect that lived within us between Kevni and Rose. In many ways this framed picture might look a little dark and sad to others. And yes this painting originates from a dark place, but to me it feels victorious. Mostly, it demonstrates a great love in the midst of the evil we lived in.

Black Flower –
The Scene of the Crime

i never even knew i had a voice. no one ever asked me what i wanted. i never mattered. i was always here since the play tryouts, but no one ever cared about me except Daryl, and i hate him. everyone inside runs from me and everyone on the outside hurts me. i never really get to leave. i never feel like i am in control. i am this stupid body. i am just a bunch of parts connected by skin that i hate. what little girl body ever knew this could happen to her?

being given a chance to talk here feels strange. nobody ever even looks down at me, and now they want to hear what i have to say. i don't even like looking at me. what i see, if ever i dare look in a mirror, is not pretty. i see a dirty, bloody, smelly body, with scraggly hair that has been chopped all uneven. i see baggy clothes to cover everything. i see a lot of fat, and an ugly face that has never really smiled...

i have all the body parts i was born with including ears. i heard what Daryl and his gang said to me. my ears will always burn after hearing all those bad words and the names they called me. his words are where i learned how ugly i am. i heard them talk about this "pathetic" body. if i am so pathetic then why did they pay so much attention to me? attention i never asked for. i just wanted to be left alone. i never wanted to be touched the way those gross hands touched me. they invaded every inch of my skin with all their parts. i didn't know people were allowed to touch people like that. they maybe didn't have a mom to teach them right... i thought bodies just played, ran around and had nice hugs. i thought bodies pumped their legs real hard when swinging on the swings. bodies held their baby dolls. i thought bodies held hands when you went for walks. i thought legs and arms danced silly to music in the living room. i think being a body probably use to be ok.

while everyone else inside got to leave the garage, i could not. i felt everything and took all the awfulness without a sound. my mouth was never allowed to have the voice part of a mouth. no voice box allowed... nobody told, and so no one ever saw the damage to me and my parts. they were all very good about washing the outside skin parts of me. it was everyone else's job to scrub off the crimes done to me. i remember thinking you better use that smelly bleach that makes my eyes tear, to clean me. ivory soap can not be good enough... some of this dirt i know never really came off. so, i usually just curled up in a little ball trying to hide myself from sight. if you really want me to speak, let me just tell you a few things... but first, you did say Daryl is a dead Daryl, right?

i see this body in parts, so i guess i will tell you a little about each one, as unimportant as they are. and why i hate each part...

i hate my feet, because they put on red PF Flyers and walked over the wall, across two yards to the garage. they walked in there so may times. when i took off the sneakers, the feet stepped on that dirty, oily floor. most of all, i hate my feet because they did not run away from the garage when everything turned so dark.

when Daryl tied my wrists to the table or to secure my arms around the pole, it felt so tight, i could feel my fingers go numb. i thought maybe they would fall off. i tried not to move, because if i did those ropes would make marks. nobody wanted Little Kathy's parents to see those marks. having my wrists tied feels horrible. my arms could not cover my naked chest. i wished someone would cover me up. nobody did, ever. so ashamed... i remember thinking, "please untie me." this body can be very still. that did not happen for a very long time. when Daryl was convinced this body would not fight or run, he finally left my wrists alone. i did learn to like our friend Emma. she taught Little Kathy to finger dance. when Emma was around, my fingers did not feel so cold, and i admit they looked a little prettier. i let my hands open up instead of looking like i might punch someone. (Emma, that was such a good trick.) i still couldn't cover myself, but it was nice to think about something else. ballerinas are pretty. i am not.

since i am talking about the ropes, i guess i should talk about my ankles. talking about the ankle part of me really makes me want to curl up in that ball. i wanted to actually turn into perfectly round ball. sure, you could throw a ball around, but you can not get inside of it. a ball is all closed up. it has no open places to put things in. i admit these legs were not very cooperative when they tried to tie my ankles to each side of the table. every inch of this body fought against that. somebody had to help Daryl tie me down the first time. i was really strong when i had to be. this was one of those times. they did not seem to be very mad though. they laughed like this was a game. i did not ever win this game, no matter how many times i tried. finally, i just gave up. this was the beginning of so much shame. i really started to my hate my parts after this happened. i did not know what was gonna happen to this body, but i already felt squirmy and cold. my skin just wanted to shrink to my baby doll's size or maybe even an ant size. really, i just wanted to disappear. invisible means they can reach to touch me, and poof i would be gone. safe... i wish i had a magic wand.

if accidentally my voice popped out, some part of my body would get punished. he liked to punish my hairs. my hair is brown with a little red in the sunlight. our mom curled it pretty with these pink plastic things called spoolies. so our hair had curls especially when we went to school or church. things looked prettier on that side of the wall... in the garage it just looked ugly. those hairs hurt when they pulled them. i don't like my hair. sometimes if i was bad, Daryl would get his cigarette lighter, hold my hair tight and put that fire right next to it. i thought he would burn all my hairs off. what would i do if he did that? how could i go home with no hair? what would i say about where our hair went? then he would just laugh, pull out some hair from the underneath and burn it with that fire, right in front of my nose. yuck, that smells horrible. i learned how to be very quiet and still, because i wanted to keep my hairs.

my poor blue eyes. i use to think my eyes were the pretty part of this body. the color is just like my daddy's. that's why blue is my favorite color. all good things are blue. the sky is blue. the blessed Mother's dress is blue. i like blue dresses. the walls in my bedroom are blue. i really like blue... before Daryl, i thought my eyes looked happy in the mirror. now they don't. my eyes sometimes even hurt just being open. they also seem to be darker. the blue is not quite as light anymore. i think they changed color because of the ugly things they had to see. my eyes want to close, but Daryl doesn't let them. he said, "KEEP YOUR EYES OPEN!" so i did what he said. just when i thought my eyes had seen the worst thing ever, they saw something i could not even imagine.

i remember when my eyes started to get darker. it began in the garage, when i saw Debra with her all grown up body. everything looked so different from this body and i knew i should not have been looking. but even worse was when i had to see Daryl's private man parts. they were too close to my face. i know that was just the worst, because i couldn't even breathe as i watched him come at me. seeing can make you very afraid. i felt like if i was a good girl, i would have closed my eyes, but if i did, something really awful would have happened. so i chose to be bad.

at the outside place i wanted to just scratch my eyes out of my head, because there i saw things that made me feel as evil as he was. i saw him hurt a couple other little kids, and animals too. i couldn't hide my eyes because my hands were tied to the bench. i couldn't help anybody because my feet were tied too. if he saw me close my eyes, then it would be my turn to sit on the stone altar. that was the worst place to ever be... so i watched. i wish i could figure out a way to make what i saw go away. how do i not see what i saw? when i would finally get back to the house, i could see how dark my eyes got. thankfully, my dad's still were that pretty blue i remember. finally, now i can close my tired, abused eyes.

the next parts of this body i have saved for last. i thought maybe i could forget these parts. i never want to talk about them because they make me feel so bad. i wish people didn't have to have them, or at least not me. i think i could live without a mouth. i don't get to say what i want anyway. i definitely could live without my private parts. i don't think anybody really needs them. i don't like anything that ever happens to them. my mom said no one was supposed to see them except me because they were private. i was gonna keep that rule, until Daryl. then i had no choice. he made me show them.

what i didn't know is that there was a place in a girl's private parts that bad people could put things into. who would ever do that? and who would ever want to do that? why did it have to hurt so much? that part felt like there was a big knife poking at it. the rest of my body felt suffocated. i held my breathe hard hoping that maybe it would hurt less. that never worked. the rest of my body could not help but try to fight. i could not make my body stop fighting or shaking, but Daryl could. he lay his knife right next to us and showed it to me if i didn't stop. i guess that dirty knife made me freeze, like when i hear the words, "Red Light." i love playing that game in our back yard... i don't need private parts to play "Red Light, Green Light." the rules in that game are clear, pretty easy and you don't get hurt. you just run and stop depending on what color they called out. if you get caught moving when the leader says, "Red Light"all you have to do is start at the beginning again with no punishment. that's cool. the best part of the game is that there was an end. you cross a finish line and the game is over. with Daryl, there was no finish line and i never dared to run.

i don't like my girl part because it bleeds sometimes and that really scares me. and what do you do about that? well, Debra told me i could use this cloth pad to hold there. being a girl body is horrible.

the very worst thing about my girl private part is that sometimes it plays tricks like Daryl. when my whole body is crying the most, from what he is doing to me, when i am smothered by this big body on top of me, when they are pushing and pulling at me, i feel like my body will just rip in half, right down the middle. when everything is moving so fast, and all i want to do is run away, i would get this strange feeling down there. a feeling that you could almost say was good. NOT GOOD, YUCK... even this body betrays me. it does something i do not want. when this happens my stomach wants to throw up and tears come out of my dark eyes. my body parts seem to be all confused. i feel embarrassed, i feel like the very worst little body. i don't even have control over the one thing i thought i really owned. i am sure i am about to blow up, or die when this happens... no time to pray, and then, like magic it would stop. but Daryl didn't... i never knew what was worse, what he did, or what this stupid body did. i wish it was just one of those really bad dreams that come in the night time. if this is what happens when you have girl private parts, i wish i was a boy. NO, big boys are bad.

the last part of me i am gonna talk about is my mouth. i know i need a mouth to eat, but i don't feel much like eating anyway. i do like the taste of the food that Little Kathy's mom makes. she cooks everyone very tasty meals and great cookies. Daryl never has snacks in the garage. he only gives soda that taste funny. i don't like his soda. and then he tricks me and makes me drink my own pee. i am so embarrassed to say that. it makes me feel like throwing up. i have to tell my stomach not to do that because that will get us in trouble. why does he make me do that? Little Kathy begged him not to make her drink that once and she never asked again, it just got worse.

in my house and at school, i get to talk, but not on the other side of the wall. i never get to say many words there. it is a rule. you have to be quiet like in the library. i never used to feel like i had to throw up, but since my Mondays with Daryl, i feel that gaggy feeling all the time. i can't even brush my teeth without gagging, and my toothpaste tastes nice. but now my toothbrush makes that gag happen every day. Daryl and his friends put things in my mouth that i know should not be there. just thinking about it takes all the air out of the room. i can't breathe. i know i have to go to the dentist to keep my teeth healthy and clean, but i don't ever want to go. i don't want that nice dentist to put his hands near my face and especially not in my mouth. if i get to grow up to be a big girl, maybe i can say i am not going to the dentist ever. i hope my dentist doesn't feel bad. he is a nice man, i just don't like his hands near my mouth. i will brush my teeth three times a day. i promise. do you think the toothbrush can brush all the yuck out of my mouth? i hope so.

ok just one more part. the skin part of me. that skin part must be very strong because it is everywhere, and it holds all the other parts together. that is a very hard job. skin feels everything. it really is where all the leftover feelings live. my skin feels damaged every time he touches it. he leaves his smell there. he leaves my skin wet and yucky. so yucky, i never think i am clean. a hundred showers could not clean this skin. i always wonder how do you clean inside my skin?

Daryl even taught other parts of me how to cut this body's skin. he taught the others to cut just a certain way. he had a certain symbol he liked cutting. i don't like that symbol at all. it looks mean. my other parts hated to do this at first because they thought it hurt. hmmmm, they thought it hurt? what about me?! after they did it a few times they seemed to like to do it. maybe cutting the skin helped them feel better. i didn't understand that at first. but now i guess i get it. sometimes my hands want to do the same. we all have to remember where to cut though. we don't want anybody to see what we cut. i feel sorry for this skin even though i really do hate it. this is so confusing.

i just want to go back to the way it used to be.... i liked when i had nothing to hide. i kinda remember the Mondays when my whole body did not hurt, when i did not bleed, when i didn't have to be sure my cuts were hidden, when my mouth did not have to lie, when i got to just drink that cool pink lemonade. i liked when i could just pee in my toilet and nowhere else and when nothing burned down there. i want to go back to swinging on my swings and playing in the sandbox in our back yard. i want to wash only mud pies off my skin. i want the only blood i see to be from a prick after i touch the rose bushes. pink roses look really pretty on the mud pies. i am very good at making pretty mud pies.

i wish i could trade my skin with somebody else, but i know nobody would want mine. they probably wouldn't like my other body parts either. so i guess this is for me to keep. so i will just keep washing it, over and over again.

Caryl... The Last Day

i started to make my plan for the next Monday. i don't plan to share this with the others inside. they will be too afraid to help me, and i know this plan is the only way out. six years is long enough. this body is older now and i am just done. there is nothing more left here to hurt. he took everything already. i don't even feel angry anymore. i feel nothing. i am done protecting the others. they all have hated me most of their lives anyway. sometimes i sound just like Daryl to them. i know i repeat his hurtful words everyday. i am and i always was the constant reminder of the rules. they followed the rules because i said so. i scared them with my voice. my voice hurt just like his. isn't it better me than him? i took over when nobody else could deal. i really was the only one with any fucking power. i can make pain stop with the cut of a pocket knife. i don't need a fucking stick. i have my own way to make things happen. everyone thought i was just as mean as him. they are probably right. he never hurt me, not a chance...

i never liked the garage. i liked going to the outside place better. it was farther away from Little Kathy's house. i could make noise and didn't give a shit. i knew all of his tricks. i tricked him. he didn't trick me. i know he thought i was just like him, that i actually liked him. he thought i would stay in his little group forever. he thought i would do this forever. he thought i would keep everyone in line when he was not in their face. i guess he is right about that one. that's why everyone hates me except maybe daryl. ask me if i care!

this summer has really been the worst. there will not be another one. not another day. only a few more hours. after today, no more rape. no more torture, no more disgusting laughter, no more stick, no more motorcycles. no more games i never really win. no more filthy, dark van. no more dark hole, no more green box, no more lying on Monday mornings. no more soda, no more god damn pee bucket. he will never cut me again. he will never make me put anything in my mouth i don't like, ever!! he will never see any of us in his pathetic garage or at the outside place again. i don't care that he will keep hurting others. i now know i can't make that stop. i tried. we will never cross over that wall again. i know what this will mean, but i have never felt so relaxed.

so, i take one last walk over the wall and already know the van will be waiting for me. do i even bother knocking on the garage door? i am like a clock. 10 AM and i am here. the door opens for the last time and he doesn't even know it. i really like that i am keeping a secret from him. i hate that he knows everything about me. not today... i pee in the bucket and drink my soda. i hand him his gun. each step my last. he skips a few steps of the morning ritual this summer. he no longer makes me hand him the ropes. he doesn't pull my shirt up over our head anymore. none of that is necessary. we know the fucking drill. we know the consequences, and that fucking soda helps now. after we go down the driveway and get off our street, he lets me sit in the seat by one window. does he not care that now i know how to get to the outside place? does he not think i might show somebody his secret place? does he think that i will never have the guts to tell? well none of that matters. i am never, ever going back there after today. my secret. the best secret ever.

i get out of the van. whoosh... so many flashes of hor-rible. my legs shake... "NO! everybody stay down. i am gonna do this alone." i will follow my plan and walk this walk one last time. i try hard not to imagine how many times this body climbed this fucking hill... i won't allow him to hurt us anymore, so my legs just keep climbing. i am glad the leaves are still on the trees. no one should see this. that sounds funny when i say that because, really, no one has seen a damn thing in six years. what makes today any different? EVERYTHING is different today. tomorrow there will be nothing to see or hide...

i have no doubts that my plan will work. i am not afraid. we get to the top of the hill. there it is, the clearing i know so well. there is no need for ugly pictures to remember this place. every inch of this Hell is burned into my eyes. this must be what Hell looks like. most people think it is all blazing fire. nope. Hell is made of this altar built of stone, wooden benches, dirt holes and a fire pit. somebody just like

Daryl lives there. big trees surround this Hell hidden far away from anybody. if you dare to scream, no one can hear you. my voice would just get lost in the trees and earn me an "I told you so" punishment. that scream only lives in my head. i wonder if i will still hear the scream after today. will i just go straight to Hell after today? you know, the real Hell. Little Kathy never did confess this sin out loud to the priest, and i don't think God ever heard her silent confession. it is too late now. Little Kathy cannot be here today. no turning back now.

here goes nothing... i act like it is any other Monday. i go take off my clothes and lay them by the tree. wouldn't want to get them dirty. oh, but that will not matter anymore. what does he want me to do on my last day? sit on the benches and watch first? sit up on that stone table and wait for the others to get up the hill? go climb into Rose's hole? he no longer has to lift this body to drop me in. i just drop down myself. i always thought i would die there in that hole but did not. i remember begging him silently to just do what i feared when i stood down there. i learned after many visits to that ever shrinking hole, that the threat of this being my grave was a lie. it became a lie when i begged to go there...

i have always pictured my skin to look like the rough, thick bark on the big trees that circle me.. "Good luck getting to me, asshole!" i wore that bark like a robe. you can't hurt my skin. with that robe on i do not feel pain. my trick. my secret. today i do not even wear the bark robe. it will be over soon.

my speech is all set in my head... a couple other guys come into the clearing. good, the more the merrier. it does not matter what they think anyway, because Daryl is the boss of them. what will they think when i am gone? will they care? who will they take filthy pictures of? how will they sell pictures, if there is no one to take them of? how will they get their drugs? too bad! i like that ending...

who will take the final shot? will Daryl keep that promise to just bury me alive? he had threatened me with that for as long as i can remember. will they strangle me with their ropes? will they just cut too deep, like they did with the animals? what will be my lethal punishment for what i am about to say? it doesn't matter anymore. i am sorry for what will happen to Little Kathy's family... i secretly pray that Daryl does not keep those promises, but there is just no other way out. i cannot live any longer in this Hell. i cannot live in two different worlds. we would belong nowhere if we ever told the truth, and how would we ever tell the truth and live anyway? i would never say this out loud, but i cannot turn out like him. i know i am all tough and nasty. that is how i helped the others. but somewhere way inside i know there is something that would not let me grow up to be like him. i no longer can follow his horrible rules. finally my need to find a way out of here outweighs the fear of my life ending.

"GET UP ON THAT ALTAR!!!" that harsh voice jerks me from my thoughts. i can't move. i won't move. can i just run back down the hill? no! this is done. i am done... i have never defied him like this before. i say, "NO!" (out loud this time). gosh, that sounded good. "NO!!! i won't get up there." i pause, take a big, deep breath and say, "NEVER AGAIN!!" somehow, my words must not be loud enough, because nobody moves.

"YOU DO WHAT I SAY OR YOU KNOW WHAT WILL HAPPEN TO YOU!!!! KATHY, DO YOU HEAR ME?" hmmm, he used our name. what is that about? sorry i am not Kathy, i am Caryl... i do take a step backwards and feel the stone altar on my back. i did not plan on taking that step, so i step forward again. my arms just hang at my sides. i do feel that familiar fear from somebody. deep inside, i feel impending doom consuming me, coming from the fear of what is to come. i pull my shoulders back and think, i must be even stronger. this is the one time i can really protect us forever. this is our way out. i will not back down. i can be the hero here. the hero we have always waited for, that never came. i hope Little Kathy's God is watching... maybe Little Kathy can ask for mercy as i complete this one last act. because i know that what i say and do next will make Daryl end my life, i feel like i am ending our life. i'm not sure if i am actually saying a prayer, but I could hear the words, "if you must God, banish just me, not the younger ones." i am not really sorry for what i am about to do, but there is no other way out...

i take one more giant step forward and talk right into Daryl's face. i can smell the smoke and beer on his breath. i see clearly his green eyes. i have not seen those eyes in many years. they were always impossible to look at. but today, i look. i look him right in the eyes and say, "Daryl, this is the last time i am ever coming here with you. i am never going back to the garage. i will never look you in the eyes again. you will never touch my body again. you will never take another picture of me. you will never take my glasses again. i will never drink your drugged soda again. i will never do what you ask again. i will never again watch you hurt others. your stick has no more power over me. i promise never to tell a soul what happened to me in the last six years. and you can go ahead and kill me now. you can punish me in any way you want. you can hurt my family. you can do whatever you want to me, but i am never coming to you again. so, i am gonna walk over to that tree, get my clothes, put them back on and you will please take me home now."

...and i do just that. i start to shake again, as i try to slip my feet into my shorts. i fall to the ground. i pull up my shorts and put my shirt on. next my socks and sneakers, and still no one moves. their silence scares me. what are they thinking? i try to shake that feeling. i stand up, break the rules, and close my eyes to him... i am waiting for my punishment. i think, "ok, take your best shot!" and i pray it works fast. barely breathing, i am waiting to feel his bullet, my throat cut, or a rope around my neck... i wonder if this is over? am i about to leave this hell? for a brief second, i feel glad and have accepted my consequence. then his hand yanks my arm and i hear Daryl say, "GET THE FUCK DOWN THE HILL AND INTO THAT VAN!" i think, no wait, you are supposed to shoot me. i think it should be much darker out here. the sun is so bright. why am i still breathing? if i get in that van, will i really make it back to Little Kathy's house? maybe this is just one last trick. Daryl must think i just want to go home. does he know what i really want is to die? maybe that is what he thinks, and he will not let me die. maybe he thinks i don't really mean what i just said. well, he would be wrong, because i am never coming back no matter what. i am ready to accept whatever comes next.

only silence on the way home…the loudest silence i have never heard. a silence still filled with questions. no one said a single word. why are they so quiet? is he creating a new plan to keep me with his group? is he going to shoot me in the garage when we get back? or is this really over? the ride back was at least long enough for all of these questions to bounce off the walls of my brain, but no answers ever came…only silence.

so for the last time, i get out of the van and he just stands there watching me leave. i dared to turn my head and look to see if he was watching me, or even worse, if he was going to follow me to where i needed to go next. that's when I started to run as fast as my trembling legs would go. he never followed me. i ran right to the stream. all i wanted to do was wash the smell of the van off of my body and simply stand in the cool water. in six years did he ever notice that i never crossed back over the wall immediately to run safely home? i kept turning my head around to see if he was going to follow me this time. maybe his plan was to follow me and just kill me in the woods. maybe nobody would ever find my body there. unbeknownst to him, he would would have granted my wish. the years of torture would be over and i would be dead. mission accomplished…

well things did not go as planned. i am still breathing. i am still alive. so i walk back to Little Kathy's yard. my feet are heavy and i walk slowly up the driveway. Fear again flushed over my skin, thinking maybe her parents and brothers are the ones that are dead. i see her dad's car. maybe Daryl got to them while i was still at the stream. maybe i should just run away. Daryl is being way too quiet.

why was i not beaten to a pulp on the ground, hidden by trees up on that hill? this is when the real terror set in. it is the not knowing what is coming next that scares me. is my new fear going to live in me for the rest of my life? will i forever wonder when the other shoe will drop? when i least expect it, will that be the moment he keep all of his promises? i guess that cannot matter now. what is done is done, but i am still never going back. as i approach the kitchen door, i hear laughing from the open window of Little Kathy's house. i quietly apologize and whisper to the others inside, "i really tried." as i put my right hand in my pocket, and feel Little Kathy's rosary beads, i think, "do these things even work?" Shaking my head, i hear myself say, "not today."

i tell Little Kathy to go on inside, they must have lunch waiting for her. i wonder, will she even know not to go back there next Monday? i guess i will have to help her with that...

What do I do now?

...everything feels a little fuzzy, but i think i am ok. i sneak quickly through the kitchen to the bathroom to do a skin check. no blood to be seen... i whisper to myself, "it's a good day." my skin looks like a regular kid's skin... ok, i'm safe to let my parents see me. the kitchen clock says twelve o'clock. wow, did i go to the garage today? is it Monday? i don't feel so good. i find the church calendar on the wall. that doesn't really help. i am all mixed up. am i in trouble? something just doesn't feel right. then the kitchen door opens and i see my dad's smile as he comes into the kitchen. it is lunch time. i guess the coast is clear, and i didn't even miss lunch.

i know sometimes that Daryl's soda makes me feel a little out of it, so maybe that's why i feel so strange. i guess i can't do anything about this feeling now. maybe some food will help. my dad sets up the TV trays so we can eat. i am glad to be home. another Monday over, i think...

...wow, that was a fast week. my brother Jeffrey and i got to do some school shopping. i love getting new clothes for school. the hard part will be making up my mind which dress to wear on the first day. none of the kids on the street really like going back to school except for maybe me. it feels like the Fourth of July to me. freedom from pain. freedom from my summer hell. freedom from having to go over that wall again until next summer. it will be over for another year. just one more week. maybe i should wear red, white and blue to celebrate...

how can it be Monday morning again? dammit i have my period. it feels like i just got rid of that. i really don't want to go to the garage today. God, just one more Monday to hate. one more day to hang my head and avoid his ugly face. i don't really feel as scared as usual today. maybe i am just so used to this recurring nightmare...

next week i cannot return to the garage and he knows that. school starts. i love school... but can you imagine if anybody from school ever found out about this? they would call me bad names, and they would be right. oh well, i can't worry about that now. i have to walk over that wall one more time this year, and be done with this for a while. my legs are barely shaking at all. i am in junior high now. school work will be harder, but i might have fun being a cheerleader, if i make it. even though i can't do those jumps as well as the other girls, i would like to try out. it sounds like fun being a cheerleader, because i get to yell and scream a lot, and it is ok. the kind of noise you make in the gym is really loud. other kids join in, because they are happy, and want their team to win. if i make it through tryouts, i get to wear a cool red and grey uniform to school. i don't like the idea of tryouts, though. that makes me feel really nervous. maybe Marie will go for me. she never had to go to Daryl's tryouts. she really is the one that does everything at school anyway. she is smarter than me. the kids at school would make fun of my shaky legs if they saw me there. just thinking about that makes me want to run to the bathroom. can't do that now though... i have to go in the pee bucket in just a few more steps. later today maybe i can practice some of those cheers i saw the older girls do last year. i am really dilly dallying now. i best not be late getting to Daryl's...

i am standing in Daryl's driveway, and i don't see the van. could it be in the garage? the sound of quiet makes my heart start to pound inside my chest. the weirdest thing is what the garage looks like today. the door is open a crack, and i can see inside the window. the curtains that were on that one smokey looking window are gone, and i can actually see through the glass. i find it really hard to picture Daryl or the camera guy washing that filthy window. it must have been Debra or maybe their parents finally saw how grimy it was. this cleaned up garage looked prettier than ever before, but did not scare me any less. i walk right in, mostly because it must be 10 o'clock, and i can't be late. once inside, i look around and it has all changed. there are no gross smells of pee, gasoline, beer, or whatever else that ugly smell was. everything is as clean as a garage can be. Daryl's garage is really the only one i have ever been in though. it seems like someone had a tag sale because the garage also looks empty. i look for my ropes, and don't see them anywhere. i walk slowly to the far end of the garage and see no guns or knives on those shelves. did the police come? did i tell someone? am i supposed to get to the outside place myself? there is no soda on the table, because there is no table. you can actually fit a car in here now if you wanted to. my head hurts, and i rub my eyes hoping that would take the pain away. i am so confused. what am i supposed to do? Daryl, where are you? is this another trick? God i hate new tricks... i feel jumpy, and keep turning around looking for someone to pop out at me. i wish he would just get here, so i could relax. boy, does that sound crazy. i look in the other corner and even the green box is gone. where did he put that, and when did he do all this? does this mean i can just leave today? i don't dare, because this really could be a trick. so i am just gonna sit on the only chair in here. i hate this chair, it is disgusting. i guess i will just sit here until i am supposed to leave, and maybe i won't get in trouble.

i notice my headache just gets worse as that big hand on the clock takes its sweet old time. i can barely open my eyes, so i close them. Daryl is not here. he can't punish me for closing my eyes if he is not here to see...right?

it is really quiet sitting by myself on this stupid chair and i start to hear a voice inside. the voice is kinda like mine, but a little rougher. could this be Caryl? my eyes pop open. she might not like me closing my eyes. she always made sure we followed Daryl's rules. eyes open, no problem.

it is Caryl... why is she talking to me? she thinks i am a baby, because i am always scared and i shake a lot. boy, if this is really Monday, it's a real strange one. she asks, "Little Kathy, why are you here?" i answer, "well it is Monday, you know we always have to come here."

...and then Caryl starts to tell me what she did last Monday, which i can't remember at all. as she tells me this story, my head starts to pound harder. i really can't keep my eyes open another second, but Caryl doesn't seem to mind. maybe she has a headache too. maybe Rose is listening now... Rose has a hard time keeping her eyes open. i have no words of my own in my head. all i am feeling is fear. is this a trick? i think Daryl is gonna walk into this garage any minute. i'll be in trouble, but at least my Monday will make sense. i am frozen in the chair listening and wondering if i am actually in my bed having a bad dream, or possibly a good dream? i don't like this. nothing feels normal. i am all mixed up.

Caryl continues to tell me what she did at the outside place. she explains to me every step she took, and every word she said. all i can think is how brave she was. i could never have said those words to Daryl. she told him, "NO!" my legs shake just thinking of what he must have done next. i was wondering how she is even here to tell this story. is she telling me the truth or is Daryl putting her up to this? i just know he is gonna walk in that door any minute and we will both pay the price. i open my eyes just a little and look around, but no Daryl. all i feel coming through that door is a warm breeze.

it seems so strange sitting here quietly with no one poking at me or trying to hurt me. i still know i can't leave until the clock says it's twelve, so i just sit. could what Caryl did actually have set us free from Daryl and his friends? i don't feel free or safe. i feel like nothing has changed. all my body parts still feel awful. they feel dirty and wrecked. i feel like Daryl hears everything i say. i always feel like he is watching me and can read my mind. could it be possible to not think like that anymore? what would it be like to never let him put his body on mine again? can my ears forget his words? i hear them all the time in my head. could I forget his yucky smell? would food actually taste good again? could i maybe eat and not get sick right after the food goes down? maybe, i could brush my teeth without gagging... that would be so nice. when i gag like that, it makes me cry every single time.

is it twelve o'clock yet? can i really go home now? i glance over at the alarm clock. two more minutes. i take one last look around. funny, it doesn't look like it used to, but i still see all the things that happened here... one more minute. so i get up off that chair. i think i should kick it to the floor, but i am still afraid to break the rules. just walk away Kathy. walk away and pray Caryl made it stop. all of a sudden i hear a loud bell ringing. the sound startles me and i can't figure out what it is for a second. i spin around to see where it is coming from. it is that stupid clock. oh my God, turn it off quick. maybe that clock is just like mine in my bedroom. please, turn it off, make it stop. he will come. make it stop. i run over there and shut it off. thank you God, it is just like mine. ok, twelve o'clock, run before he finds you here.

i step outside the door and feel the sunlight on my face, and squish... i stepped on something and fell forward slipping on it. Kathy you are so clumsy, just go. scrambling to my feet, i see what i stepped on. it looked just like that little bird from the green box. but it could not be him. he died a long, long time ago. oh God, just please get me out of here. as i am running down the driveway, to cross over to the stream, i hear that familiar laugh. the one i hate so much. no words, just a laugh. is he watching me? i will never be free from him. i start to cry, and i run as fast as i can. i can hardly see, with my eyes flooded with tears. i knew i could run to the stream with my eyes closed, so i keep moving. i need to get down there, not to wash, but to hide. i need to find my smile before i go back home. i feel sick. i really don't think this is over. what do i do now?...back to school tomorrow.

Part Two:
Journey to the Light

My 38th Thanksgiving

I love the smell of turkey with all the fixings cooking while surrounded by my family. The joyful sounds we make while preparing to sit down to Thanksgiving dinner are so comforting. No matter what life brings us during the year, we gather and make these same dishes that have been prepared on this day in November every year. I am grateful sitting down to this meal made with love by the most special people in my life. This Thanksgiving, as always, we took a moment to thank God for our family and of course the chefs that created the feast before us. On this day, I could hear the laughter and taste the abundance of my favorite meal, but inside, something was off…

This was my 38th Thanksgiving, and I felt like I was underwater, holding my breath. Each sound I heard was muffled. I wore a smile that pained my face. I stumbled through the day with no feeling in my body. I was so confused by this feeling that I just wanted to be home with my son tucked in bed, music on, and me frozen on the couch. I wanted to be cocooned in a soft blanket. I had only swallowed one glass of wine before dinner, but felt weak and wobbly like I drank four.

I went through the Thanksgiving motions I had memorized over these 38 years. After eating my favorite meal, I frantically pushed myself from the table, to barely make it to the bathroom. The food poured from my body and I knew I needed to get to that safe cocoon I yearned for. At least now I had an acceptable reason to leave the festivities. No one would question why I was leaving if I was physically sick. Still feeling like I was under the ocean searching for air, I somehow drove myself and my son home just a few miles away.

Hearing my kitchen door close behind me, I exhaled with relief. As I locked the deadbolt I immediately felt the privacy of my apartment. I remember pulling the kitchen shades down to ensure not being seen. Finally, I kissed my son Timmy goodnight and tucked him into bed. Feeling safer with that kiss, I crawled onto the couch grabbing the blanket already there waiting for me. Soft music was playing. I guess I had left it playing while we were gone. Needing just a little light, I lit my favorite candle. I wondered, how can the smell of pumpkin pie come out of a candle?… On that drive home from my aunt's house, I doubted I would make it home to this safe spot. But, it was all good now. Exhaustion took over. It was hard work keeping that smile on my face for this holiday. Deep sleep came like a rescue team…

Screaming, with no sound, I found myself on my couch, blankets ripped off, pajamas gone. Sweat covered my naked skin as I shivered from the cold simultaneously. The air had been sucked out of my living room. Something was crushing me. No, it is someone forcing his body on top of me. I could not see his face. NO! NO! NO! NO! Stop! Please don't hurt me! Please stop, you are hurting me… My arms were tied down. I can't move under this power that is on me, and inside me… Then I hear myself praying, "Hail Mary full of grace…..", over and over again. I can taste salt. My tongue is bleeding. I cannot get off the couch. I hear a voice, "Wake up Kathy. Just wake up!" I try to sit up, and break away from this overwhelming force that has enveloped me. I wake up! Who is talking to me? Who helped me wake up from this horrible experience in my dream? It was so real; not a dream. What just happened to me? My body hurts between my legs. I feel wet and gross. My wrists ache. I shiver like I was naked in the snow. Where is my blanket? My cocoon had been ripped apart, and I do not feel like a butterfly. I cannot fly away. I lay crushed on the couch.

I realize I am on very shaky ground. My thoughts go to finding my phone. But, who do I call? Certainly no one in my family, I would scare them to death...

Just a couple months before that Thanksgiving, I sought out a therapist. I had been crying a lot and a friend mine said, "If you don't find a therapist I will find one for you." He felt there was something seriously wrong with me and I needed to sort some things out. I thought, ok I would like to feel happier. He was right, I should be happy with my little family of two. I had been so blessed to deliver my only child, Timmy four years ago. The day he was born really was the best day of my life. So why am I so sad? I was not sure I wanted that answer or to start therapy, but my friend was pretty insistent. Deep inside, I knew he was right and did exactly what he said. Thank God I did, because I definitely need help this Thanksgiving night.

So, I dug out my therapist's card from my wallet, and with trembling hands I dialed his emergency number three times, and hung up. Did I honestly want to make this call? No, yes, no, yes... I really didn't know the answer to that question. I let it ring and thought, "Is this really an emergency? Did my new therapist, John really mean

I could call this number? What defines an emergency? When is the fear and pain great enough to use this number? Was this that moment he was talking about? So many questions flooding my brain and I had not one single answer.

In therapy, John had discussed sending me to a shrink, and getting me started on an antidepressant. I clearly was depressed. Every day I had to drag myself from one place to another. I cried a lot, and didn't eat anything but string beans and drank insufficient amounts of water. I coined this diet program, the string bean diet… I deliberately cut into my own skin, often. I stubbornly refused to take medication, because I was sure I didn't need it, until this Thanksgiving night.

John did accept my emergency call. By the time I heard his hello, I was crying and shaking so hard my rings made a racket banging against the phone. He could barely translate my mixed up words between sobs, as I blurted out the pieces of this dreadful Thanksgiving. I begged him to make an appointment for me to meet with that damn shrink he had been talking about. Hey, if a pill could fix this mess I was in. Right now, I'd take a bucket of them and be done with this. I wouldn't need therapy, because this pill was going to magically save me from the terror I was trying to escape. Yes a pill! What took me so long to figure this one out? I administered pills every day at work. Maybe some pills could work for me too.

With John's promise to set me up with a psychiatrist, and that I could go to his office in the morning, after a long silence, I was able to safely say good bye. I remember thinking he was letting me hang up first, giving me the choice to end the conversation. John had an immeasurable amount of patience. I finally said goodbye and peeled the phone away from my ear technically severing the connection.

Still fearful, I looked from room to room for my perpetrator that only existed in my terrorizing dream. Somehow, I believed he was gone but I did not feel safe.

I think this was the day that I truly started my therapeutic journey to healing my resurfacing past wounds. This was day one of finding my way out of a dark, scary maze of what had been six years of my little girl life.

Turn the lights off please

I started journaling in between sessions with John. This was a good suggestion. I had journaled in the past and found it helpful. Not knowing how challenging journaling would be at this time in my life, I thought this would be easy enough. I created a simple little plan in my head to pick up a journal again. I planned to get a journal with a beautiful cover to disguise what I feared I might write after that Thanksgiving nightmare. The foolish part of me however, thought this might make therapy sessions easier for both me and John. Maybe, I wouldn't have to say any words. Therapy could just be like "Show and Tell." Hmmm, no problem. Just hand in the journal at the beginning of the session and let him read.

A few months into therapy as I started to trust John, I wasn't so nervous about going to my sessions. I was more comfortable sitting across from him in his office. Thankfully I hadn't had anymore nightmares like I had on that November night. The Zoloft the psychiatrist put me on had really started to take effect. I remember that moment very clearly. This feeling when the medication started to work was like a window had opened up, and a fresh cool breeze brushed by my face, allowing me to breathe again. All this in just eight short days. Again, I thought a magic pill was great idea, until the darkness crept back inside my soul. Most of the time, I felt a constricting pressure in my chest. I was dizzy and frozen in place, afraid to move through life. I wondered, how long do you think I can hold my breath? The answer to that question was, a very long time...

One morning, while I was journaling on my bed in front of an open window, I found myself writing down the forbidden story of Little Kathy's worst day in the garage, that very first day; the day of her first big secret. She had been sworn to secrecy by the most evil man ever and here my hands were writing it down, in ink, in a book with a beautiful cover. This surely was against Daryl's rules... The tiny words, now written on the paper were funny looking, and got smaller and smaller, till you could almost not read them. As my right hand wrote, I felt that familiar dream feeling I had as a little girl. I always described it as "that no way out feeling." It was a suffocating feeling. That tight, choking feeling in my throat made me gag...I felt, surely my life was about to end and fought the urge to hide in my closet to continue writing. Secretly, even from myself, I had made a comfortable little space in the closet of my bedroom. This space was filled with some pillows, a blanket and stuffed animals, a small flashlight, rosary beads, M&M's, a magic wand, and pocket knife. I do not remember building this secret hiding place. It was like someone had snuck in and built it for a sweet, but very scared little girl. At first, this discovery was a bit disturbing, but here it was, and the cozy space sure looked inviting. So in I went.

Once inside my hiding place, I continued to write fast and furious with everything misspelled and hard to read. Inside my belly, it felt like a volcano was starting to shake before it erupts. "Do I keep writing? Do I run? Do I slam this closet door shut and stay here until the coast is clear?" Suddenly I knew what I had to do. I grabbed my new journal and stumbled to the bathroom just in time for the volcano to explode into the toilet. I threw up until there was nothing more inside. I closed the bathroom door and tore the pages out of this all-telling journal. Next, I watched my hands shred each page into a pile of what looked like snowflakes. Only one letter allowed per flake. No one could ever put these words back together again. Dripping with sweat, I thought, I didn't tell. I didn't tell. I'm sorry, I'm sorry, I'm sorry… From the bathroom floor, these words played on repeat in my head for hours. I wondered, how would I make it until tomorrow?

The next morning, there I sat in the lobby of the counseling center waiting for John to walk down the hall to get me. It was 10:00. This day I felt an overwhelming need to hide from the other patients waiting for their sessions to begin. Surely, they did not have anything uglier to tell their therapists than me. Feeling incredibly exposed, I wore layers of heavy clothes to cover me. Thankfully, it was winter and I probably didn't look too out of place.

John was running over, as he sometimes does. I didn't like that, but I prepared for this wait by bringing my latest self help book to read. I am pretty sure I read the same sentence twenty times and had no recall of any of it. Comprehension was not really part of my plan. I simply did not want to chat with anyone and the fake book reading protected me from socializing. I felt a person sit down in the chair right next to me. This body felt much too close to me. His elbow was touching mine. Damn, I usually put my purse on that chair. I thought, they must be having a group therapy in the next hour, there are too many people in this waiting room today. I gave a slight glance to my right, because this man smelled like he hadn't showered in weeks and reeked of smoke. If I didn't need too see John so desperately, I would have walked right out that door. I could feel that panic feeling sneaking up on me. My face felt hot, while my hands felt cold and damp.

I did feel bad for the man, his shoes had holes and no laces. I noticed his shoes because I couldn't look up any higher than his feet. I didn't want to see his face. Maybe he was just down on his luck or maybe even homeless... I rearranged myself to the left, and then I saw it. This guy with worn out shoes, smelling of beer and cigarettes was holding a tall wooden walking stick...Frantic for John to rescue me from this waiting room, I froze like a statue in my chair. Everything in me wanted to run, but instead I didn't move a muscle. My reality at that moment was that I understood Daryl had been dead for many years, so how could he in fact be sitting next to me, his elbow touching mine. It didn't make sense to me, but I was sure it was Daryl... Who else has a stick like that?

All of a sudden, without warning I found myself picturing the day I heard Daryl died. I felt dizzy siting in my chair still waiting for John. I couldn't feel my arms or legs as I kept leaning further to the left away from this man with the stick. I was remembering me standing in my childhood driveway hearing neighbors talking about what happened to Daryl. I was in my twenties, home for the summer from nursing school. Ironically, I remembered receiving this news while I was standing right next to the very wall I had stepped over for years to go to the garage...I recalled feeling nothing when I heard how he died. I heard the words. The story was interesting, but I just stood there with nothing to say. My neighbor was very animated as she told the news. He was in the back of a convertible, but not sitting in the seat. He was on top of the back seat, where the seat meets the trunk of the car. The wheels squealed, the car sped off and he fell off the back of the car to the road. He broke his skinny neck and twenty-four hours later... done. Over for him, not for me.

I notice my left leg was shaking out of control. I had no idea how I would stand up when John finally came down that hall to get me.

I tried to focus on the anticipated safety of John's office and forget that Daryl was touching my body again…

Finally, I take a breath at the sight of my therapist. I don't remember John opening the door and letting me in. My only thoughts were focused on that ugly walking stick in the waiting room. I could only feel that violent jolt of the stick in the middle of my chest. He seemed to have poked a hole right into my soul striking the fears and shame that Daryl had planted there long ago… With each strike of his stick, he reminded me who was boss. He reminded me that he owned me. He held all the power. I was nothing but a bad little girl who now did whatever he said. That stick reminded me of the garage, of the smell of oil, smoke, beer, and the ugly thing he called sex. What hurt the most is that stick reminded me of where I longed to be… on the safe side of the wall.

Now in John's office, I cautiously allowed him to close the door. John had somehow earned my trust. John asked me to look at him and breathe. Then, without revealing any name or secrets, he reverently told me the story of the man holding the stick. He said that this man's stick was almost the only thing he owned… I had not seen him limp into the counseling center before he sat next to me touching my elbow. My nose was in a book. Somehow, after a while, John proved to me that this man's stick was used to help him walk, not to hurt me.

Once the walking stick crisis was averted, I felt the pressure of the previous day building up inside again. That huge volcano still active inside me needed a place to explode. My body trembled because it needed to pour out some painful hot lava. My problem then became, how could I let these words come out with John looking right at me. I didn't want him to see the dirty, shameful person that went back to the garage more times than I could remember, doing things I still had no words for. Now that I was in his office, all I wanted to do was runaway again. How would I reveal those words I tried to write in the privacy of my closet? I had destroyed those pages for a reason. Would I tell him that after I wrote those words in my journal, I vomited from disgust and then showered, rubbing my skin raw until it hurt? That after I wrote those words I had never spoken before, I cut my skin as if that is what I was supposed to do? I was sure it was not possible to let him see my face as I confessed this very small piece of my story.

After a long silence and many tears, I pleaded with him to turn the lights off. If he did that, his office would be totally black. There were no windows to allow for sunlight. I knew if he flipped that light switch he could not see my face. Genius, I thought... John tried to explain to me that I could share anything with him and that he would not judge me. He promised that whatever I had to share would not change how he regarded me. I thought, but you have no idea how horrible I am... This banter went on for a while in my head. Finally he said something that made sense enough to change my mind. It was simple. In order for him to be sure I was safe, he needed to see my face. At least that is what I heard. He agreed at one point to some sort of a compromise, but the lights stayed on. That was one battle I did concede to.

So with his chair facing mine in this little counseling room, I was now going to take the biggest risk of my adult life. I was about tell someone I had only known for a couple months that when I was six, I walked into this neighbor's garage, thinking I was trying out for a play and then walked out an unholy, pitiful, shame-faced girl. That this girl played a disgusting game where she took off her clothes and allowed this person, a neighbor, a bastard, an ugly, scary, dirty, hateful, bad man to do things to her that she did not know any-one ever did to anyone. Being so innocent, she did not know what the words sex, rape, assault, or the very least, molest meant. What she realized that day was that there really are no words or complete sentences to describe what happened to Little Kathy...me.

The heavy floodgates were cracked open just enough. Some of that hot lava was allowed to drip out. That day, John respectfully began to hold me up as I began to tell my story. My little voice for the first time had been heard. A few times over the years prior, I tried in little ways to tell, but never was quite loud enough to be heard. I am not sure those efforts to tell had ever really produced sound...

For a very brief moment after saying those softly spoken words, I remember a tiny bit of relief. My brief extended exhale was fol-lowed by panic. I immediately wanted to take it all back. I wanted to cut all my words into pixie dust and throw them away, but these words were not written on paper... What had I done? My very first words of this hidden truth had been told. The forbidden secret had been exposed. I just broke the number one rule. My head jerked around when I was startled by this screaming in my right ear. "DID I NOT TEACH YOU ANYTHING BITCH? YOU KNOW WHAT HAPPENS IF YOU TELL!!" Had John just yelled at me? I looked up at John from my lap where I had torn a huge pile of white tissues. He didn't look mad, but this familiar voice in my right ear was very mad... Had I not thought of what might happen if I told John, even in this most private room almost thirty years later? I knew the rules. What had I done? OMG, what will happen to John?... I should have never told.

A War of Words

it is so hard to fall asleep at night. every night, when it is time to go to bed my legs start shaking just a little bit. when my head hits my pillow and i dare to close my eyes, the noise begins. i hear those ugly Daryl words loud and clear, over and over. i can almost feel his breath on the side of my neck just above my ear. i really only hear the words in my right ear, because for some reason, he chose that ear to yell into. while we were in the garage he yelled softly, but then he came closer, so i was the only one that could hear. he didn't want people outside the garage door to hear him. i don't think anybody would hear him anyway, because his brother always mowed the lawn while i was in the garage. i used to love the sound of the lawn mower, but not anymore. i don't even like that cut grass smell anymore. when i here that sound or smell the fresh smell of cut grass, my ears ring and hurt, because it makes me hear Daryl's horrible words instead. how does that happen? feels like a trick to me. the only good thing about hearing his words when he is not really there is at least he is not breathing right in my face. i hate that smell much more than the tricky smell of grass.

he uses all the words that are probably on the bad list. some words i think he made up, because i never ever heard them before. they must be really bad words, because of how he says them. they are mean and sound dirty. if his friends are with him at the outside place, they laugh and say their own words, if he lets them. they can be loud there because it is in the woods where nobody lives. nobody can hear... i do wish somebody could have heard these words. maybe they would have come to see what all the noise was about. some of the yuckiest words he said were when he was doing bad stuff to me. i hated those words the most, because just like the smell of the cut grass, when i hear those words inside my head, i feel him right on me. sometimes when i am alone, i still feel his horrible skin on me, and i think i am there at the place i hate the most. i can't get away from his words, his body, or the place that i heard them spit into my ear. yuck, yuck, yuck... at night, when i open my eyes, laying on my own pillow, safely in my pink bedroom, i still have to try to find my way back from the outside place. it feels all mixed up. i don't feel safe anywhere, even in my bed, with my parents sleeping just downstairs. gosh, i wish i could just go tell them about these bad words. my parents never say those words, ever. they never even raise their voices very much. they say nice words. they smile and give good hugs. i love to be in my house... i hate when Daryl sneaks inside my head when i'm not looking. sometimes i wonder if he is really there, living inside my ear.

...he says, " SHUT UP, SHUT THE FUCK UP, YOU KEEP YOUR MOUTH SHUT, DON'T TELL ME NO, STOP MOVING, LAY STILL, STOP YOUR FUCKING SQUIRMING, NOT A WORD. I DON'T WANT TO HEAR ONE SOUND OUT OF YOUR MOUTH, NO CRYING, NOT ONE TEAR, JUST DO WHAT I SAY AND SHUT UP, YOU ARE A FAT PIG, YOU ARE AN UGLY, SLUT, HOAR. THEY ARE GONNA LIKE THAT PICTURE YOU DIRTY GIRL, DO YOU LIKE THE WAY THIS FEELS? YOU ASKED FOR THAT. MOVE AGAIN AND I WILL CUT YOU. WHAT WOULD YOUR MOMMY AND DADDY THINK OF THIS? DO THAT AGAIN AND I WILL CUT YOUR HAIR OFF. FUCK YOU!!! OPEN YOUR EYES. SHUT THEM AGAIN AND I'LL TAPE THEM OPEN. YOU CAN NEVER GET AWAY FROM ME. I AM THE ONLY MAN THAT WILL EVER BE WITH YOU. NO ONE WILL EVER LIKE YOU. NOBODY WILL EVER LOVE YOU. YOU ARE SO UGLY. YOU ARE ONLY MINE. YOU BELONG TO ME. YOU ONLY ANSWER TO ME. YOU WILL DO WHAT I TELL YOU. TAKE OFF YOUR CLOTHeS. PEE IN THAT BUCKET. NOW DRINK. YOU TELL ANYBODY AND I WIL KILL YOUR FAMILY, EVEN YOUR LITTLE BROTHERS, AND THEN I WILL KILL YOU. SEE THIS KNIFE, IT IS REAL SHARP... I WILL KILL YOUR LITTLE KITTY. I WILL SEND ALL THESE PICTURES TO YOUR FAMILY AND THEY WILL SEE HOW BAD YOU ARE. THEY WILL SEND YOU AWAY. THEY THINK THEY HAVE A GOOD LITTLE GIRL. HA HA HA HA!!!! YOU ARE PATHETIC. POOR LITTLE KATHY. I WILL BURY YOU RIGHT IN THAT HOLE IF YOU DON'T SHUT UP. DO YOU THINK THOSE BEADS HELP YOU? YOU CAN PRAY ALL YOU WANT. NO ONE CAN HEAR YOU..." and so many more words i can't make go away. they will just always live in my head, no matter what i do. i wish i could cut my right ear off, but everybody would see that and want to know why i did it. obeying Daryl's words is the only safe thing to do. i just hate hearing him when i try to sleep... will i ever sleep again?

at night the words are the loudest because i am alone and the house is quiet. i want to just run away, but i still would have my ear on my head, and i know that no matter where i run, the words would still be there. his words bring the ugly pictures to my eyes, and the pictures bring the yucky feelings. i just want to die. i can't get away from him. maybe he is right. i do belong to him. i will never be safe again.

when all this noise starts, it scares me. it's like i am right there in the garage. i can't take it. i thought when i crossed back over that wall back into my yard, i could be safe for a few days. how does he get in here? so i try to block the sound out. i pick up my transistor radio, put it tight against my right ear, and turn it on loud enough to hear, but soft enough so nobody else can hear. i am supposed to be sleeping. i pray for the radio station to play my favorite songs that me and Amy sing together. i make believe we are walking around the block in the sunshine with our radios pressed against our ears. my transistor was black and her's was white. this was one of our favorite things to do. we were always smiling and singing with our music. thinking about that makes me happy for a few minutes anyway, and then i hear his voice again. how does he do that? oh God, here it comes again. please make him stop. i put the radio down, because it is doing no good at all. well, maybe just for a couple minutes... i pull my tiny tears doll closer and reach for my rosary beads in the bed. maybe whispering my rosary softly out loud will block out this awful sound. i pray my Hail Mary's until my mouth is dry. if i stop, even for a second, the voice returns. i might as well be saying the alphabet or my multiplication tables. i know no one is hearing my prayer, because his mean words never stop... and then i realize the sun is out. thank God, it is morning. i am glad it is time to get up. i hope the noise of the day will keep me safe from his words for a few hours. i am just so tired...

Little Kathy does tell about those unforgettable words the best, because she heard them in her ear as they were said. I know those words very well because they never really stopped. His voice always lived in my head. There were years that I was able to block them out almost completely only to be replaced with a recurrent nightmare that began during the time I was being assaulted. This nightmare seemed to be the worst during the warmer months when the triggers of Daryl's assault were most present. The biggest trigger was the spring air… The first smell of spring, and my anxiety starts to escalate. After so many years of therapy, I have learned a lot about my triggers, but these feelings of fear and sadness just seem to sneak up on me and take hold. One big clue to me that the calendar has entered spring time is this nightmare which has nearly been impossible to describe, even now. There are no words in this repetitive nightmare, only feelings, which are almost worse than hearing his voice. The only words I have come up with to share to describe the nightmare are what my parents have told me that I reluctantly told them when I was little. So this is my best effort of finding words to describe this experience. I have always called this nightmare, "The Dream Feeling." I called it that, because the feeling came to me when I was asleep, and awake.

The descriptive words I came up with are: "Awfulness, Being eaten by a whale. No way out. Being buried alive, Suffocation. A space so big and empty that I am lost in it. Everything feels bigger than me, even though nothing is there, Being eaten alive. My arms and legs falling off. Being blind and unable to find anything to hang on to, Barely breathing. No air in this space. No colors anywhere. The ground dropping from underneath my bare feet. Panic. Get me out of here. Stuck in one place and unable to run…"

And that is about it. There are no buildings, rooms, people, or spoken words… just this awful feeling that jolts me from wherever I am, whether it is walking out the door into some fresh spring air or sound asleep in my bed. It is the most unwelcome guest.

I have spent my whole life since I was six running from the dream feeling in different ways, starting with Little Kathy's efforts of playing music in her ear, and blocking Daryl's words with her own words in prayer. Once I got into therapy, I begged for answers on how to make this indescribable dream feeling go away… I realize this was a big request, and like Dorothy in "The Wizard of Oz". I know now, that I am the only one with the power to rid myself of this demonic feeling and somehow find my way to safety… In therapy, questions about this dream feeling needed to be addressed. John's answer, until I could really face my demons was to replace these words and feelings with more positive ones.

One afternoon while writing this book, I took a break and was rummaging around in my closet to find a book and instead I found this beautiful box. The decorative box was covered by a backdrop of old fashion ornaments on a Christmas tree. The top of the box however, was covered neatly with a page out of a magazine. The magazine photograph was serene, with a winding river surrounded by fir trees, and a path to walk on. Some of those trees were barren, but still beautiful. The colors in the background were pale pink and lavender. I became both curious and excited at this interesting find. Taped onto that picture were the words, "Breathing Space." I turned the box over, to examine it further, and I found these words taped to the bottom. "You are not helpless, you aren't lost, and you don't have the right to give up on yourself." Then I remembered decorating this box a long time ago, but had no idea what could be in it. I opened the box and found a piece of crinkled yellow legal pad paper. When I saw the handwriting on this yellow paper, I knew right away who wrote this. It had been John's attempt to give me some new positive words to hopefully help win this battle of words in my head. These positive affirmations were attached to a Contract for Safety. The contract was written on the same type of yellow paper, but was not crinkled. It was smooth and looked official. The contract was signed by myself and John. On the other side of the contract was a list of things I was supposed to attempt to do over that weekend in November, so long ago. God bless him, he tried so hard to keep me safe on his weekends off and this was an attempt at that. Well, obviously, I honored the contract not to hurt myself, and I am proud I was strong enough to do that.

What I want to share with you are some of the affirmations I know I read over and over again that weekend, and many times after that. It is interesting that this paper is in very poor condition. I must have crinkled it up in a little ball at some point in disbelief, and then tried to flatten it out again. There are 25 of John's affirmations with one added by me at the end.

*All my feelings are valid.
*My feelings matter.
 I am important.
 I love myself.
 I accept myself.

I approve of myself.
I am just as important as anyone else.
I deserve love.
I am loving and lovable.
*I deserve good things.
*I can give voice to my feelings.
I am never alone, God is always with me.
I always walk in the light of God.
* I deserve to be treated well.
I can have the kind of relationship I want.
* I am a good person.
I have a lot to give.
*I deserve to be happy.
I make good choices now.
I am willing to let go of the past.
I let go of negative thinking.
I forgive myself.
I forgive all those who have hurt me.
*I am willing to change.
and I added,
* "I love to dance."

I remember when I read this list for the first time. I thought, "Are you kidding me?" Those were some really strong words, and half of them I totally did not believe. John had said it wasn't mandatory that I believe them. I did know in John's heart, he believed them, and for that time in my life that felt good enough. Back when John wrote these words, simply taking that paper home helped me feel less alone. I knew he took a lot of time making this handwritten list. The little stars next to some of the thoughts indicated the affirmations that I might have believed to be true. The others seemed ridiculous at the time. I couldn't imagine ever taking them into my heart. I guess that is why I crinkled the paper into a little ball.

Shortly after that, John created a tape with these affirmations, and many more, spoken with his voice accompanied by a background of soothing music. This tape was like a meditation for me during those nights when Daryl's words would not stop and I could not fight back alone in the dark of night. It really was John's voice against Daryl's. Thankfully, sometimes John's voice won the war of words, and I finally could get some desperately needed sleep.

John also created little signs for me with affirmations written on index cards. I took these cards, and placed them in inconspicuous places around my house. They were in places that I really needed them. They were next to my bed, inside the medicine chest, behind a mirror in my bathroom, in the closet where I hid sometimes, in the sunroom on my easel where I painted, and in the kitchen where the sharp things were. All this was about our safety, and armor against Daryl's words until I could really face my demons, and walk through the pain of my past. I am forever grateful John took on the challenge to fight these words with good words and reminders of God's love…

Today in the year 2021, Daryl's words do not live in my right ear anymore. They do visit sometimes. Then, the playful part of me, who loves "The Wizard of OZ"; thinks of what Glinda the good witch says to the wicked witch of the West. "You have no power here! Begone, before somebody drops a house on you, too!"… And sometimes it works.

Because There is Always Another Answer...

When I was a child there were so many times that I just wanted to die. I knew it was not the right thing to do, but I felt so hopeless and could see no other way out. I am lucky that somehow even with the huge secret I was keeping, I did not follow through with all my plans to end my life. I didn't think there was any place to turn, because I had to maintain that silence for the safety of all that I loved. Even with my fear-based, sworn silence, I was blessed with a family that loved me and I did have a sense of safety there. My family was the light in my very dark tunnel. I believe between my newly found inside parts and that safe side of the wall, I survived. WE survived... I am very grateful that somewhere way down deep, I found the strength of spirit to escape the pull to suicide and make it to adulthood, where I could safely ask for help again and again.

I kept many journals during my therapy years. Sometimes, out of desperation, I wrote several times a day just to stay alive. While I was writing this book, I found a page torn out of one of those journals

I had surrounded myself with as I wrote. I still don't know how or when I found this page, but I found it to be very important. The title at the top of the page got my immediate, undivided attention.

Suicidal ideation and the planning of my death was a very frequent occurrence during my trauma years, and then later during the healing from that trauma. In my daily journaling, suicidal thoughts were written about more times than I can count. I couldn't understand how sometimes these thoughts would pop up unexpectedly in the middle of what appeared to be unrelated topics. What I do know, is that all I wanted was the unbearable pain of my memories to stop. This chapter is about one of those moments in time. I start this chapter with the exact words from the torn out journal entry. I remember writing it with the encouragement of my therapist, John. I needed to have a page to grab, written in my own hand, to remind me of the reasons why I should not kill myself. Here is that page.

Reasons not to kill myself.

Because I love Timmy. He loves me. And he needs me to be his mother.

Because I deserve to live.

Because I won't let Daryl win.

Because my life has value even when I can't see it.

Because it was not my fault.

Because I will feel better eventually.

Because if I die today, I will never again feel the joy, freedom and strength I feel when I run.

Because if I die today, I will never again feel the love of my family and friends.

Because the seconds do not cease passing to the next... Because even if it feels like time has become an unbearably heavy stone, it is not. All I have to do is endure this weight and get to the next second.

Because the will to live is not a cruel punishment, even if it feels like that at times. Life is a precious gift.

Because I owe my inner children. They are the reason I am here. If I die today, I will erase the meaning of their suffering and incredible endurance. That is a great loss.

Because I already have the skills to find my healing path. I have done it over and over again.

Because I deserve Peace that will come after this battle is won, and it will be won. One minute at a time...

Because I am furious that I have suffered the pain of his evil and filth.

Because it is critical that I survive.

Because, you say it will get better. You say, I will be happier and know real love. You say, there is nothing gross about me. Because, you say I am lovable. Because you care about me. Because, you say I'm worth listening to. Because, you say my hands are clean and not tied anymore.

Because, you say I can use my voice.

Because I really want to know my little Girl inside... She must be very strong.

Did I believe all these reasons when I read them at times of need? No, not all the time. What was important at the time was I knew John believed these reasons to be true. And I trusted him.

This section of my story is broken up into parts, because each section is how I fought the daily thoughts of suicide and won. It's a look at the obstacles and gifts along the way.

And so it begins, my fight for life

I had been in therapy for a couple years. Twice a week I would meet with my first therapist, John. In the very beginning of therapy it was torture to drag myself to the counseling center, but as time moved on I wished I could be there every day. No amount of therapy seemed like it was helping. What I mean by that is, therapy got a lot harder before it got any easier. I had to first learn to trust this therapist enough to share my awful truth about what happened to me as a little girl. I had always remembered part of this history, but I had stuffed it all pretty deep. Saying those first words about the garage were almost impossible to spit out. Because I had so much practice, I was a master at hiding my past. In retrospect, I wished I could have just kept everything tightly tucked away. Now as I sit at this computer typing, I thank God and my inner strength for finally letting me find my voice. I do really believe, not opening this Pandora's Box would have killed me for sure. Little Kathy was the first to be scared silent and she set a very good example. I guess as an adult, I became desperate enough to dare to open up that rusted and tightly locked box. After verbalizing those first truths, I miraculously found that I was safe in telling John. I acknowledged the truth that because I told him, the ceiling did not fall on top of us, and we did not both instantly die. It became clear to me that John did not run, hide, or vomit at the sound of my voice. He did not tell me never to darken his door again. He supported me by listening intently to my words. He never judged me, but most importantly John believed me. He did not do what Daryl said someone would do if I told. He stood by me through very tough times.

Little did I know the hard work had only just begun. At that time, I didn't know there was so much more to tell. I also never imagined or would have chosen to actually feel what happened to me decades ago. When I was little I had perfected the art of dissociation.

I learned to protect my heart and my mind from insanity. Now, with this outpouring of my memory, each word became so painful. I had no idea a person could feel so much pain and still survive. I did not want to believe this happened to me. I certainly never wanted to say the words out loud. Once this secret box was pried opened, it unfortunately was too late to close it shut again. Everything inside me seemed to be pouring out like a raging river. With this deluge came all the fear I held tight within me. My main perpetrator was long dead and buried, but I still feared him as if he was still walking the earth. His words, his threats and promises were as real to me now, as they were when I was six. Walking out of John's office became a great feat. While dragging my feet, making my way to the car I was sure I would be grabbed from the parking lot, thrown into a van and kidnapped. I knew that those perps that were still among the living would come for me. I had broken the cardinal rule. I told… In my brain I was six again and Daryl was the boss of me. This may sound outrageous or even crazy, but this fear was very real. I was now in for the fight of my life. There was no returning to my commitment of silence. My words could not be undone. I really did tell. The worst part was, I was very sure Daryl knew.

I struggled with every waking move I made after that session. I was a nurse and a single mom. My son Timmy was about four years old at the time and the real light in my life. I had a great family and a few good friends. Long distance running was my ongoing obsession and doubled as a stress reliever. Timmy and I had a spacious, comfortable apartment which I could support on my own salary. My appearance was that I had a normal life. The outside view of me in no way matched what was going on internally. I literally felt my body and soul were being ripped apart, struggling to make my way through the horrific trauma of my past…

I stopped eating except for maybe string beans and water. I started cutting my skin in hidden places, just as I did when I was a little girl. My cuts were in Daryl's design. I now know that his cutting design, is the "Anarchy" symbol. I know that because I Googled the origin of this symbol that I occasionally saw on the backs of stop signs. He used this symbol both right side up and sometimes upside down. I remember the day I read the definition of this symbol for the first time. That definition spoke of sexual perversion, suicide and doing only what you wanted as a group or cult. One definition described who commonly used the symbol. The definition also spoke of hard rock music and drugs. Being an adult reading about this made me think that Daryl's picture should have been placed right next to the definition, since it described him perfectly. A part of me thought he must have created this symbol in the 1960's. The sight of this demonic looking symbol struck hard in my soul and would instill fear whenever I saw it in public places. I only knew it as Daryl's sign. That fact made me think he could still be around. Even though I hated and feared this anarchy sign, I still impulsively scratched it into my skin in hidden places. I guess it was one of my deeply implanted lessons I carried with me.

Once, I made a mistake while cutting and my secret got let out. I cut this hideous symbol into my hand. I didn't remember doing it. When I went to therapy the following day, I was upset and embarrassed that my artwork was visible. I shamefully took off my bandage and showed John the back of my hand. Again this was a secret only revealed in John's office. Together, John and I had to come up with a safety plan to prevent this unhealthy impulsive act. Developing a safety contract was a tall order because I literally didn't remember doing it in the first place. Some part of me inside had done this. Because I felt out of control where cutting was concerned, coming up with healthy steps to stop the process felt overwhelming. Before we actually came up with a strong safety plan, I did truly promise to tell him if and when I cut again.

From the very beginning, John always felt I needed more support outside of his office; maybe a close friend or family member. He was, of course, right, but in my mind that was not happening. Again, I fought for control of this decision. Opening up to anyone else terrified me. The fear that something bad would happen to anyone I told still raged on. The fact that John was not annihilated by a man with an Anarchy symbol on his forearm didn't convince me it was now safe to tell those I loved.

I was definitely leading two lives. On one hand I was a good mother, I held a good job as registered nurse, went to work on time, and kept a clean house. In retrospect, I have been told I appeared normal. What people didn't know was once Timmy was tucked comfortably in bed, I was sucked back to feel the feelings of my past trauma. These resurfacing feelings would just engulf me without warning. I felt powerless to shut them out. This unwelcome purging felt like air rushing out of a balloon after it had been blown up way too tight. The enormity of this experience resembled an emotional hurricane. The force of my trauma's angry storm knocked me to my knees. The days of having a rare unnerving flashback were gone. The quiet at the end of the day became a distant memory. The truth had been unlocked and was here to stay. I was going to have to face my demons.

Regardless of the pain, I kept going to therapy. Sometimes I would come home from John's office and feel some relief, but it was short lived. I did eventually agree to see a psychiatrist and get started on some medication for depression and the acute anxiety I was experiencing. I fought the idea of a psychiatrist tooth and nail, but deep down I was willing to try anything. Could an extra pill or two help this increasingly destructive pain? The antidepressant I had been started on when I began therapy did help give me more energy to move from one place to another for a while. I could almost pinpoint the exact moment the Zoloft kicked in. On the eighth day I swallowed my Zoloft, I felt like someone opened up a window to allow me to breathe. Then the Buspar I was prescribed helped my hands from shaking. It stopped the speeding feeling I had acquired from the high dose of Zoloft I was now on. Eventually he added Ativan to the mix to help during times of panic.

What I haven't mentioned yet was that once I started to tell my story in therapy, the nightmares I had been having most of my life turned into huge night terrors. For me, this was filled with screaming, sweating, and as the name says, terror. The sleep walking I thought I had escaped, started to resurface again more frequently. This was intolerable. I feared sleep and didn't get much of it. Adding sleepless nights to the mix was making it hard for me to function at all. The psychiatrist then started me on Restoril at bedtime and that did help somewhat. I did not like the idea of being on all this medication. I knew about Daryl's secret medicine he slipped into the soda he made me drink. This made part of me wonder if all medicine could be another trick.... Who was this psychiatrist anyway? I decided to trust John and took my medication as ordered. However, deep down I knew I now had a way out of my tortured existence if necessary. I now had pills to hoard... This was the beginning of my backwards safety plan. I would never breathe a word about this secret. Being a nurse I knew what words I had to avoid, to keep these pills coming, and did just that.

I pushed on through the remembering, saying the words out loud and believing I would just move past this. Quickly I realized, it was so much harder than simply having a voice for what happened to me. I had to also manage my everyday life of a working, single mom. It appeared I was doing that except for the fact that I was losing a lot of weight. In my head, anorexia became my friend. "Look what I can do?... You cannot make me put anything in my mouth I do not choose." Somehow, shrinking in size felt comforting to me. Being a size two felt awesome. Being a runner, I thought being lighter was a good thing anyway. At first people said, "You look so good Kathy. Are you loosing weight?" I had the perfect response. "I am running a lot. The weight just seems to fall off." Slowly without admitting it, I knew I was getting weaker. However, my determination to be in control of my food consumption was my strongest new super power, and I liked it, a lot. Having any power at all felt like a life saving gift. So my string bean diet continued. I always fed Timmy a good meal and I would pick at my food, to hide my decision not to eat. My mom, however, did not like to see me so thin. One time we went shopping for a dress to wear at an upcoming wedding. My brain thought I still wore a size eight or possibly a six. Through my clouded eyes, when I looked in that full length mirror, strangely I saw maybe a size ten or higher. Immediately I judged myself unfairly to be fat and ugly when I saw my image reflected back at me in the dressing room. I felt embarrassed, confused and claustrophobic in the fitting room that day. My mom brought an endless stream of decreasing sizes of the same beautiful dress and handed them to me through crack in the door. I had been hiding underneath baggy cloths for a while. I thought I could disguise my incredibly shrinking body from her. In a way I didn't want to hurt her, but mostly I didn't want her to try to stop me from hanging tight to my only super power...

Then she opened the fitting room door before I had my dress on and saw my ninety something pound body. She put her hand over her mouth, in shock at what she saw and started to cry. My story of running extra mileage was not going to fly here. This dreadfully honest visual terrified her. I could almost see her heart breaking. My mom thought I was dying of some horrible disease. She was probably right. It was just not the disease of cancer she was thinking. That moment scared me to death. Even though I had hidden the trauma in my life and lied to keep it a secret, I basically shared everything else with my mom. Very ashamed, here I stood, half naked with stark bold evidence that something was seriously wrong with me. Urgently, needing to protect myself, I was about to lie to her again. I was not ready to tell her my secret. I was forty something years old and still terrified she would be hurt physically if I told her. All Daryl's words were screaming in my head. When we got home, she sat me down and we did have a long talk about my weight loss. As painful as it was to lie yet again, I did. I tried reassuring her that I was okay and that I was just stressed. Adding one lie to the next, I explained that I had increased my running mileage and must not be eating enough. I promised to eat more and assured her I was not hiding any horrible diagnosis from her. What I knew that day was that my secret could not be hidden much longer. After we said goodbye that day, I knew she would share everything about our shopping spree with my dad. Therefore, I also knew this discussion was far from over.

40 Years Old, I Agree to Tell my Parents

Dealing with the past continued to get more difficult as each week passed. The feelings I was having did not seem to be compatible with life. Each day was a struggle. I was occasionally missing work. Sometimes therapy was at 4pm and I was scheduled to work at 11pm. If my session had been exceptionally difficult I was responsible enough to stay home. Being unable to focus at my job was not safe. There was this one co-worker and friend I knew was always looking for extra time. She knew I was going through tough times. All it took was a phone call and she would fill in for me. That inconvenient, last minute act of kindness was a gift I would never forget.

John continued to bring up the fact that more support outside his office was critical. I fiercely fought back against that. During that time my parents were keeping constant contact with me. The dressing room scenario opened my parents eyes and I was never far from their sight. My hiding skills were diminishing. They called every day and babysat Timmy when I was at work. They were extremely supportive without me ever telling them how much I needed them. I began to see the worry in their eyes, as they demonstrated their love for me.

In one of my therapy sessions, John did not let me avoid the discussion about the necessity of telling my parents. It was springtime. John had already gone through one spring and summer with me and knew what those seasons triggered for me. As soon as the weather started to warm up my worst triggers began to surface. Other than a few random visits to Daryl's garage, all my trauma took place in the warm months. I remember hating this particular therapy session with a passion. The terror of telling my parents was still very much alive. John did not back down, and while I hated that at the time, I am very glad he pushed me to tell them before the triggers of spring began. So I agreed they would be told, but it would be done my way. I needed a way to share the information, and still feel like they would be safe after they found out the truth. John and I collaborated on every detail while creating this plan. Somehow after several sessions, we came up with a way to tell what happened to me and still keep everyone safe from Dead Daryl's threats.

After much deliberation the disclosure plan was put on paper. It looked like a legal contract written on yellow legal paper and filled with stipulations. We agreed that John would actually tell my parents, so I didn't have to say all the words. My fear of payback from a dead man was like fire in my gut. Also, I did draw a distinct line in the sand in about actually giving my perpetrator a name. To me, saying his name out loud during this process felt like a death sentence. Once John told my parents I was sexually assaulted when I was a young girl, I would then answer the questions I could. Therapeutically, I am sure John would have preferred I tell my parents directly, with him merely present for support. I, however, was simply not strong enough at that point. Because John believed I desperately needed my parents support concerning this enormous issue, he felt any plan that revealed the truth to my parents, was a good plan.

My challenge was getting them to John's office without totally scaring them to death. On a designated day, I stopped by my parent's house with the intention of deciding on a date and time to meet at John's office. That afternoon, I nervously settled myself into our family's old black rocking chair in their kitchen. I chose that spot to take on this difficult task because of the comfort this chair possesses. The history of the rocker felt important on that day. That, and I chose the closest available chair before my wobbly legs buckled. I didn't realize how scared I was until my butt hit the chair. I wished I had my yellow legal paper scripting what I was supposed to say. I remember thinking why am I so afraid to invite them to a therapy session? That really was my only mission on this day, but I was already anticipating the enormity of what was to come. Trying to appear calm, I focused for a moment only on my body sitting in this sturdy old chair. I appreciated the decorative cushions my mom had placed there. My back felt supported, and God knows the back and forth motion of the rocker was soothing my escalating anxiety. My arms fit perfectly onto the cool wood that the chair's arms offered. The wood felt smooth because the black paint had been worn off from my parent loving arms resting there. I knew all three of their children, and now their grandchildren had been rocked to sleep by this old relic. I guess maybe I wanted to feel all of that as I began to roll this ball of truth down a hill into their laps. Would there be a way to stop this ball from rolling if it became too painful? Was there any turning back after this family therapy session?… I felt myself rocking just a little bit faster, envisioning any old rocking chair moments I could recall. Taking a deep breath in, I wondered, when are we too big to be rocked by a parent in a chair such as this? Quietly, my adult body yearned for that.

Disguising all this drama from within, I casually asked my parents to come with me to therapy that next week. To my surprise, they agreed immediately, but my mother looked like she might cry as the request came out of my mouth. She moved from the other side of the kitchen island coming closer to me, looked right into my eyes and said, "Kathy, you are scaring me." Because I had noticeably continued to lose more weight, she again asked me if was dying of cancer. I compassionately told her no, but I really needed them to join me that coming Monday.

Thankfully, that was just a couple days away. I know the anticipation of this session was going to be as horrible for them as it was for me. Their warranted interrogation did not stop with her first question. Had I been in their shoes, I would have had just as many urgent questions. Eventually, my mom bravely asked me if somebody had hurt me. I absolutely knew what she meant by that, and she was right on target. This one question knocked the wind right out of me. I remember thinking I might slide right off the rocking chair which was no longer in motion. I don't know why, but their obvious curiosity was not part of my plan. I had no idea how to field these questions. Finally after tears and hugs, I did say a few words I had not planned on. I told them that when I was a little girl someone did hurt me, but

I just couldn't say anymore till we were in John's office. As I think back, that was so unfair to them, but at that moment I was not strong enough to pursue this any further. I remember one other very difficult question my mom asked me that tore my heart out. She very somberly asked, "Was this person anyone we love?" Pausing, I generously promised her that the answer was, "No." During that most incomplete conversation, I remember promising that we would all get through this, and that I trusted John to help us. As expected the next couple days were tough, but not as hard as that life changing session.

So once again I got no sleep Sunday night. I really didn't know how this therapy session would play out. What I did know, was that my lifelong secret was about to be exposed to the two people I promised not to tell; ever. I wondered how high the price would be for breaking the most important rule of them all.

Crawling out of bed that Monday morning, I felt like I was running on empty after chasing sleep for eight hours. I awoke bug-eyed, nauseated and shaking like a leaf. I took my morning medication and counterproductively grabbed a large coffee. I searched for some kind of balance, and desperately prayed to get through this extended therapy session. I had balked at the idea of tacking on an extra 30 minutes to this meeting. My thoughts were to get in and get out with as little pain as possible. Who was I kidding?

There we were, sitting in the waiting room at the counseling center. I introduced my parents to the nice secretary at the desk which somehow lightened the tension a little bit. Watching John come down the hall to get us, made this part of my journey a reality and I wanted to puke. This may seem like a lot of drama for what was about to happen. For me, what I was about to do, felt as scary as walking into Daryl's garage.

Our therapy space looked different that morning. John had brought in more chairs to accommodate all of us. I chuckled to myself thinking, there are so many others here with us. I could already feel the fear coming from the kids inside. We all appeared to get comfortable, but the anxiety was running high. Thankfully John stepped right in and began the session. He guided us cautiously through to the end. John followed our plan just as we had discussed. He said, for me, the words I could not get out. My parents cried. I remember sitting glued to my chair, with my legs shaking uncontrollably, and wondering where I was going to get the courage to speak one syllable. On one hand, I wanted to undo the words already spoken by John, and run out of the room saying, I made this all up. I wanted to take back every word I had told John, and live my life out in silence, as I did for the 40 years of my life. What I was feeling was that I had just severely hurt the parents I loved so much. Why did they have to know? Couldn't I just do this all myself? I went through it myself, and survived… But the words had been spoken, and could not be unheard. I was going to have to walk through life in a different way now. My secret was told. With Pandora's Box now wide open, I knew my parents would now have a million legitimate questions I had no idea how to answer.

In that ninety minutes I did not tell them who it was. I did reiterate that it was no one from our family. My dad really wanted to know who the perpetrator was so he could kill him. My mother was grateful that it was no one we loved. I told them that I was about nine when it happened and that it happened only for a couple years. I know this was still lying a little, but their faces looked so anguished, I could not dig this knife any deeper. I couldn't really tell them about Daryl's lure tactics, because then they would know the name of my perpetrator. I realized Daryl was dead, but his parents were not. Also his two siblings were still alive. The realistic fear of my dad approaching them terrified me.

There was one more absolute that was included in making this revelation a safe one. I made a huge request of my parents. I begged them not to tell another soul about what we had just shared with them. I felt terrible about this request. Just as I needed support to heal, now they certainly did also. I needed time to work through the reality of finally telling my parents. In the end as rough as it was to honor this request, they respected the pace of my journey out of silence.

John helped guide us through the next part of the session. He calmly invited all three of us to share our feelings. With tears falling on my dad's cheeks, I remember his strength assuring me he would have made the assaults stop. At one point, my parents were facing each other as they questioned how they missed all this. They wept that these crimes happened on their watch. My heart broke to hear these private words between them. I knew just how hard Little Kathy and the others had worked to protect our family from Daryl's evil threats. In my adult heart I knew my parents would have gone to the police so many years ago, but in those dark days Little Kathy simply could not tell.

That is about all I can remember of that session. I know John somehow pulled us together, so we could make it back home. We both assured my parents that between therapy, medication, and their support, I would work through my past in a healthy manner. I think they left the counseling center cautiously reassured, however, I was not convinced. I was still of the belief that we would get into an accident on the way home, that our homes would be burned when we got there, and that we would die during the night.... I guess I knew telling my secret was the right thing to do on one level, but I underestimated the depth of my fear which had just escalated beyond my imagination. When I hugged my parents in the parking lot, I was aware my world had just changed forever.

Once I shared my trauma with my parents they did exactly what John expected. They were there for me with as much support they could give, in all aspects of my life. Mission accomplished.

Abandonment

From the dates in my journals, I find that in January, after sharing my secret with my parents, things started to change in therapy. One thing that happened was that I started to remember some of my most difficult experiences from the past. These memories were mostly Rose's. The things that happened were dark and unimaginable. Unthinkable words and flashbacks were coming wildly to the surface. At night, my private time was filled with a terror I had never felt before. Most nights, I did not figure I would see the morning sun. I lost so much time during all this, I was grateful for the rising and setting of the moon and sun. The adult parts of me would set my alarm clock many times during the day, to just get me from one place to the next. The weight of these memories was so heavy. We could not carry them alone. I went to therapy, and did really hard work, trying to get all of this out of our body and soul. This was a slow, painful process that would not be processed quickly.

As I struggled with this, apparently a change had taken place in the Counseling Center, where my sessions took place. What I was hearing John say to me the first day he brought it up was very upsetting to me. His boss had told him that day, that he was being given more responsibilities, and that would interfere with my therapy time. He was going to have to decrease my sessions, from twice a week to once. I remember feeling that hot rush of panic flow from my chest to every part of my body. This may sound a little dramatic, but all I could feel was every molecule of air being removed from his office. I felt like I needed rescue oxygen. This was an old familiar feeling in itself. "Please John open a window."

The next few random quotes are from my journal at the time when this transition was taking place. I share them with you, to give you a peak of my perception of the changes being made and how they made me feel. These quotes are in order of time, after the changes were made.

"It will be hard to see John just once a week. I have never done well with that. I don't want to go backwards. I need some consistency. One hour a week. I am afraid. John said, we could work something out with phone calls. Oh I don't know. Take a breath Kath. Let's see what happens."

"I need to talk to John, but I have this feeling he is too busy. He says, there is just no time to see me twice a week. The Andria part of me keeps repeating, 'It just doesn't matter. I don't matter. We are not important anymore'.... John just wants to cut our time down, and is blaming it on the system. Afraid to call. Not important enough. If we have a set back, too bad. No time. Unsafe. Can't seem to connect each session. Last session was too short. This is not going to work. I am feeling forgotten. I believe John's words, but if his time is filled, it's filled. I am very uncomfortable calling in a crisis. I feel like an interruption in his day. A bother."

"I feel a commitment being broken. I can't ask for what I need to heal safely."

"You said, 'Even if you got worse, I still can't see you more than once a week.' That scares me."

"Why does the Counseling Center slack, have to be picked up from my time? Let's let her go back down into the dark. Just one more needy pathetic client, (DEB 136-my privacy number). I feel like a number, not a person. Boy does that feel familiar."

"I am a wreck. I need a session with John. No one else really gets this stuff. And God, Michael (my boyfriend), should not have to deal with all this. I will stuff it all again. Oh Fuck it. Just shut down. We can do that. Go back the way it was before therapy. Shut down. Safer. Less risk. Once a week sessions open a can of worms (or snakes). The snakes run all over me, and can't find their way back to the can they came from. Then I have to leave with these snakes slithering at my feet."

"My message to John probably won't get to him. He won't remember our 3 pm Monday appointment. I want to throw up."

"You said, 'Call a Crisis line'...This will not work. There is no backup. He does not hear me. No one ever did. It's too much to figure out, with all this inside confusion, in 55 minutes. Rip me open. Mess everything up. Bring the kids out. Challenge everything. I want to die. Much easier. Let me just die, please. Why keep going? I feel defeated. I'm drowning. No one hears or cares. Thrown to the jungle...."

"There use to be time to talk about the past, and how to do my daily life in the process. Now, with so little time, I can't work on either in any depth."

"And so I took a small breath, and dared to say all my fears and concerns about the time constraints of therapy. Then came the word 'Abandonment'. John actually said the word. All of my fears and doubts fell out all over the room. I told him, I have not felt his support, whether it was there or not. All the events, and words said in the past few weeks, made me feel like I was floundering, and put back in Rose's hole.... Rose felt, 'what haven't i done right? you said you wouldn't hurt me if i did what you said. so i did. - now you throw me to a place i can't get out of. i'm afraid to cry or ask for help. you'll get mad. how do i be?'"

" Rose really said that just right. We did feel left in the hole. Alone, with no one to save us except maybe Daryl."

"My fear of abandonment is so overwhelming. No one thinks I should have this feeling. My parents didn't abuse me. My abandonment came to me in other ways. When the word is brought up, my first feeling is Rose's hole. The 'No Way Out' of the hole. The no one will rescue me, from the hole.The where are my mommy and daddy?? The silent scream, of the hole. The no one can hear me, of the hole. The useless hope, of the hole. The dirtiness, of the hole. The leave me there to die, of the hole. The need to die, of the hole. Then the trick of the hole. Daryl reaches down to help me get out. Does he care? Does he like me? Am I safe now? Rose says no."

"Therapy sounds exhausting and hopeless. How do we even go there to-morrow? Don't even know what to do, say, or feel. Too much. Too little time."

"I don't need this kind of therapy. How can I do this? I feel worse when I leave, knowing that is it is 6 more days until I come back. Can't get to the next Monday. So maybe I shouldn't go at all. I feel defeated. I'm drowning. No one hears or cares.Thrown back into the jungle. I hate Mondays."

"No safety net. To me, it feels like I have nothing to hang on to. Calling you doesn't even cross my mind at really bad moments. I don't feel wel-come to do that. The feeling is, you are too busy. You might as well be on vacation. That is what I feel like between sessions. Before, I could feel safe with your words, and what I saw in your eyes. Now I don't see your eyes the same way. Your voice sounds angry to me. Today, I left your of-fice and cried for another 15 minutes. I couldn't even leave the parking lot. I would have gone directly to cut myself, but I didn't want Michael to see the mark. Is it a good thing to leave therapy in worse shape than when you came in?... AND IF YOU SAY THAT IS MY CHOICE, I'LL SCREAM!!"

"One more week until spring begins. Nothing will happen like the past. It is 1995 not '65. I know that, but the smell of Spring goes right to my center. First the smell of the air brings a flash of a happy little girl, picking flowers in her yard. Then my next breath is linked to torture, and shame. I want this to stop. I want to be like other people. I want to feel whatever spring fever is... That is what happened today, when I walked through my yard, and saw all the early crocuses. I thought briefly, what a pretty color and then began to cry, and struggled to breath. I felt that shaking in my legs, again"

These entries in my journal were intertwined with entries dealing with abuse issues, and then special moments with Michael, work, and Timmy. I was dancing as fast as I could, trying to live my life, but was slowly starting to feel like I was on my own. I was losing my lifeline. I know now, that was my perception at the time. I guess that is all that mattered in retrospect. The memories and effects of my past were so overwhelming, and challenging them alone felt impossible. I realize after reading back in this journal, the feelings of abandonment I was experiencing within the current situation were triggering the feelings from my childhood trauma. My abandonment started when Rose was lowered into the hole. She felt like her parents were so far away, even though she went home to them after each encounter with Daryl. Her fear and silence isolated her. The limited number of therapy sessions with John brought her aloneness to the surface, and actually given a word. Abandonment felt unbearable.

A Walk in the Park?

My nightmares got much worse. I essentially had slasher dreams repeatedly about my parents being cut up, and left to die. I dreamt about being assaulted over and over again. Waking up terrified, sweating, and crying became a nightly occurrence. John had made me a tape of his voice with calming words and affirmations. In this tape he assured me I was safe. This tape lived next to my bed all set up in the tape player. All I had to do was press play and listen. This was on many nights, and got me through until morning and the blessing of daylight. John's safe voice kept me from giving up in the middle of the night. It certainly helped me more than my medication during that time frame.

I know this will sound crazy, but in the middle of this nightly drama, I actually was reacquainted with an old friend from my past. What is even more startling, we somehow became boyfriend and girlfriend. Much to my surprise, I let him into my isolated world with only a slight reluctance. The fact that he had already been a trusted high school friend some 20 years earlier, allowed me to grant him early entry into my tightly locked heart. His face, his voice and handsome presence said safety to me. Almost instantly this relation-ship brought some happiness, relief and dare I say respite into my life. I enjoyed everything about this unexpected rekindling. One of my fondest memories of jumpstarting our relationship took place sitting in his bedroom which doubled as his office. It was a large room that felt comfortably casual. It was complete with a sitting room which felt safe, even though there was a bed on the other side of the room. That day we shared some wine, listened to great music both current and historic for us. The important part of this afternoon is that we talked for hours. I remember sitting on a chair, wearing his sweatshirt, with my feet up on his desk. There were just enough windows scattered in this spacious room to allow for all the air I needed to breathe. As this timeless encounter unfolded, I remember asking myself, "Where is my panic?" As I secretly smiled at my pri-vate internal conversation, the only answer I came up with was, "Not here and not today."

Michael had a beautiful dog, named Bella. She was ever present, making us always a threesome. Historically, I was always a bit afraid of dogs, but she was so calm and sweet. Because she was always so close to me, I figured it was a sign that she liked me, or she was covertly protecting her dad. My real take on Bella was that she had learnt her gentleness from Michael. That thought made Michael even more attractive in my eyes. You could see the unconditional love Michael had for this beautiful, golden brown Vizsla. I admired their relationship. My observation of this truly said something to me about the man I was sitting face to face with. I caught myself smiling as I listened to Michael's voice speaking so gently to her. I felt blessed to have an unspoken microscopic look into Michael's capability of earning Bella's love and trust, which is exactly what I hoped for in a relationship. I wondered, could I really trust that much? That day I learned not to fear Bella and welcomed her snuggling against my leg.

That first afternoon enjoying Michael's company made me feel like maybe I was normal. During those hours of intimate conversation, I told him the abridged version of my past. Somehow skipping the chit chat of college stories and business moves in his life seemed ok. By the end of that Saturday, he knew I was in therapy and involved in a group for survivors of childhood sexual assault. He also knew what medications I was on. All of that seemed okay to him. I had not yet gone into any real depth of what had happened to me. And did I really have to? Everyone had a past, right?…

My new developing relationship felt delightfully strong, and I sincerely believed it could grow into something lifelong. One spring day shortly after we started dating, we decided to go for a walk, on a marked trail in the woods. This trail was actually located on a map about an hour away from his house. It had a sign designating it as a known trail with a name. There was a small parking lot with instructions and restrictions listed on a park sign. All these things gave me comfort by indicating that this was a well known place. While we were parking the car and looking at the entrance to the wooded area, I did notice a slight familiar shaking in my legs. I acknowledged this nervousness by placing my hand gently on my left leg. I thought that might calm Little Kathy and give her some comfort, allowing me to enjoy this afternoon walk.

I longed to feel normal. In therapy, I had learned techniques to help hold me in the present. I learned that if I encountered something triggering a memory from the past, I should try to see how both situations were different. I thought to myself, "I got this!" I went right to work on this mental exercise. In my mind I set up two columns, a "Present"column, and a "Daryl"column. Daryl's place in the woods definitely did not have a sign, with a name, or a parking lot. In the present, I would be walking next to a man that I felt safe with. I was never safe walking the wooded path with Daryl. With Daryl, I had a t-shirt covering my face and a belt around my waist like a leash. On this day, Michael would gently hold my hand. My other hand would hold loosely Bella's leash. I could see the two columns in my head and they were totally opposite. Recognizing the differences of the past and present slowed my heart rate and stopped my left leg from shaking. I actually felt a smile forming on my face as we unloaded the trunk. Maybe, this could just be a sweet nature walk.

So, off we went carrying our picnic lunch we had packed in a small backpack. The walk into the woods was so quiet and enjoyable. Even though the mere smell of spring is always a big trigger for me, when we started out it felt like a little piece of heaven. This was not a hike. We did not have to climb any hills. I was glad about that. Climbing a hill in the woods, would just be one more emotional challenge to file in the past column. One thing I knew for sure about this adventure was, if it got to be too much for me, we would just turn around, go home, and it would be ok.

About half way through the walk I noticed that Michael had gotten a little quiet, but I thought he was just taking in the pretty surroundings. As we got further into the woods, I sensed him physically guiding me. He went from quiet to very talkative and pointing out different pretty things he was noticing as we walked. I thought, how sweet he is. Then he said we should probably turn around and look for a spot to rest and eat our lunch. It was mid afternoon and I was getting a little hungry. The lunch we packed was light, healthy, and contained all safe foods. My anorexia continued pushing it's way into the day.

On our way back, again Michael kept guiding my steps. My women's intuition for some reason questioned what he was doing. I remember seeing an inviting clearing up ahead. I thought it would be a pretty spot to lay down our tablecloth, and eat lunch. I started to walk towards the clearing, and I felt him lightly tug my arm. He said he saw a better place a little farther down the trail. Even though it was unlike me to stand strong, and say what I wanted, I did. Gently pulling back, I said, "Let's eat over here. Bella likes it here."

As I stepped into the clearing, I saw what Michael was avoiding. What stood before me, was what he was trying to protect me from seeing. He was hoping he could get me out of these woods, having only experienced a nice walk in a park. Instead, he knew, in a flash I was about to fly like lightening back into my past. And Michael was right.

We could see that people had spent a lot of time in my chosen picnic spot. In front of me, there were beer cans, pieces of clothing scattered on the ground, and a couple camp fires made of rocks. Even before I got close enough to see details, I had an idea what I would find. In my mind I had already seen a place just like this. I could feel it in my body first, which by now was shaking like it was 20 degrees, not 65 and sunny. I felt drawn to the trees that surrounded the clearing. On these trees were pictures carved into the bark. There were also pictures, painted in red, on the same trunks. The picture that cracked my protected heart wide open was of Daryl's symbol. The anarchy symbol was carved everywhere.The other pictures were stick figures of people with weapons. On one tree there were red lines, painted horizontally across the tree, from the bottom of the trunk traveling up to where the branches were. I moved closer to the center of the clearing and stood in front of an old campfire surrounded by old stones. As much as I wanted to get away from this spot, I felt an uncontrollable magnetic pull to move closer. I wanted to see what this place was. It felt so familiar. The familiar feeling made me dizzy and short of breath. When I was close enough to smell the remnants of an old campfire, my stomach felt sick. My legs weakened like they had no muscle at all. When I looked down into the ashes, there were remains of something other than timber. Something that had bones...

By now, Michael had a good hold of me. I am sure he just wanted to pick me up and get me out of there in one piece, but I had been sucked into this space and I was going nowhere. The next few minutes were a mass of confusion and chaos. My efforts to stay in the present were now failing terribly, no matter how hard Michael tried to have me focus on him and Bella. I wanted to run, but my legs would carry me nowhere. I felt them buckle underneath me. I did not feel safe at all, now on my knees. I was sure Daryl would show his ugly face at any minute. My stomach hurt and I heaved like I would vomit, but nothing came out. I felt like I couldn't hold my urine. In one brief moment, I felt so many things. Terrified, like

Little Kathy, angry like Rachel, and fearing death like Rose, all at the same time. I did push my self back up to standing and started to run towards the car. Something immediately switched inside. I stopped dead in my tracks and ran back to fight someone that was not there. I think Michael had taken my lead by now, and just tried to keep me from hurting myself. At one point when we were both feeling Rachel's presence (the angry part of me) I remember Michael handing me a rock, which you might think was dangerous. What I didn't realize was that Rachel was scraping the tree bark with her fingernails, trying to remove the red stripes. Inside WE knew what those red horizontal lines meant. To Daryl and his friends, each red line was like notches on the belt of a pedophile. This was a rapist's score card. So, as Rachel tore at this red paint with her fingers, Michael handed her the rock, to protect my hands. I remember him telling me to try to use my voice as WE scraped at the bark. I do believe sound came out of my mouth that day. I don't remember if I said words or screamed. In retrospect I think I was being very brave, even though I am pretty sure I looked like a person having a full mental breakdown. He coached me a bit, which helped because having an angry voice was not my biggest strength. This release went on until exhaustion took over. I fell to my knees and cried into my hands. Sitting on the ground, Michael held me as I wept. When I was finally calm he helped me to my feet. He gathered our stuff, found poor Bella, and we made it back to the car. Once in the car with doors locked, I had no words for what had just happened. I felt confused, like I was lost in a fog. My head was killing me and I just wanted to disappear.

Afterwards, I couldn't remember the details of this unexpected disaster. This had been the worst flashback I had ever gone through. Later that night, Michael and I slowly tried to untangle what had happened earlier. After hearing him talk to me about what he saw me go through, I felt ashamed and embarrassed that I was unable to stay present. It was discouraging that all my defenses had been shattered. I was compassionate enough with myself to understand I had never been exposed to such intense triggers before, but I still just felt defeated. I was feeling more like a victim than a survivor once again. Afraid to ask, I wondered, what must Michael think of his girlfriend now?... Was I ever going to be free of my past?... And who would ever want to live with anyone like me?... One of Daryl's best lines was, "NO ONE WILL EVER LOVE YOU!" After that day, I was sure Daryl was right. I never did sleep that night. I was so afraid of what nightmares I might have. I did not want Michael to have to comfort me any more that day. Normally, I hated to leave his house when the weekend was over, but this Sunday I wanted to get back home. My confidence had been seriously damaged, and I feared I would just break into a million pieces. That was not going happen in front of this man I loved. Stuffing all of this away sounded like the best plan. The only place I might choose to talk about this would be in John's office. I seriously questioned, would I make it alive to my next appointment? Could I hold my breath that long? During Daryl's assault on me, I learned that breathing brought tears, and I could not safely have them until I got to that appointment.

Get to the Next Second. Just Try...

The next couple weeks were the worst I had ever lived through since I was a little girl laying on that altar. I don't remember much about the days between that Sunday with Michael and whenever my next session was scheduled for. I lost so much time. I had flashback after flashback. I did not eat or sleep much. I was dry heaving and experiencing diarrhea throughout each day. I was sure I was just going to die. Then one day not long after that walk with Michael, I remember calling my parents, lying and telling them that I got called in to work. I needed them to take care of Timmy, not because I was going to work, but because I did not feel healthy enough to be present for him the way he deserved. I promised myself, I would get the help I needed while Timmy was with them. I sincerely meant that promise, that I almost didn't keep...

Once I had Timmy safely in my parents care, everything just spiraled down. I could not rest, and yet didn't have the energy to reach out to John like I should have. I felt totally engulfed with the fear and pain of my past. I reviewed in my head all my sins that could have brought me to this terrible place. I had told the secret to my parents. I broke Daryl's #1 rule, and was paying for it. I was obsessed with that thought, and knew I would not win this battle. Daryl was stronger than me. I knew all of his friends from the motorcycle gang, had not died. Still living in the same town I was brought up in, I had seen them around. They were older and all ugly as ever. They were still riding motorcycles with their faces covered with bandanas. I felt like it was only a matter of time before they broke into our apartment, and it would be over. With that thought, I felt unable to protect Timmy or my parents.

I found myself curled up in a ball more than once in the closet holding my rosary beads tight in my hands. I felt the need to get away from the terrorizing noise in my head. I had no idea how or when I crawled into my hiding place. All of us inside were just trying to get safe. Cuts were starting to show up on my skin, and I was having some unscheduled vaginal bleeding. I obviously was hurting myself, but had no knowledge of those assaults to my body. When fully oriented to my surrounds, my only thought was to end this unbearable existence. I knew suicide was supposed to be the wrong decision, but I felt like I was no good to anyone and that me being alive would eventually get my loved ones hurt. I knew Daryl's promises would be kept. He already took one child from me while in my body, and I feared for Timmy's safety. As I write these words I understand just how sick I was at that time. The PTSD caused by my past was at it's very worst. I couldn't see myself regaining any control of these symptoms. I could't take it anymore. My Son deserved better than this... and I had to protect my parents. I had no hope of being strong enough to work at my job as a nurse that I had taken such pride in. How could I take care of anyone else, when my best thing was hiding in a closet, with rosary beads in one hand, and a knife in the other? I could no longer think of one person to reach out to. Who would want to listen to these crazy thoughts? If I told Michael, why would he want to stay with me. Could I really even get better? That day I thought not...

So my plan to end my life began. I knew I would not end it with a lot of blood everywhere. I did not want my family to find me in a pool of blood. The easiest course of action was to use my pills. I always had that thought in back of my head since I started taking them. I knew if I could not tolerate the healing process after such trauma, I had a way out. That monthly refill gave me great comfort. With unsteady hands, I took out all my pill bottles from the shelf in the medicine cabinet. I remember dropping them twice in the bathroom. I got one of my journals out. My plan was to write a short individual letter to my parents, to Michael, and John explaining why I was about to do this. And then of course one for my precious son. Oh God, how would I write that letter?

With my pill bottles all lined up on the bedside table, I very calmly took off my clothes, took a hot shower, applied my favorite lotion to my scarred skin. I already knew which dress I would wear. It was the beautiful black dress, I had worn the night I was reacquainted with Michael. I didn't have the energy to put on the little makeup I usually wear. I knew I could not lift my arms to fix my hair, so I didn't. Sitting on the edge of my bed I emptied my pill bottles one by one. Having just been to the pharmacy I had a full supply of everything. I counted out 90 tablets of Ativan, 30 tablets of my sleeping pills, 30 tablets of Zoloft, and 80 tablets of BuSpar. Certainly that would do it. I always had a big glass of water right by my bed, and it was full. The phone was sitting there too. It felt far too late for a phone call. No one could help me, not even John who I had once trusted to get me through this for a couple years. I knew I could not be helped now. Daryl had me all over again, just like he did when I was six. He may not have been standing in front of me, but he was always in my right ear, as loud as ever. So there would be no distress phone call that I had promised to make at times like this. That ship had passed.

My next task was to write my four goodbye letters. I felt totally numb, almost sleepy as I prepared to die, until I picked up my favorite pen. Putting pen to paper had always been an easy way to express my feelings, but this was not just a journal entry. The letters I was about to write were going to hurt the people I loved the most. I began to cry as I wrote, starting with John's, then Michael's, my loving parents, and then the most important one, Timmy's. I took a couple Ativan to help me through this part of my plan. I dreaded Timmy's letter the most. I loved him with every fiber of my being, as broken as it was. Sitting there, for what seemed like forever, my hands shook as I held my pen hovering over my journal, but no ink was ever put on the paper… Every moment I had spent with my son in the 5 years before was flashing through my crowded, confused mind. I remembered every minute of Timmy's delivery into the world. I actually could smell his newborn skin. He was my gift from God. Even with the complication of being left to be a single mom, he brought nothing but joy to my life. He was that light at the end of my very dark tunnel… Did I just think that?… How could I leave him alone without a parent? I knew my parents would raise him with love, but they were not his Mama. Thoughts began to sneak into my head that maybe this was not such a great plan. I had always put Timmy before me. Could I put him first now? Could I try one more time to survive my personal hell? Could I stop the process I had started today? Could I find some crippled strength to pick up the phone just a few feet from my reach? I looked up from the tear stained paper, saw my pills lined up so neatly waiting to be swallowed, and took one short little breath. In my head I could hear my inner voice say, "Just try."

As if watching my body move, without feeling I dragged myself from my bed, took off my pretty dress, changed into my tiny pair of jeans, now baggy on my body and struggled to pull a warm sweater over my head. I felt so cold. I hugged my shoulders, not out of caring for myself, but to get warm. With my hands still shaking, I returned my pills to the appropriate bottles, and walked barefoot into the kitchen. I saw a slightly bloodied steak knife on the counter. I knew where that had been, because I could now feel some familiar pain on my upper thigh where I must have cut. I cleaned the knife and put it away. I picked up the phone, sat on the kitchen floor against the oven door so I wouldn't fall, and dialed the memorized seven numbers that would connect me to John. Saying a quiet prayer that I was doing the right thing and that he could help me, someone answered quickly. I told the secretary who I was and that I needed to talk to John. I told her it was an "Emergency." It's funny, I had been very close to this spot many times before, but never knew what the word "Emergency" really meant. When did I feel I was in enough trouble to call it an emergency? I guess this was that moment.

John picked up the phone. God only knows what I said, but he got the message. I do know I told him part of what I had started to do, and that I could not get through this alone. In my heart I thought he would just say come to my office, but that was not the case. I must have told him too much, and he said I needed to go to the hospital. Hospital? I can't go to a hospital! Once again, I remembered Daryl saying I would be locked away for being crazy if I told what he had done to me. I was not going to a hospital. I hung up the phone. Without pause, John called right back. I answered after deliberately listening to it ring several times. I told him my litany of reasons why there was no way I could go to a psychiatric hospital. John had a supportive answer for each reason. Losing my job and my son were my main fears. Then of course, there was that pesky Daryl instilled fear, that the doctors would never let me out of the psych ward, once I was locked in there.

Together, John and I came up with a plan on how this was going to work. I fought him every step of the way, but somehow we agreed on a plan to admit me to a nearby psychiatric hospital. He did threaten to call an ambulance to come get me if I did not commit to safely getting myself to that hospital. I know now, he was mandated to make this happen, in the light of my suicide plan, and having the means to kill myself. But most of all, I know he cared about my safety, and believed I could survive this journey with more support, starting with hospitalization.

The plan went like this… I would call my parents and tell them I was okay, but I needed to go to the hospital for a few days. I needed to know Timmy would be safe with them and discussed how they would tell him why mommy was not around. That was the worst part. I told them they could call John if they needed to. I then called Michael, and asked him to drive me to the hospital where they had a bed waiting for me. He worked right in town, and I knew he would come quickly. I hated having to ask for this kind of help from him, but he was loving and respectful about all of it. He knew what I had just been through on our walk in the woods. He had a glimpse of the fear I was living with. John told me to keep the phone with me as I prepared to go to the hospital. He reminded me he was just a phone call away. My thoughts now were, how will I tell my story in this hospital? It was so hard to open up to John, and now I was going to have to do it again. I was scared to death.

Packing for this unwanted vacation felt overwhelming. How do you pack for a Psych hospital? The first things I grabbed were Sara bear, my blue shawl, and my rosary beads. Anything else didn't seem to matter. I did pack a few pairs of jeans and tops, underwear, and toiletries. I wanted stuff to do my hair which actually sounded hopeful from where I was standing, but packing was making this unexpected journey a little too real, and all I really felt was hopeless...

I heard that dreaded knock at the door. It would be Michael. Normally, I felt like running to the door when he knocked, but under these circumstances I wanted to act like I wasn't home. After pausing at the door and taking a deep breath, I slowly opened it. I felt embarrassed, inadequate, and lost. My boyfriend was about to drive me to a psychiatric hospital. Pathetic, was the only word I could come up with... To my surprise, the word he had in his mind was brave. I disintegrated into his arms, as he held me up. He said, "You are the bravest person I know. I can only imagine how scary this is, but you are doing the right thing. Thank you so much for making the right choice, and asking for help." And with that, he picked up my small suitcase, I held Sara bear in my arms, and we walked out to the car.

It was about a 45 minute drive to this hospital. I had never seen the facility before, didn't know where it was, and had no idea what to expect. I relinquished getting me to this place to Michael. I felt so scattered inside, I could not even complete a full sentence. What were we going to talk about while he drove anyway? Rehash what I wrote in my suicide note to him? Thank God I had torn all those notes into tiny pieces and thrown them in the trash. Both my parents and Michael had a key to my apartment and I would never want them to find any evidence of my failed suicide plan. Any more exposure at that point was more than I could handle. All I remember visually about that drive was this big, old looking, bridge we had to pass under to get off on the exit to the hospital. To this day, passing under that bridge brings up that scared feeling I had as we neared our destination that spring day.

Once we navigated our way from the parking lot to the intake area, part of me wished I had swallowed all those lined up pills back in my bedroom. I tried however, to focus on Michael's words before we left the house. This was me being brave. The intake person allowed, with my permission, Michael to stay for this part of the process. They already had some information about me, told to them by my therapist and the employee assistance person, from where I worked. That EAP was protecting my job, and my privacy. I have to say he did a good job because no one at work ever knew where I had been, except for the one person I told. After the endless questioning, we discussed my immediate plan of care. I would first be placed in what they called their ICU. This placement was purely for my protection, until my suicidal ideation resolved. My room consisted of a twin bed and a very big observation window, so I could be under constant observation. Someone also sat right next to me. This seemed like overkill to me, but I guess they knew best. The staff of course took my toiletries, hair dryer with the long cord, and anything else that resembled a hurtful item. We contracted for safety on paper. They promised they would not tie my wrists unless absolutely necessary for my safety, or the safety of others. Holy shit, with that promise, I was officially terrified. What they did say however was that they did have a blue, padded time out room to keep me safe if I needed it. I agreed to that, making a mental note that I like blue. I appreciated all this information and the intake person's honesty. And so it began, Michael and I said our goodbyes. I starred into his eyes, silently pleading with him too take me back under the bridge to the highway… This goodbye was very difficult, but this social worker was kind and assured me, as did Michael, that we could visit, when the doctor said it was ok.

Triggers and Gifts in a Psych Hospital

I stayed at this hospital for 13 days, with one pass to go home for Easter Sunday. I will never know how they let me out that day. I guess because I did not really tell them what was going on inside. I made myself appear safe enough to leave, with the contract to return that night… I truly was an Oscar winning actress.

I don't remember much of my hospitalization, but there are a few important moments I would like to share with you. These were some unexpected gifts that seemed to make a difference, and helped move me toward taking my life back.

During the time I spent in the ICU section of the hospital, the staff would gather us all up, to go outside to a small unattractive courtyard. Most everyone was just happy to go out and have a cigarette. Part of me was afraid to got out, but I wanted to get some fresh air, and emerge from behind these locked doors. It was the second week in April, and the weather had been unusually mild before I was admitted to the hospital. Everyone around me was glad winter was over. For me, my most difficult seasons were just beginning. Just breathing spring air, was enough to throw me back to the time in my life that put me in this place. Someone mentioned it was cold outside and to dress warm. I grabbed my jacket, my shawl, and tucked Sara bear under my arm. When I stepped outside, I was struck by eye squinting sunshine, and snow falling on my face at the same time. Without a pause, I burst into tears. I found an empty picnic table and sat down. With tears on my cheeks, I dusted off a couple inches of snow accumulation which made me crack a smile. Carrying around so many confusing feelings, I wondered what my face looked like to somebody on the outside. I didn't want anyone to see me cry like this, but impossible not to notice. Were we not in a psych hospital? The staff member always at my side, offered me tissue, and I told her I would be okay, feeling comforted by the snowfall. I didn't want to go back inside. After sitting for a moment and letting the snow melt from the heat of my cheeks, I was able to identify two feelings. Gratitude and surprise. Snow had always made me feel safe, and protected. I still experience that feeling even now. The safest time of the year for me is always winter. In the winter, school protected me from visits to Daryl's garage. Snow meant a warm house and my favorite homemade soup. It meant being all bundled up, playing, and building snowmen with my dad. It meant sliding down my friend's backyard slope, screaming all the way. In the winter, I did not have to feel hot and sweaty in a garage, while being touched against my will. I also knew I would not have to climb that hill in the woods to Daryl's awful place. Snow meant freedom from my perpetrator... And on this day, in the Spring, here I was at a psychiatric hospital, among strangers and an unexpected snow squall appears as I walk out the door for the first time since admission. This in itself felt like a small miracle.

Mostly this crazy, short lived snow storm brought a smile to the faces of some very sad people in the secured courtyard. It felt a bit like recess in grade school. I was probably the happiest person out there that day, but this was disguised by my tears. That was ok though. This genuine smile was my first in a very long time. I simply wanted to be in this moment, and that sounded like progress to me. Then this older, disheveled man came and sat at my picnic table. He scared me a little, but also amused me when I saw he had two lit cigarettes hanging out of his mouth. He must have seen the question in my eyes, and said, "They never give us enough time out here for two." Hoping he wouldn't come any closer, I smiled politely and said nothing. I probably looked a little strange to him too. Here was this grown woman, sitting outside in the snow, wrapped up in a shawl, holding tight to a teddy bear.

He asked me who my friend was, pointing to her with his yellow stained finger. In my quietest voice, I said "Sara bear." He replied, "Hi Miss Sara bear. How about we build a snowman. No, let's build three, one for each of us." In an instant my tears dried up and I started to laugh hysterically. With our bare hands, we built three little snowmen. These snowmen were pretty frail looking. We did not have much to work with. There were no top hats, carrot noses or pretty scarves, like the days I built snowmen with my dad. Our snowmen simply had blades of grass for arms, and pieces of hay for legs. Three little snowmen on the picnic table marked a changing moment in my life. To this day, I cry when I share this very private and pivotal moment. This very interesting character was definitely sent into my life, as was the surprise snow day. This most unusual snow squall reminded me that I could feel safe. Also, I learned that this unkept man, smoking two cigarettes simultaneously, with striking clear blue eyes brought me pure and simple joy that I so desperately needed. I promised right then and there, to file this moment in my safety plan for life. The other thing that this 20 minute experience did for me, was give me a piece of my faith back. In the midst of my present chaos, I truly believed God had interceded, and brought all those pieces together, for both of us maybe. Our snowmen didn't last more than a day, but we did see their remnants when spring reappeared at our next outside recess. Somehow, all this made breathing the spring air just a little easier.

After three days in ICU, someone felt I was ready to be moved to the Trauma Unit. It was known as a dual diagnosis unit. There was an interesting combination of patients there. Most were adolescent age patients, with drug addictions along with trauma issues. There were only a few private rooms and I was fortunate to be placed in one of them. Possibly my age had something to do with assigning me to a private room. I clearly had twenty years on the other patients. They all looked like I could be their mother. I wondered, what was I doing here? While I checked out my new home for the next couple weeks, they told me as I improved they would allow my son visit me in my room. He had to be accompanied by my parents, and that sounded amazing. I cannot tell you how relieved I was to hear this. Instinctively, I scanned the room to see if Timmy would like it. I wanted him to know that I was ok and in a nice place. His visit gave me something to look forward to. It immediately became one of my goals. My favorite part of the room was that it had a closet big enough for me to crawl into when I needed to be safe. I thought Timmy might like the closet too.

There were long lists of therapy groups and activities to attend throughout the day. That as I recall, felt scary at times, but also turned out to be helpful. They administered our medication at specific times. They monitored my food intake because of my eating disorder and low body weight. I earned privileges by complying with my plan of care. I did learn quickly how to play that game and say the right things to gain extra privileges. That was actually a welcome distraction from my internal struggles. The staff continued to watch me very closely. A staff member rounded on me every fifteen minutes for about three days after my transfer into this unit. After the isolation I had created in my home life, all of this attention felt very exposing and uncomfortable.

There were times when my internal younger parts came out onto center stage. During that first week, I didn't seem to have much control over my internal power struggle. I also couldn't really tell you why that happened, because the memory of my early hospitalization remains foggy. What I do know is I spent a great deal of time in the time out room. That did not feel like a bad thing to me. I found comfort from the blue padding on the walls and floor in that quiet isolation room. I felt protected as opposed to punished. I heard some of the patients talk about the "Blue Room" as I fondly called it, with distain suggesting it was similar to being put into solitary confinement, like in a penitentiary. This misunderstood room became my favorite place. I remember wishing I had one in my apartment. In the Blue Room I felt totally safe.

When flashbacks would develop, and they did often while I was in the hospital, I knew I was safest in the confines of those softly secured walls. In that room I remember female staff members sitting next to me handing me tissues. They gave me enough space and allowed me to stay safe when I was dissociated. The best part however was knowing that Daryl was not allowed in that room. Eventually, I recognized that Daryl had no power over me in my favorite room. With the realization that I was safe, the staff became more lenient with their supervision. They started sitting outside the time out room and watched me through a window when I needed to be in there. During these time outs, I could let myself rest and just let life move past without me. Learning how to relax was a big step. Being on guard most of my life was exhausting and required so much of my energy. The Blue Room was spacious enough to breathe, and safe enough to really let go. I could cry in private if I wanted to or I could ask for someone to come inside and listen to me. The staff eventually had to really decide when I needed to be in this room, or when I was just trying to escape everything around me.Thinking back, that is probably exactly what I was doing. Finding a safe place to be was an accomplishment. Knowing the Blue Room was there for me when I needed it's safety made me more courageous. Knowing safety was just a few steps away, allowed me to participate in the activities the program had planned for my treatment. The choice to do the hard work I was avoiding was made easier by the safety of my favorite room.

Building jigsaw puzzles was historically something I always enjoyed. Something about fitting the right pieces together was very relaxing to me. I could get lost in the process for hours if allowed to. At the halfway point of my stay in the hospital I was given a privilege of building puzzles in my room during down time. My mom had a passion for jigsaw puzzles as well, so she made it her job to make this happen. She supplied me with puzzles she thought I might enjoy. Michael sanded down a large piece of plywood to do the puzzles on. This was great because this flat wooden surface was not heavy which mad it portable. I could make the puzzles on the floor or up on my bed. I could even carry a half made puzzle into the day room if I wanted to. I really appreciated my new privilege. I was also very touched that Michael went out of his way to make me a portable table. As I finished one puzzle after another, I remember feeling real joy when I stepped back to view my good work. I was proud to complete a task that actually looked beautiful. I admit, maybe I became a little obsessed with putting these pieces together and creating such pretty pictures in the end. This daily project did start to feel a little therapeutic even though in the beginning "puzzling" as I called it seemed like simple, mindless, entertainment.The interesting, but not yet obvious thing about putting together jigsaw puzzle pieces was that each piece reminded me of me, and all the different parts inside me. Putting the pieces together weirdly began to feel healing as well as comforting. I may not have mentioned this before, but I have 19 puzzle pieces inside. At that time we were not ready to totally fit together like the puzzle on the table, but thankfully we had started to work together towards a common goal of staying alive.

As I look back on my hospital stay, the most profound experience I had, was at a Narcotics Anonymous (NA) meeting. I never understood why I had to attend these meetings in the evening. I did

not do drugs and rarely drank alcohol. This however, was a require-
ment on the unit, so me and Sara bear went to all of them. These
meetings were a bit scary for me because Daryl and his gang did
drugs. They had bought those drugs with the money they made selling the pornographic pictures of me being assaulted by my perpe-
trators.The guy running the meeting was skinny, and had tattoos on
both his arms. I thought, do they really expect me to sit here with
so many triggers staring me in the face? Yes, was the answer to my
silent question.

And so the speaker (John) from the NA group began to tell his
story. I sat my self down as far back in the room as possible. I did
not want to be to close to any of this.What I really wanted was to
disappear or maybe sneak back into my room with the door closed.
Ironically, the speaker was asked to give his presentation standing
right in front of my bedroom door so there was no getting back
in there. As he was telling his story, he confessed that because of
his addiction, he did anything he had to do to get money for the
drugs he needed. He very transparently went on to tell us all his
sins and crimes against the innocent to get his next fix. It really did
sound like his private confession while he spoke to this small crowd.
He did sound sincere, so I started to really pay attention. As he got
deeper into his story, he said, "I sexually assaulted young children.
I sold the pictures taken during those disgusting acts, so I could af-
ford my next fix." He continued to say, "I didn't care about anyone
but me, my drugs, my power, and my pleasure." With that, I almost
passed out cold. My body began to shake uncontrollably. These few
powerful words made me physically ill. The past was being flashed
before me. I held my breath, but my tears fell anyway. A staff member noticed my reaction, and came to sit by me. I wanted to run, but
at the same time I wanted to stand up and scream at him from the
back of the room. Instead, I just sat there and listened to everything

he had to say. He cried as he told all his repulsive truth, and then shared how he changed his life around. In a very quiet repentant voice, he confessed that he no longer abused children. He got clean, served some time in jail, and was now trying to give back by telling his story in forums like this. His goal was to help other addicts, not do what he did, and make their stay here, the beginning of a clean and sober life. Obviously this was a very hard story for him to tell. As I sat there, I had so many mixed emotions. Fear always led the pack, but a close second was this rage I could feel building inside me. In a way, I was seeing Dead Daryl standing up there, however Daryl never had any remorse or paid for his crimes against me. In the midst of my confusion inside, someone announced a 10 minute break. Without thinking, I did something extremely brave and way out of my comfort zone. I took Sara bear, wrapped my shawl tighter, and walked up to this speaker, not really sure what I was about to do. The staff member followed me closely. She didn't know my next move either. I am pretty sure she was trying to talk to me, but I had my own words in my head and did not hear hers.

I found myself face to face with John who greeted me with kindness. I was a little afraid to look him in the eyes. I was terrified they would be green like Daryl's. In a split second, my words poured out of my mouth. I told him what Daryl had done to me and why, which echoed what he had just shared in his talk. Courageously, I finally looked into his eyes. I did not notice their color. What I saw was, his eyes were filled with tears. He pulled up a chair and asked me to come sit down with him. My voice was filled with fear, anger, and one big question, which he could not really answer. This question was, "Why did Daryl do this to me? And why me?" I began to sob. Many words came out of his mouth, but what I guess I needed to hear was one specific thing. He began to apologize for his own sins against children. He also said, "I am sorry he did this to you."

He made no excuses for Daryl concerning his possible addiction or need for drugs. He said Daryl was evil and wrong. He reminded me over and over that the things Daryl said to me were all lies, and in no way what happened to me was my fault. Leaning in closer, he said that he had faith that I was strong enough to get through the aftermath of this past trauma. I snapped back at him, "How do you know that?!" He looked me right in the eyes and said, "Look what you are doing right now. First you came to this hospital to save your life. Now you walk up here to talk to someone who reminds you of your perpetrator. In my eyes, you are one of the bravest women I have ever met." He told me how glad he was that I came up to him, bringing with me the face of a young girl he had hurt once, and now was all grown up. He was given an opportunity to say how sorry he was and I had listened. That somehow felt good to me. In this moment of great honesty, I felt like I started to have a voice, and I was being heard. I did want him to see my face. I wanted to be that little girl face. I wanted him to apologize to her. And he did. I knew that moment would never come when Daryl would apologize. He was dead, and even if he was alive, he never would have done what this brave man just did. On that day, even though I didn't want to hurt John's feelings, I told him I would never forgive my dead abuser. However, I did accept his apology to his victims, in their honor.

By now, the staff member that had been standing behind me had left us alone. It was almost time for the meeting to resume. He asked me if he could give me a hug. I cautiously did accept his hug. While he very gently held me, he thanked me for taking that long walk up to the front of the room to share my truth with him. Knowing we had both been gifted by this honest encounter, I thanked John as we embraced. Once again, I was experiencing a pivotal moment in healing, and I was truly grateful. Starting back to my chair, I felt very dizzy. My head felt like it was in a vice. It hurt to just keep my eyes open.

I found that staff person, and asked if I could go rest somewhere. Somebody was in my Blue room, so she escorted me to my room. The team moved the meeting farther away from my door. With tears falling, soothing my eyes, I fell into a deep unbroken sleep, until the next morning. One of the first in my entire life...

Many times during my healing journey, I have felt that words could not describe my feelings inside. Words just seemed inadequate. It was very frustrating to me that I could not express myself, when it came to certain emotions. On occasion while journaling, I drew pictures when my words ran out. These pictures were all very cryptic, but it did articulate what I was feeling. I however never pursued the idea of using pictures or art to help deal with my feelings as a tool. Well, this psychiatric hospital thought this was a great idea, and I therefore had to walk into my first Art Therapy group. After the first meeting, I sensed art could help me safely express myself in a whole new way. These meetings were not as easy as just sitting down to paint a picture and then move on to the next group. We chose our own particular feeling to work on with any medium we wanted. That felt like a tall order, but I noticed that painting worked better than saying the words I couldn't give myself permission to say out loud. Then came the second part of the activity, when we were asked to share what feelings came up as we worked on a project. I never thought an art class would be so emotional, but I discovered it was. Once other patients in the room shared, it made it a little easier to take my turn. I begrudgingly learned to love this thing called art therapy. I noticed it felt similar to the passion I had for fitting my puzzle pieces together in my room.

I literally could not draw anything beyond stick figures in the past. Much to my surprise, some creative part of me suddenly blossomed out of nowhere and I could paint. After a couple classes, I wanted to paint every spare minute available to me. I felt like some-one flipped on a light switch, giving me a freedom I had not known before. I especially liked working with watercolors. I discovered how strongly some colors made me feel. I also discovered, I hated working with certain colors, and loved painting with others. Black and red scared me immediately. Purple made me cry in deep sad-ness. Blue made me feel safe. I found that even when I was painting a painfully intense picture, I wanted to incorporate the dark parts among some beauty and light. It was truly like painting both sides of the wall. Those painting so often screamed volumes about my double life. There were different components and meanings involved with each painting. In the early stages of this new emotionally creative outlet, I was often surprised by the finished product. Many times I didn't even remember how or when I created the painting. When I was painting time seemed to have no meaning. Often I would get lost in the act of putting paint to paper. Time consistently escaped me while I sat in my creative space. After a while, I would look up at the easel and there sat a painting I couldn't recall painting. This doesn't really surprise me, as I think back. I realized that all parts of me needed this wordless, creative outlet. Many of the inside parts of me felt that painting a picture was a not so secret way of telling without really telling. For them, the good part about that was that they could save their pictures in a hidden box. They found comfort in that. Painting became one of the gifts I took home with me and was most grateful for. What I didn't know then was that art and wa-tercolors would become such an an integral part of my life.

During my stay in the hospital I was given time to rest and re-cover from the initial acknowledgment of what had happened to me so long ago. In a way I took a break from the real world, as I tried to get my feet back under me. I was given space to hit a type of reset button. I learned how to stay off that dangerous, slippery slope I had almost crashed at the bottom of just a couple weeks before. I learned new, creative, survival tools to work with when I got home. I realized this walk was far from over. I believed this hospitalization is where I learned that my feelings would not kill me. I recognized that my feelings were just that, feelings. Many of the exercises presented to me in the hospital were about learning to trust others, but mostly trusting myself. I knew I had to focus on my healing first, but still have a daily life, with a son, my job and Michael. The thought of challenging this balancing act scared me to death. Having about 5 more days in the hospital before my scheduled discharge date, I still had time to work on my preparation for going back to the real world. My goal was to heal and safely live my life in unison. Boy, that still felt like a lot to ask, but I started to feel like I had more energy to give it a try. I started to believe that I could survive this journey.

Please, Just a Little More Time

The piece of my hospitalization that I have been avoiding is how it all effected my relationship with Michael. Looking back on this part of the story, 25 years later, is a lot easier than it was to live through. I have a much better understanding of what happened now, than I did then.

Right up until our walk in the park, a couple weeks prior to my admission, Michael and I were really connected. I believe we both felt like our relationship was solid, and blossoming into something long lasting. I was amazed in the midst of my healing, that somehow Michael and I became a couple. I felt blessed that the gift of Michael was bestowed upon me and would last forever. I was given this place to fall and actually felt loved for simply being the woman I was. I felt happiness and excitement with a man, I had never dreamed possible. The feelings of acceptance, safety, and comfort were things I needed deep in my heart. We shared a solid friendship history from high school that was never forgotten by either of us. This friendship was a strong base to allow me to move forward into deepening our relationship.

Michael and I were reacquainted at our 20th high school class reunion. A couple of my therapy sessions during that time were spent finding the courage to even go to this reunion. I needed to feel confident that some of my inside turmoil could be contained long enough to get through that upcoming fall event. I had never told any high school friends what had happened to me in grade school. Michael and I were very close friends during all 4 of our high school years, and I never leaked out any evidence of what had happened to me as a child. As I prepared for this reunion, my therapist convinced me that no one would be able to tell I was raped as a child, walking in that door, and certainly this topic was not appropriate conversation for this venue. The reunion was supposed to be a four hour event that I surely could live through. John assured me if I was really uncomfortable there, I could just leave. Now that sounded like a plan. All the preparation in therapy paid off, and I finally made the decision to attend.

As I look back in my journals, this preparation for the big night, was not as easy as buying a pretty new dress. I was on a mission to look as care free and happy as I could. I was doing such hard work in therapy surrounding the past trauma in my life, that I had to come up with a fool proof way to disguise my internal chaos. From where I was sitting, this big event was more like a masquerade party than a reunion. As I looked for something to wear, I had a few goals that were a must for me to comfortably go to the reunion. My dress had to have long sleeves to cover my scarred arms. It had to be conservative to make me feel sufficiently covered and not exposed in any way. During my dress hunt, I realized it could not look too happy. First, I tried on a selection of colorful dresses. They did look beautiful on the mannequin, and the store attendant thought they looked perfect on me. When I looked in the mirror however, the dress lost its beauty in my eyes. I felt like an imposter and had the attendant take them all back. I did finally find a simple black dress that seemed to be made just for me. I had never worn a black dress in my life, but this dress seemed to match my insides better than the others. It simply looked like a pretty, little black dress with flowing layers giving me room to breathe in. I was sure many other women would be wearing black for this semiformal event and I would fit right in. I do have to admit I felt pretty in the dress I had chosen.

Next, I created a script in my mind of appropriate things to talk about over cocktails and appetizers. Certainly, I could not talk about the two years of intensive therapy I had just survived. My life had been consumed with night terrors and flashbacks. (Definitely not party conversation). In my mind I would stick to my nursing career, my son and long distance running. Someone was bound to find one of those topics interesting.

Fortunately, I still maintained contact with a couple friends from back in the day. Since I did not have a date for the reunion, they asked me to join them and I agreed immediately. I was very grateful for the ride. The thought of walking into the venue alone was terrifying. Their gracious invitation made this grande entrance much less stressful. When we walked in together, surprisingly my fears dissolved. I noted that as a small victory and was grateful.

I was amazed at how many of my classmates showed up. I saw the faces of people I truly enjoyed so many years ago. Eventually, I noticed my smile felt natural instead of forced. I began to breathe easier and I noticed my legs were no longer shaking under my black dress. When I walked up to the bar, I saw one of the people I had hoped would be there. It was my old friend, Michael. He had aged very nicely. I thought what a handsome man he had grown into. We hugged, very happy to see each other. That night we spent a fair amount of time talking. As I recall we went to an after party and continued to get reacquainted. Surprisingly, there was no denying I had a great time at the reunion. In the end, the event was nothing like I feared it would be. I actually felt like a normal adult. For those few hours, I almost forgot about my tortured past and really enjoyed myself. When the nights coming to an end, Michael asked me for my phone number, and said he would give me a call sometime. I hoped he meant that, but if not, it felt nice that he even asked. I left the party feeling proud of myself. I remember thinking as I was getting back into my friend's car, "All that fuss for nothing."

Well, obviously he did use my phone number, but it took him 10 months to dial. He had been working on his life too. By that time, I had given up hope that he would call, but I hadn't really been waiting by the phone either. I was pretty busy just living. I was a single mom, had a full time job as a nurse, and was busy getting my emotional life into one piece. When he did call, I was delighted. I of course wasn't home, but I think that was probably for the best. Listening to the message he left created a teenage like fluttering in my stomach. I admit, I called him right back. After three rounds of phone tag, we finally got together and our new rekindled relationship began. This turn of events was such a welcome surprise. He was a very busy man with his own business to run. We definitely had conflicting schedules, but we both wanted it to work though that challenge and we did.

I saw our relationship like this beautiful diamond in the rough. As I reflect back, I remember this relationship very clearly, but still felt compelled to search my journals to read exactly what I felt at the time. I was brought right back to those wonderful days, and found myself smiling as I read. He let me lead our dance in the early days. Going to fast in the beginning might have scared me away. What I read though, was that it was harder to go slow than I had thought. Feeling cared for and loved, was something that had been missing from my life for a very long time. I clearly realized I had never felt this way before. Reading further, I felt validation that I had not just imagined this love relationship. We had loved each other. Our focus was on the same page, as we grew closer. Flipping through my journals, I discovered an entry that described how I shared a snippet of my trauma history with him. The words I wrote touched my heart deeply as I revisited them. This is that entry...

"What he knows about my past...It happened on the street I lived. It was a neighbor. There was more than one abuser. It is very hard to go near my childhood street. I usually avoid that street. Rapists don't kiss... rapists hurt you. I am very present when I am with Michael in an intimate way. A couple sexual positions are still scary to me. (He understands). I use to clean myself, after what they did, in that stream across the street from my house, before I returned home..." (What I need to interject here, is that the Michael owned a business located right next to that stream, on the corner of my childhood street.) And this journal entry continued... "He knows that his business being located there, has made that area feel just a little bit safer. He held my hand while I talked. He moved his chair closer to me when he could see I was a little teary. (So was he). He is good. He told me he would call me in 2 days after we talked, because he wanted me to have some space, to see how I felt about sharing my past with him. He said that he would call me on Monday. (and he did) When he called me, as planned, he said he had been afraid he made the wrong decision in waiting a day to call. He was afraid I might think he was loving, and leaving. That's what amazes me. I didn't feel panic or fear of him leaving me. I think I truly trusted him…"

I knew there was no hiding such a big secret, in a love relationship. One of the things we did best was our long talks. They were open, very clear and honest. There were no emotional games in this relationship. Going to his house on weekends felt like a trip to some private island. Our alone time made me feel whole, like an adult woman, regardless of what was going on in my internal world. Even when it came to sexual intimacy, I trusted him enough to actually welcome that in our private world. And loved it. He was a gentle, patient man in every way. I felt safer than I ever imagined I could feel. I acknowledged that I had intimate adult love feelings with Michael. I describe in my journal exactly how those unique private feelings traveled through my body. They seemed to begin as a warm feeling deep in my chest, moving from there to the rest of my body. I felt them with my soul. I could clearly see how different choosing to make love, is the exact opposite of what happened to me when I was a child. This opened my heart in a way that would change my life. What I discovered, was that it was possible for me to feel safe, and free enough to love totally.

The seven months that followed our first date were everything I could have hoped for. Of course nothing is perfect, but this felt perfect enough to me. We did talk about making this a permanent relationship a few times. We both shared our deepest feelings with each other and our love was very evident. This felt hopeful, and I just continued to enjoy the present, one day at a time. This happiness made my therapy work a little bit easier. Of course my past did not go away just because I had love in my life. I did have difficult moments in Michael's presence. This was not something I could, or wanted to hide from him. He responded in those moments with love, gentleness, and respect for my whole person and the process of healing.

We enjoyed doing things outdoors with his sweet dog, Bella. We enjoyed hiking, and tried to fit that into our weekends whenever we could. Our love for hiking of course brought us to that traumatic day in the park. That will forever symbolize the collision of the two lives I was leading. It was an example of both sides of life splitting wall. As beautiful as I see nature, Daryl created evil triggers for me, within the backdrop of Mother Nature's beauty. On that spring day in 1995, I was not yet healthy enough to conquer the enormous triggers and flashbacks that casual walk laid before me. As I see it in 2020, the safety of having Michael there ended up being both good and unfortunate...

For the few weeks after that experience, in my heart I believed Michael had seen a little too much of what I felt no one should see. He saw the real aftermath of what the 6 years of Daryl's assaults had done to me, in living color. It was the first time I really started to worry that he might be questioning the strength of our relationship. I worried he might think twice about being in relationship with someone who was only a couple years into her healing journey from childhood sexual assault. My old fears that I was not good enough started to resurface. My anxiety worsened as my fears grew into monsters, and the flashbacks that started in the park repeated themselves over and over again. That's when I spiraled down to a place where my fight for survival no longer felt like an option. I was giving up. I am forever grateful I did the right thing, by asking for help when I did. On that day when it counted, Michael did step up and stand beside me getting me to safety.

As I shared earlier, Michael brought me to the hospital in crisis that spring day. What I did not share, was that when I was signing into the program I named him as my contact person, as well as my parents. When he signed the consent papers, he wrote his relationship to me, as fiancé. That one word filled me with hope and promise that this relationship was solid, and we would make it through this complicated time. I voluntarily admitted myself to the hospital to get safe, and then doing the work of dealing with my past. My goals were to gain strength, find a little hope, and reach a place that living was not such a struggle. I wanted my life back.

The first week in the hospital I felt a strong healthy support coming from Michael. He still seemed like the Michael who truly loved me. I trusted the words he said before I was admitted to the hospital. Those sentiments gave me hope, and the belief that coming here was the right decision. After the first week in the hospital, I was rewarded with a day pass on Easter Sunday. Michael came to pick me up and we spent the day with my family. I was glad to be released for a few hours mostly because I wanted to spend time with Timmy. I do recall not feeling fully present and a bit uneasy that day. Being out in the world again felt a little intimidating. I did feel like I was dancing as fast as I could trying to appear as sane as possible. I knew everyone there loved me but deep down, I perceived myself as the elephant in the room. My progress was not going to be a dinner topic. I really only had a few hours on this pass, so after dinner Michael and I snuck away before we headed back to the hospital. We stopped by my apartment for a little quiet time. I hated to admit it but that was the first time I felt a twinge of doubt about our relationship. Michael was quieter than usual which made me wonder if something was off.

On our drive back to the trauma unit, I remember thinking maybe our relationship within this setting was too challenging for him. Was he really strong enough to walk this walk with me? I had gained some real confidence after the first week of hospitalization. I was sure I could get better. I thought back to how far I had come in just a short period of time. Michael's visits were always enjoyable, and always left me feeling like he could see my progress. But after that day pass, as much as I tried to deny it, something felt different. The change was almost undetectable, but I could sense it. He was a bit more quiet and introspective than usual. In my eyes, he appeared to be thinking about his words before he said them. Doubts about our relationship started to creep into my head. I shut those unthinkable doubts down, the best I could. Surely, I was just being paranoid, not having faith in the power of our relationship. I trusted him completely, and tried to focus on the power of our relationship. As positive as I tried to be, I felt the ground shaking beneath me. What was it I was sensing?

The next day he came to visit as planned. I remember putting on my best face, even fussing more with my hair and choosing more carefully my cloths that day. I was hoping he would see how well I was doing. My discharge date had been set earlier that week at my progress meeting. I was scheduled to be released in just a few more days. I was excited to share that surprise with him. I also told him about the healing experience I had with the NA speaker just a few nights before. That experience felt like a milestone for me and I wanted to share that with him during one of our private visits. He genuinely sounded proud of me, but again I felt he was distracted as I told him the story.

Something still felt a little off even during the first moments of that visit. I couldn't figure out what it was until the last 10 minutes of visiting hours. I could feel some anxiety as our visit was coming to an end, but definitely not prepared for what was about to happen. Out of the blue, with no prelude, the most devastating words

I could have imagined, very quietly came out of Michael's mouth. Tears were coming from his eyes as he spoke. I felt suffocated by a creeping sense of impending doom surrounding our space. Frozen in my chair, I wanted to shut down this bad ending I felt coming at me like a freight engine. At that moment, I actually thought I was going deaf. His face looked very sad and I could see his lips moving, but I could not hear what he was so delicately trying to say. I am sure not wanting to hear had something to do with that.

What I eventually heard was, Michael asking for space from our relationship. He said maybe someday we could work this all out, but right now he did not feel he was strong enough to be in this relationship. He said, and I quote, "Love should not be this difficult." I definitely and very clearly heard those six words. We were sitting in a corner craving some privacy. We held each other as we both cried. Even though I had been sensing a change in him, I still felt blindsided by all this. The moment felt surreal, like this may just be one of my bad dreams. What my body could not deny was the swell of emotion in his. I could feel the tears falling from his face onto mine. Those tears are what made this nightmare a reality. We paused to breathe for a moment as the clock ticked in the background. It was at that point, I wondered if he had talked with the staff, prior to dropping this bomb in my lap. Any security I had been feeling about going home in just a few days was obliterated in that ten minute discussion. My heart felt like it was being torn open. I had hoped that by coming to the hospital for help, I would leave with a better grip on my personal life, which Michael was a huge part of. The next thing I knew they were making the announcement that all visitors must leave. Tonight, I was sure that did not include Michael. Did they not know my world was falling apart before my very eyes. They were pretty tough about visiting hours and I was no different than anyone else.

My closing words, as I made efforts to say goodbye with some sense of dignity were, "Please Michael, I just need a little more time."

As we separated and he walked out the door, I disintegrated to a puddle on the floor. Someone must have guided me to the blue room for a timeout, and some privacy. I wept for hours in my welcomed seclusion. The tears shed were filled with pain, sadness, loss of love and again abandonment. Mostly, I felt like I was not good enough. I covered my ears to block the sound of Daryl's old lies mercilessly screaming into my right ear. His voice reminded me that I was damaged goods. The other words I heard repeatedly were my own. "Please, I just need a little more time. Can you not give me that, Michael?" Sitting alone in that time out room, just me and the Kleenex box made sense, because I looked as alone as I felt. Obviously, I was not as healthy as I had thought. In just a matter of hours, I was planning how I would self injure again. All my promises to ask for help when feeling unsafe sounded like total bullshit to me now. Who really cared anyway? I did not want to stay in this hospital another minute. Revealing my self injurious thoughts would definitely buy me another week here. That was not happening. I was so out of here. These dangerous thoughts would become my newest secret.

My brother and sister in law came to see me the next day. As the three of us sat squished side by side on a couch really made for two, I remember thinking they were literally holding my body together while I was crumbing.

There were not to many journal entries during this time. That does not surprise me, because I had no words to match my overwhelming chaotic feelings. The few entries I did find, I thought might shed some light on what was really going on the two days after Michael's visit:

"Last night, and all day yesterday was really hard. Spent the whole day in pain. Crying and crying. It was good that Tom and Felicia came to visit. I felt so much support from them, as the three of us sat squished together on this really small couch. It felt good to be close to people that loved me no matter what. Can I get better and just be me? Hopefully, Michael will love me enough to want to be together forever. I can't imagine my life without him. I could never just be platonic friends with the man I am so in love with. And so I would also lose my good friend. God please help us... A feeling I need to work on - I need to feel good enough."

"Feel like total shit. I want to cut so bad. I fucking hate everything and everyone except Timmy. I want to hide. I don't want to feel the disgust and rage inside me. It's awful. I don't know how I will get through this. How will I be any different when I go home? Just file all this fucking shit. Nothing good is gonna be for me. I don't want to see anyone. I hate. I hate. I just want some peace, but there is none for me, ever. My life, who cares? I hate I hurt I hate I hurt I hate I hurt..."

"Tonight I feel like I am fighting for my life, AGAIN. A life I never had permission to have. Permission... Give myself permission? So what... Where will that take me? Trying to be me. Me is not good enough, and it never will be. I don't want to see anyone tonight. I can't stand myself. I can't stand my life. Except Timmy. Oh I love my family, but I need more. I need a newly made family of my own. All my life I always wanted just the basics. A husband that loved me, a child, and a home to live together in. I almost thought I had that. Now, I wish I had not taken that risk, and opened my heart to those possibilities. Only to be hurt. IT DOESN'T MATTER."

" I am going home tomorrow. I'm scared and very anxious. I am afraid to even write my thoughts down, for fear of being kept here. I am not sure I will ever feel like living...."

"I am leaving today. We're scared. How do we be? How do I be? How do I close this book, and walk out that door. I was suppose to be leaving with Michael. My brother Tom is here to bring me home. How do I hold this together? One step at a time..."

So, Tom and I made that drive back home. I remember wishing it would take hours, because I had no clue what my game plan was for when I reached my destination. When I opened my back door, I was comforted to find that my house was spotlessly clean with flowers in the kitchen. My parents must have come in and prepared for my homecoming. My overdue bills had been paid. My grandmother even paid my rent that month, such a gift to me. All this, to help me with a fresh start. As I got settled in, Tom offered to stay for a while. I promised I would be ok, and contracted for safety. I just wanted to be alone in my own apartment, take a short nap, and wait for Timmy to arrive. We embraced for a few moments. That long hug felt like me hanging on for dear life. My goal was not to look to far ahead, and just stay in the moment. I felt proud that I survived, and came home to my son. I, however, did not envision this day looking like this, filled with so much sadness. After watching Tom leave, making sure he was down the driveway and gone from my vision, I then slid down the wall that was holding me up. There I was, crying on my kitchen floor, just like the day I went to the hospital... or maybe these tears were a little different. I noticed that strangely the tears I was crying on this day seemed to feel ok. How could that be? They just poured from my heart, down my face, onto my jeans, and I did not judge them. They were no longer impossible tears. My arms were wrapped around waist, and my legs laid straight out on the floor. I noticed I wasn't curled up in a ball. My body gently rocking in a comforting fashion. It dawned on me, I might be taking care of myself, and that was a change for me. A good change.

This acknowledgment of survival brings me back to my list of reasons to live. Every reason will always be extremely important. They remind me of everything I have and want moving forward. By staying alive, I honored my family that love me. I recognize now that they will always be there for me. I know I am not alone even when I feel lonely. But most of all, by not taking my life, I give honor to my young parts inside that fought like hell to make it to 1995. And Daryl did not win... I feel like the score card changed the day I chose to live and that put me ahead. I promised myself on that day, I would not allow my perpetrator to take my soul away ever again.

In closing this chapter, I firmly believe giving up is never the right answer to intolerable pain and hopelessness. After years of silence, I now know if I use my voice and ask for help, I can find another answer. This answer will never be easy, but the outcome will be much better than the alternative.

The Blue Box

I enter this chapter with great sadness and reverence. This part of my journey began with "Rose's worst days." Healing from the fact a baby was formed as a result of Daryl's evil still makes my head drop and heart ache. I amaze myself to think I can actually open up enough in these next several pages to tell this part of my truth. Not writing this part of the story would be fair to none of us.

I have confessed this, the ugliest of sins, in a silent chant more times than I could count. The picture of this sin, that only I could see in a hidden corner of my heart, was painted black. That lack of light represented the gaping hole that drained my heart empty. It did not seem possible that any amount of penance could heal this mortal wound. I literally felt lost in the woods, miles from the clean waters of absolution. No words could ever really express the level of shame I carried for decades regarding the creation and loss of Sara.

When did this healing begin? I think maybe it was the creation of Candy. Maybe she was God's gift to us. Her fearless disregard for the consequences of her compassion and her protective nature may have helped Rose take the first step out of a guilt ridden darkness.

Candy miraculously came to Rose, took the bloody remains from the pee bucket, and frantically buried them with as much grace, love, and dignity as she could. She did this in the face of evil, filled with terror at what might happen next. Candy, no less vulnerable than Rose, stayed focused, with her nakedness, on her hands and knees, trying to hold Rose together while she bled. I cry as I remember her efforts to protect Rose and somehow give honor to the sacred remains of this piece of them... These are the moments that I revel in my own personal strength of spirit and creativity. As I remember that day in the woods, I can barely breathe in awe of our courage to retain the soul God gave us. I envision Candy's tears falling into the dirt, while digging a hole to bury this little spirit, she had named Sara. Her body was still bloodied from what Daryl had done just minutes before. And so, my breath is swept away even now as I write. Allowing myself permission to even imagine a moment such as this in the life of a 11 year old girl is unthinkable. Recognizing that this was me... I weep again.

Even in the midst of terrifying confusion, Candy being the calm, nurturing, creative part of me, formulated a plan to remember where she was burying Sara. She was positive that one day Rose would want to come back for her. She silently made a promise to be by her side when that day came. Together, they would somehow find an appropriate place to bury her. A holy place... Even at such a young age, they knew that Sara deserved an honorable resting spot.

~

One spring morning, about 3 years into therapy, I opened my eyes and took a deep breath of the fresh air coming into my window.

I felt that familiar love/hate relationship of being enveloped with the first hints of spring. With that breath, I felt the immediate pull to do something I have been lured to do before. This time the magnetic pull came from deep inside of me, and not from Daryl's dark side of the wall. This call from within, dragging me from the comfort of my bed, reminded me in some ways of my son tugging on my nightgown trying to wake me from sleep, because he had a nightmare. Once the cobwebs in my head cleared, I recognized that it was Rose urging me to open my eyes. She usually doesn't present with such enthusiastic power. That morning there she was, front and center at the crack of dawn, begging me to take her to "the outside place." She was adamant that today was the day she wanted to go get Sara. Without question, this broken part of me captured my full attention. I appreciated that Rose did not just secretly steal time and then take this on herself. It was however crystal clear to me that today would be the day we would go back to that awful place. I thought, Candy was right imagining what Rose may want one day…

During a therapy session a few weeks prior to this urgent request, Rose struggling with her words, took a huge risk to reveal her darkest secret. She confessed to John that Daryl put a baby in her and then made it go away. Being sworn to silence, with the punishment of unimaginable harm looming near, her hair hung in her face trying to cover her shame. Speaking no louder than a whisper, she used only the necessary words to make sure John understood her secret. She would not have said it twice. Rose did feel a momentary sense of relief by telling the truth, but almost immediately was overwhelmed by the fear of punishment from her perpetrator. See, Rose never believed Daryl was dead. John and I both tried to convince her he was gone, but she knew better. She still heard his vile words in her right ear every day.

I knew if I told John what we were thinking about doing, he would tell us it was not a safe plan. Because in our eyes this was the right thing to do, I knew we would not reveal our rescue mission to anyone. We were going to "the outside place" regardless of John's concerns. In the end, it was our decision to make. I also knew that Rose would not let me sleep until we scooped Sara up from that evil ground. Since the day Rose shared the memory of Sara in therapy, the idea of retrieving her remains never left our thoughts. Even being the adult, trying to be the wise one, picturing Sara buried in that awful place was more than I could bear. With that heartbreaking visual, I knew this journey to retrieve Sara had just become a high priority secret plan.

My question was, how was I going to get us there? I was aware that only Caryl knew the route to the outside place. She had that memory safely tucked away for us. Convincing Caryl of anything was not as easy as you may think. She swore she was never going back to that disgusting place, and here I am asking her to do exactly that. She was definitely aware of Baby Sara. What happened to Rose that day was one of the last straws that pushed Caryl to become the brave warrior part of us. She vowed then, to end Daryl's reign of terror once and for all.

Strangely, without too much persuasion or a whole lot of Caryl attitude, we gathered a shovel, plastic bag, a shoebox, the car keys and piled into the car. I smiled as I remembered thinking, "I need a bigger car." As we started toward this vile place, the entirety of me was shaken up. Our internal turmoil was crazy loud and made it nearly impossible to focus on the road. This was not an easy Sunday drive and I never needed a GPS more. Could there possibly be an address for something named "the outside place?" I tried to reassure myself this was a rational scheme, but as we approached the city line, I had my doubts. In the back of my mind I comforted myself with the knowledge of my appointment with John the next day. Yikes, how was he going to respond to hearing about this fiasco first thing on a Monday morning?

I knew this 20 minute drive must have been dangerous, because when I turned off the engine and put the car in park, I had minimal recall of the drive. This trip was a psychological nightmare in the making, but to Rose it was imperative that we travel this journey to get Sara that Sunday morning.

It had been thirty years since we had turned right onto this bumpy road. The jolting from beneath the wheels of the car snapped me into the present. Was this a real road? Are we in the right area. There may have been a street sign, but I hadn't noticed and wouldn't recognize it as the right one anyway. This road resembled a path in the woods or a gravel driveway someone didn't want to pave. I could now see what I once could only feel from the floor of Daryl's van.

Somehow, we did find the miserable, hidden place. Driving down the road, I did recognize some of the familiar markings that had been burned into my memory. The nagging pain in my stomach made me acutely aware we had reached our destination. I reluctantly parked the car on the side of this narrow road. It was lined on both sides with pine trees that stood like a huge privacy fence. It didn't seem fair that Mother Nature had a part in keeping Daryl's secret. I hated those trees. In that moment I was reminded why the smell of pine straw made me so uncomfortable, but still I got out of the car.

Walking up that hill, weaving in and out through the woods felt like stepping behind that dirty curtain in the garage, so many years ago. With all that natural camouflage, I realized why no one ever did discover what was happening to me up here... Before getting too far into the woods I looked back to remember where my escape vehicle was. I must have been so focused on climbing up the hill that I missed the clearing on the other side of the dirt road. I was a bit startled by what I saw, but there it was, that scary old cemetery I tried so hard to forget. It looked smaller than I remembered, but that is all that was different. It still had those black and red symbols of hate spray painted on the ancient gravestones. I stood there paralyzed looking at this frightening scene. I consciously pushed down the memories of what happened beyond that stone wall that surrounded Daryl's cemetery. He had told me the place was haunted, so I was glad it was daylight. From my view on the hill, it seemed ironic that there was so much sunshine lighting up the cemetery. My forty something year old eyes saw green grass and sunshine. My gut however was shaken by a sudden fear of ghosts. We had come too far to be scared away by the ghosts that may or may not have inhabited that place. Barely breathing, I looked back up the path knowing I was going to have to climb this overgrown hill to reach Sarah's temporary gravesite. I reached inside myself, counting on Caryl to help out here. She was the oldest, and had walked this path last. My brave but reluctant 12 year old inside would have to get us to the scene of the crime. The terrain had changed so much I wasn't even sure I was on a real path. Would any one of us inside succeed in navigating this tangled maze? As my legs were getting scratched during this climb, I wondered, how did a little girl ever make it through all these sharp bushes. Noticing the blood on my ankles, I started to panic. I wondered if Caryl could find the right path, or even worse would we get lost and never find our way home? This very well hidden clearing in the woods we were searching for contained the worst pieces of my childhood nightmare. Slowly, we trudged on, placing one foot in front of the other with Caryl in the lead. I may have looked like a middle aged woman hiking in the woods, but I felt all the feelings of a scared young girl. Trying to protect myself

I interjected a little musical humor. With a quivering voice, I sang a little tune, "Lions and tigers and bears. OH MY!" As I repeated this little ditty, I was stealing from the "The Wizard of OZ" soundtrack, I wished I was back hiding behind the couch trying not to watch that part of my favorite movie… Instead Little Kathy's legs shook like always, as we climbed. Rose hung her head, walking, slowly praying she would not trip, just following the leader. Caryl tried to speed things up, to get this over with. I hadn't noticed, but Rachel had joined us, continually asking if we were fucking crazy. And Candy, was her usual patient self that understood what her job was.

Together, we did find the infamous and unforgettable clearing. The moment I laid eyes on this spot, my hand rose and covered my mouth prepared to vomit. I felt the nausea rise quickly, and could taste stomach acid in my mouth. I tried to swallow it back down, but without skipping a beat and tears dropping onto my cheeks, I puked all over the ground. I thought to myself why the hell did you do this alone? I took a deep breath and tried to ground myself. This was tough because for the first time since Caryl said her final goodbyes, I was in the physical presence of my past. With my legs shaking the way they were, I felt like an earthquake was about to swallow me whole. Looking up from the circle of puke at my feet, I wiped the vomit from my chin. Gripping tightly to my shovel and shoebox, I realized I was looking strait at the ugly, moss covered stone altar. My body revolted and I was forced back in time, slamming strait into Rose's early memories. I saw her being dragged up the hill by a belt around her waist. She was wearing that little purple t-shirt over her head to cover her eyes. Then, as if not one day had passed, I felt an abrupt tightness squeeze my waist. Desperately trying to reorient myself, I looked down at my running shoes standing in the dirt. I could see there were no other people next to me, but I could feel the presence of all my young, tortured parts of me… Was I going to make it off this hill alive? I felt like there was no way out, and really didn't know the answer to my own question.

I sidestepped past the altar. I avoided that stone raping table like it was on fire. Oh God, this is awful… "Breathe Kathy. Just keep breathing, You can do this." I chanted to myself several times until I could catch my breath again. Frozen in this spot, I now understood where the images came from that I had spent hours at my French style easel recreating with my paintbrush. In that moment I reluctantly accepted an internal affirmation that those paintings were not just scenes from a bad dream. Those pictures were real. I did not imagine them. There it all was, right in front of me. I saw the real wood benches going up the incline of the land just like an outdoor movie theater. The stone altar still had that soft green moss growing on it. My thoughts flashed to that rough feel on my back, when I was forced to lay on the altar. I remember no soft comforting moss on that stone slab. Holding firm, trying to avoid the next landmark just past the wooden benches, I got my first glance of that round stone fire pit. From what I could see it still contained charcoaled remains of stuff I dare not look at. I turned away, but instantly I looked back because I smelled that burnt flesh odor. It was something my nose did not forget. Please let this be my imagination… My adult thoughts were, "Oh my God, this is really real. I didn't make this all up. I am standing right smack in the middle of my childhood Hell." I could no longer hold back the sobs from my weary heart, and was now certain I was not strong enough to do this. Everything in me wanted to turn and run back down the hill. My feet pivoted, as I almost began my descent, but then I remembered faintly hearing the words, "I am not ever coming back here again!" and wondered, were those my words or Caryl's. With that said, I felt determined to follow through with today's mission that together we set out to do for Rose…

When my head cleared, I looked up and saw the huge tree I had
been doodling and painting most of my life. As I stood at the foot of
that tree, I felt it's roots under my feet. I stepped back to look around
to find what I had come here looking for; the exact burial spot. I felt
a welcomed warmth right where I was standing. I looked up and
saw Rose's sun shining through the designs of the leaves that decorated the draping branches. I remembered Rose trying desperately
to escape through those leaves. She was in search of freedom from
whatever was being done to her on that altar. There were so many
conflicting feelings about this damn tree, its shade kept me cooler
as my back was pressed against the stone slab I was made to lay
on. That tree was just one of many that hid the scene of the crimes
against us. But mostly, I knew that a large tree stood above the tiny
grave we had come to find…

Backing up even further, I softly asked Candy, "Is that the
one?" I felt directed to a small pile of rocks at the foot of the tree.
As I moved closer again, I watched my knees hit the ground. No
longer feeling my body, my hands start moving Candy's stones
which miraculously remained marking Sarah's spot. I could see
my busy hands digging in the dirt. I knew they were mine, because
I could see the sapphire ring my mom had given me, on my forth
right finger. The hands I was watching no longer felt attached to
my body. Dirt was collecting under their nails. I felt like I was
watching some other little girl's hands. Whoever these hands belonged to it didn't really matter, they were doing what we had set
out to do. They dug and dug until they stopped. With that pause,
I knew exactly who the person was controlling these hands. The
deliberate gentle movement was a dead giveaway. Candy leaned
over to pick up the plastic bag from the shoebox and filled it with
this sacred dirt. Each movement was shaky, but slow and careful. These hands knew exactly what to do. My job was over for

now. I was no longer needed for this. Candy gathered Rose's treasure and placed it respectfully into the makeshift coffin. She was keeping her promise to Rose. Before Candy closed the shoebox, she questioned if she should also take the stone markers with her. Everything seemed to stop at that thought... The Kevni part of us had stepped forward and wanted to do his something special for Rose. Kevni always liked rocks. He liked how they felt in his hands. I think they made him feel stronger. I always recognized his presence, when I returned home from walks. I would find my pockets full of pretty smooth rocks. Sometimes, I found these treasures lining the tub of the washing machine. oops... I was touched that Kevni took the stones and reverently placed them in the box. It was his offering of love and protection. We all heard his quiet, stuttering voice loud and clear.

Once back on my feet, it took a moment to regain feeling in my body and then I heard those familiar words in my head. "Hail Mary full of grace...." This prayer continued as we looked around one last time, and finally made a daunting attempt to walk back down the hill. This was not easy. My legs felt like jello. My knees seemed useless and I was trembling like never before. A foggy feeling surrounded me, as if I was in the middle of some night terror I was fighting to awaken from. My only thoughts were, "There is no way out." So, I prayed faster and out loud to no avail. I started to seriously lose my footing. I stumbled on rocks and brush, hitting the ground more than once. I started hearing Daryl's vicious words and felt his hot smoky breath on the back of my neck. Was he chasing me?... I covered my right ear with my free hand and held my shoebox like a football with my left. No one was dropping this valuable box. I somehow weaved my way through the trees, veering off path, and finally making my way to safety of the gravel unpaved road.

Once in the car with door locked, I became more aware of my body. My cloths were full of dirt and sticky pine straw. In the rear view mirror I could see a cold sweat on my face. I seriously had no idea how to start the car. I could feel panic starting to take over as I tried to put the key in the ignition. I watched the keys fall to the floor. My head hit the steering wheel when I reached to pick them up. I tried to settle down and focus only on getting away from this place. I stopped this insane tailspin by taking a deep breath and starting to pray, "God please help me drive this damn car!!!"

The next thing I knew, I was showered and wearing clean clothes, sitting on my bed with a white shoe box in my lap. I knew what was in the box and was grateful Rose's mission was accomplished. What I did not know, was how I got home from that horrible place. My next thought was, "What do I do now?"

Monday morning came after a long restless night, and I awoke with the answer to my question. I will bring Rose's shoe box to John's office. Somehow we thought this precious cargo would be safest there. When I got to John's office I stood motionless in his doorway. I held tightly onto my tiny coffin. Never taking his eyes off me, he guided my body cautiously to my favorite chair across from his. I think John may have been in shock when I told him what we had done the day before. From the look of compassion on his face, I knew I would not have to plead with him to make space for Sarah right there in some corner of his office.

Several times over many months that followed, John brought up the idea that we needed to bury Sara in an appropriate place. Inside, Rose agreed with him, but she was simply relieved to have rescued her from that awful place. I on the other hand was not yet ready to take that next step. Since the day we last marched up the hill to retrieve Sara, I was reeling from all the pain we unearthed from this experience. Deep down, I knew John was right, but emotional exhaustion would not allow me to move forward.

With the promise to bury Sara as an ultimate goal, this precious shoebox lived in his office for about a year, until he told me he was moving out of state. His career and personal life were about to change. He was moving down south. Way south... Yes, you read that right. In disbelief, I remember asking him to repeat that last sentence more than once. I was sure my ears were playing tricks on me, or even worse, maybe one of Daryl's promises had come to fruition. I gripped the arms of the chair when this intense dizziness overcame me alerting my body to breathe. This could not be happening. Without thinking about him for even a moment, I silently screamed, "Why are you leaving me?"

In the month that followed, I found myself cycling through these five stages of grief about once a week. 1. Denial and isolation 2. Anger 3. Bargaining 4. Depression 5. Acceptance... Or maybe just four stages. I don't believe I ever made it to acceptance until about a year later. After all I had experienced as a child, how did losing John as my therapist become the worst thing that ever happened to me? He would be moving hundreds of miles away at the end of the month and somehow I had to let go of my lifeline. In my mind, this was not possible, so I did the first stage of grief like a rockstar. I totally denied the idea that this would in fact come to be. Truly thinking I could talk him out of moving to pursue a new job, and starting fresh with the woman in his life, I just refused to believe him. He kept trying to talk about closure and working on transitioning me to a new therapist. In complete denial, I thought why do you keep bringing this up? I continued to talk about the future of our relationship like nothing was going to change. John was the first person on the planet that I had told these dark secrets to and now he walks away? How could that be? Denying he would soon pack up and move was so much easier than dealing with the pain of him actually doing it. Still positive I could will this ball to stop rolling, I did not tell a soul I was about to loose my therapist. Instead, I convinced myself he would never leave me. Being abandoned by him was not an option I could survive. My mind became obsessed with old safety plans crumbling. My safety net was being shipped to another state. Who would answer my emergency calls when I was sure I couldn't take another step? I had made a commitment to him that I would not kill myself without calling him first. Together we had made lists of all my reasons to live. Did his move mean our contract for safety was null and void? And who was going to feed Rosebud?

With that thought, I remembered the most recent incident when my suicidal thoughts warranted an emergency phone call. John returned my desperate call immediately because I had not used my emergency option in a long time. As always he listened to my painful sobs and hopeless story. This time he did something different and got this creative idea to send me on a trip to the pet aisle at Woolworth's. If this was a new distraction technique, it was a good one. The plan intrigued me enough to use my very last ounce of energy. I took my portable phone and moved out of my fetal position on the floor of my safe closet. John's clear directions were for me to pick out a beta fish in my favorite color, some fish food, and a fishbowl. I wrote down John's shopping list and reluctantly off I went. What is a beta fish anyway? He said the guy at the store would help me find what I was looking for. Google wasn't around at the time, so I was just going to trust John. When I walked into the store, I looked up searching for the Pets sign. I spotted it along the back wall of the store. Once I got there, I could see there were so many different kinds of pretty fish to look at. There was a glitch, however. I had to walk down the bird aisle first. At the first sight of the bird cages, I wanted to turn around and run out of the store. Instead, I bravely scooted right past those cages to reach the little tiny fishbowls all in a row.

In the corner of the store, there was a young man scooping something out of one of the large tanks. He must have noticed the lost look on my face, and asked if he could help me. I thought, did John call this guy to warn him about me? He took the crumpled up list from my outstretched hand I was offering him, and asked me what color Beta would I like. There were so many choices, but it took a mere second to decide. Our Beta fish would be a blue and purple one. These colors were so brilliant and seemed to change with every twist this tiny creature made. The kids inside had not agreed on much lately, but this was a slam dunk of a choice. The store clerk, who I assumed was an authority on all fish, then proceeded to tell me that beta fish are a fighting fish and they are better off living alone. He did not however know whether this was a girl fish or a boy fish, so I immediately name it Rosebud. Rose, because Rose loved purple and Bud, for if it was really a boy. Since I went through all this trouble to buy the fish, I presumed it was also my job to name my little lifesaver. I could not bring myself to buy one of these miniature bowls the clerk said Beta's could live in. I was sure Rosebud would be claustrophobic in there all alone. I chose a much bigger bowl with plastic seaweed looking vegetation and a few rocks to hide behind when needing privacy. Finally, I picked up some high quality fish food, and mission accomplished. I thanked this most tolerant store clerk and carried everything out to the car. John had told me to bring all of this to his office. That was going to be the best part. Being very proud of all my choices, I was sure John would think I did a great job. The secretary at the desk knew I was coming and sent me right down to John's office. His door was open and I walked in, hands full, with a big smile on my face. Death averted once again.

John said Rosebud (he did love the name) would live in his office, and when I came in for my sessions, it would be my day to feed our pet. I accepted my new responsibility. Just one more reason to stay alive...

As my denial of John leaving weakened, I imagined my life contract being shredded into tiny pieces. I found myself fantasizing crazy scenarios of how I could lure him away from his plans to leave. All this anxiety helped nothing.

I would have to say I skipped the Anger stage and went straight to the bargaining stage. I considered doing anything to keep him where he belonged, with me. I would have sold my soul back to the devil if that is what it took. Could I possibly charm him into staying, by professing my great love for him? Maybe, I would be a better choice than whoever it was that was making him leave the state. I promised to be a better patient. I absolutely believed once I was healed, maybe we could be married and live happily ever after. Did I forget to mention that part?... Therapy can get very confusing sometimes. As I learned to trust John with things that were so incredibly intimate, my feelings for him got very muddled. During my most private moments, examining my relationship with John, I was sure of two things. One was that I absolutely needed him to be my therapist, probably forever. He knew more about me than any other person. He accepted me, without fear, no matter what I told him. He listened to me. He believed the unbelievable of my trauma. He had essentially saved my life, when I was on a suicide mission. He was my lifeline. I trusted him. I had never once entertained the thought that he would leave me. Being the same age, I just figured we would grow old together. I imagining we would one day have therapy from our rocking chairs, which would naturally morph into walkers and wheel chairs. The down side to having a forever therapist was how do you marry your therapist, and still have a therapist? I truly felt like I was in love with John. That sentence does not sound strong enough for what I was feeling at the time. This particular internal conflict was a huge problem. I had read about transference between a patient and therapist, but knew they were not talking about us. I was so mixed up. Having these conflicting feelings, I judged myself as a pathetic woman. Even now, the memory of my screwed up one-sided love affair seemed like a legitimate possibility at the time.

As our closure deadline grew near I began to panic. There was not enough time to prepare for his departure, most of that was my fault. I had been so busy running from my feelings and now there was no time for them. My panic turned into a feeling I did not do well. That feeling would be anger, the second stage of grief that I had avoided. Rachel would have gladly stepped in for me, but this felt like adult stuff. I could not bare the thought of my last few sessions with John being filled with the kind of rage I felt growing inside. This feeling was ugly, mean and selfish. So instead, I saved that anger for private moments, outside his office and directed it at me. In my mind I had driven him away, so I took it out on myself. What made me think I was good enough for any relationship, therapist or girlfriend?

When our last couple days were in front of me, I wanted to act like a well put together adult woman. I did not want him to remember me as the pathetic, spoiled child that I knew I was. Gosh this was difficult. What had happened to my dissociative powers? With all my magical thinking skills, could I not disguise this explosive anger I had desperately tried to deny?

When I entered John's office for the last time, I may have dressed like an adult, fussed with my hair a bit, and applied useless makeup, but certainly I was no older than 9 that day. The kids inside did not understand the adult reasons why this kind man was leaving us behind. As I recall, the final session was not even the usual length of time, which I did not understand then. So many tears had been cried from both sides of the room in the past couple weeks, and on this day we would simply say good bye. That session still remains foggy to me. Dissociation was now at full tilt. What I do remember clearly, was one answer to a question I had wondered about. That answer became my parting gift. With five minutes left of the session, John asked me if I could take over the full care and custody of Rosebud. With mascara already stinging my eyes, his request completely washed all makeup from my face. Unable to speak, I nodded my head and we started to pack her up. He was prepared for my answer and all we had to do was get her out to the car. I moved out with the fishbowl, fish food and my beautiful Rosebud. John had to help me with this however, because I also had to move my makeshift coffin. The hug we shared for the last time was both comforting and excruciating. And that was it. That chapter technically was over. There were cordial letters to check in with me periodically, but he moved on, and I had to work at doing the same.

My new therapist Virginia had been a substitute for John when he was away on vacations. I was never stable enough in those days to go a full week without therapy. John also had gone to Virginia for supervision. Apparently, that is something therapists do. God knows he probably did need a little help to see me week after week. Because of those previous meetings, and whatever a therapist shares in supervision, she knew me, my history, and that I was coming to her with Sarah's little coffin. John filled her in on the value of this box. Virginia was very honest about the fact that this very tiny coffin could not live in her office forever. She wanted me to honor Sara as she should be, with proper burial. Shortly after I stabilized somewhat from the loss of John, the next planned challenge was to face my feelings surrounding the contents of this shoebox. Because it took me a while to get over John leaving, I was blessed with a sabbatical from dealing with the grief around Rose's traumatic loss. My personal fear of her pain felt insurmountable. I fought Virginia tooth and nail on this one, but lost. She was right and secretly I knew it.

This was an extremely difficult part of my journey. Virginia felt Family Therapy would best help me get through this safely. I have to say at first I was not a big fan of bringing my family into the picture, but I could not come up with a good reason why including them in this process would be detrimental. Secretly, I hoped no one would come. It just seemed so much easier conquering this alone, if not easier, definitely more familiar, Virginia's point exactly. How did she know me so well so soon? Invitations were sent out and family therapy began in a blink of my eye, no more stalling. Everyone invited came, my mom and dad, both brothers and one sister in law. The idea of telling five people I loved that I had been pregnant at age 11, had my baby violently removed from my body, and buried under a tree just made me shake my head with exhaustion. I was so tired of disclosing what Daryl had done to me. This particular story was disturbing even if you were simply reading it in a book you found in a Fiction aisle, but I was about to share the saddest most dramatic thing that ever happened to me with my family. This was a heart wrenching process and it took weeks of preparation. I would have understood completely if one by one they excused themselves from the private room we were in as I revealed this long held secret. Maybe, I did not give them enough credit because the exact opposite happened. My entire family met my truth with love and support. They cried. Their tears both broke my heart and warmed it all at the same time. The only shame in the room was mine. That may have been the day that my shame began to slowly dissolve from inside my soul. Seeing their anger at the horror of what Daryl had done to me started to penetrate the wall that tightly held the feeling called shame inside my chest. Somehow the heartfelt words coming from my family made sense. With their support, I began realizing Daryl was the true owner of this shame.

As I recall, we met for six sessions, each one more emotional than the next. The day I remember most clearly was when I brought Sara's box into the room for them to see. I prepared them the best I could for this last session, but it was still heartbreaking. I continued to feel the need to protect my family. Cautiously, I let each person hold the shoebox coffin. When the box was opened, we could smell the sage John had placed in it so long ago. That scent and its memory took my breath away. With one breath I felt John's presence in the room... That comforting trigger calmed me right down. Reverently, I welcomed my family to touch everything I had put into the box to keep Sara safe, my rosary beads being the most important item. I brought the box from one person to the next. It almost felt like I was carrying my baby and asking each one to hold her. Other than the sound of crying and tears falling onto clothing, you could have heard a feather fall to the floor. This spacious family room grew smaller and felt respectfully somber, as we honored her. Sara was now a niece, a granddaughter, and if we had shared this with my son at that time, a sister. This was a very difficult day that I had avoided for 30 years. After this session was over I did feel supported. I no longer felt alone with the worst story of all, a secret no more.

With the first stage of our plan being successful, Virginia nudged me to move on to the second phase. This part of the process was an important one because I had to deal with my relentless, life altering guilt. I desperately needed to talk to a priest about all of this. The good news was, that I knew the most wonderful priest and I was sure he would help me if I dared to ask.

I had known Fr. Terry for many years from the retreats I had been on in the past. My mom was a secretary for the retreat house where Fr. Terry lived. The fact that we had a connection before this meeting, made walking up the stairs to his office just a little bit easier.

In this meeting I needed a holy man to listen to my story of Daryl and how Sara came to be. I needed to purge this deep pain of Sara's demise. I had to use the adult word "abortion" out loud. That piece of our story could not live in my head any longer without release. It was essential that my soul hear his words in response to all of this ugliness. I needed to say my confession and honestly, still wondered if there was forgiveness for me... Looking back on that day, this piece of healing felt more important than my 20 plus years of therapy.

I had gotten so lost and confused when it came to understanding my relationship with God. For many years I felt abandoned by my God. I had come to believe Daryl's words, reminding me that no one ever heard my prayers. When things got so dark in my young life, I lost sight of the light I had believed in before the darkness engulfed me. These are the things I was bringing to Fr. Terry's office.

Dealing with the anticipation of this meeting with the man whose absolution was going to free me from my own personal bondage was more than anyone should endure. Being terrified of that day and yearning for that moment of absolution was quite the inner conflict. Pulling myself together was like herding sheep lost in the woods. I felt rumblings from everyone inside. Rose with her head lowered, really felt hopeless and just wanted to go home. I could feel Little Kathy's legs doing their shaking thing. Rachel was shouting, "What the fuck?!" trying to turn this calamity around. Caryl echoed, "A monastery really?!" Sweet Emma and Lilly silently agreed to participate. Candy just seemed to hold my hand as I looked up at the big building with holy symbols welcoming us inside. Carrying all this baggage with us, were we really welcome here?

Not truly surprised by this inner turmoil we earned in our youth, I still tried to stay Kathleen, to look as adult as possible. The plain glass door felt like it was made of rock. Taking all my might to push it with one hand, I leaned in with my shoulder and got past the first barrier. I protected with my other arm the sacred box filled with my secret pain. Crossing the threshold, I was immediately surrounded by that monastery smell. There was a mix of incense that always lingered in the air, followed by that book smell from the small bookstore to the right as you enter through the main entrance. Both fragrances did soothe my nerves just slightly. This smell triggered a memory of a women's retreat I had participated in here in this building. During that retreat I remember allowing myself to let God's love in. I recognized that a possibility once again. All that, and the door had not yet closed behind me. Once inside, I realized I was here to make my confession. With that thought, I slipped back to a place where Rose and Little Kathy attempted confessing one other time. The smell was similar, but the building did not look the same. Here there were no confessionals or long aisles to walk down to do our penance. Would we actually succeed this time, or lie to the priest again? The good news was, today I did not have to go behind any scary curtain to tell my sins…

Yep, I was scared to death as they rang for Fr. Terry. How did that nice lady behind the desk know that is who me and my shoebox wanted to see? I don't remember telling her why I was here. Again, I reminded myself to pull it together, as I followed her directions to make my way to Father's office. I heard my own whisper say, "It's now or never." But just like a bad dream I once had, this floor seemed to gobble me up with each step. Thankfully, Candy held tight to my hand and guided me to my destination on the left. I stood there looking at a rectangle sign nailed on to an old wooden door. It held the name of a kind holy man with a round face and blue eyes. My memories of him were safe and calm. So why was I so damn scared to face him today? Would his eyes turn black or even worse, Daryl green when I revealed my story to this Godly man with a white collar? As I reached up to knock on the door, I paused and thought there is only one way to find out, I then heard my hand tapping softly on the door. As his footsteps approached, my heart started pounding almost as if I was running from Daryl. Maybe my heart is right on point... As the door knob turns, I looked down at myself. I felt four feet something, instead of five foot five. So much for appearing to be adult. The heavy door opens and I see no white collar. Instead, he is wearing a perfectly pressed, pale blue button down collar shirt, making his eyes even bluer than I remembered. I exhaled at the sight of him. Allowing myself to let out a breath released the growing lump I held in my throat. Before the next breath, all the feelings I was holding inside started to come out in the form of tears, drenching my red cheeks before he even let me pass into my confessional.

It is safe to say that Fr. Terry is a very patient man. Simply choosing the safest chair in the room was my first important issue. Having a tissue box near by the chair was of concern as well. I finally settle into a cool leather chair with wings surrounding my shoulders that now were located somewhere in the vicinity of my ears. I flash to my ballet teacher placing her hands gently on my tense shoulders in efforts to remind me to relax, releasing my arms to flow with ease as I danced. The Emma part of me seemed to perk up and smile at the thought. Maybe she was reminding me to finger dance. Surely, if Daryl didn't notice these relaxing hand movements, neither would Fr. Terry. All these wandering thoughts appeared to be my efforts at stalling. I took a moment to notice I was once again breathing, cradling my box in my lap. Realizing that Fr. Terry was still in the room, I looked up to see which chair he had chosen. He rolled the other leather chair closer to mine to face me without the blockade of his desk. He was far enough away that it did not feel beyond my imagined boundary. Hmm, boundary... that is a word I had only just learned the definition of. For the longest time I just called it the "B word" because I could not decide if that was a good thing or not, Yep, stalling again. I looked up from my own little world in my leather chair, and there he was still patiently waiting for me to find the courage to share what had brought me to his office. Having known him for a few years, I knew he counseled many people in need. Still judging myself, I gasped at the thought of admitting to him what had happened me. My tears apparently still fell down my face onto the shoebox, so it seemed I needed a nudge to find my voice. He leaned in and asked me what feelings were behind my weeping eyes. That tiny tug at my bursting heart was all it took. That opportunity to finally tell a priest had arrived. Out came my darkest secrets. Every ugly sin fell before him in a puddle filled with shame and guilt. My fear of telling no longer mattered. Once this deluge began, there seemed to be no end to it. With my hands covering my face, a litany of the most disgusting words I swore I would never repeat, just spewed from my mouth. My pain was raw and searing, but I felt relief. I must have looked like I just crossed a marathon fin-ish line, minus the joy that comes with the medal they place around your neck. I did not feel any pride or satisfaction that I had reached my goal. What I did feel was exhaustion. My body was so weak, I was not sure I would ever get up from the chair that engulfed me. My legs felt numb from being curled up sideways on the chair. With my face damp from tears and sweat, I felt the need of a shower.

As I opened my eyes and peaking from between my fingers, I found a pile of used Kleenex all over me and the floor. Trying to focus, I remembered Fr. Terry was in the room. Or had he left? Lifting my head, I saw that the nice man in the light blue shirt had moved his chair closer to me. I saw tears on his face. His eyes were not dark or green. They were remarkably even more blue against the background of his now flushed face. He had not backed away or run to hide. Instead, he gently asked if he could hold my hand. Was he not afraid to touch someone this dirty? The words never came from my mouth, but for one brief moment I could hear Black Flower's voice saying, "But my hands will dirty your pretty shirt." I must have indicated it would be ok for him to hold my hand, because I saw his clean cool hand reach for mine. I was not alone. Virginia was right. He was not afraid. Then he began to speak the most unlikely words… What I clearly remember him say was, "Kathy, this was not your fault. You were a little girl. What he did to you was horrific. You did not ask for, or welcome any of this into your life. You did not have a choice. You were too young. He had all the power." I remember feeling confused and saying, " But Father, a baby was conceived." And very quietly I added, "And then they aborted the baby from my body. Oh My God, I am so sorry." I began to shake uncontrollably, and I heard this wretched cry come out of my body. He moved from his chair, to his knees and held me as I wept with grief for the loss of Sara… Over and over again he assured me that I had done nothing wrong, but still I begged him to hear my confession. In my heart I felt I needed to be forgiven by God. He told me that there was nothing to forgive, but that he would be present with me as I prayed my confession. He then said the holy words I longed to hear. These words were for both me and the kids inside. His beautiful prayer was of God's love for a little girl who was brutally assaulted and taken advantage of. The prayer was for comfort and healing.

Fr. Terry kept his promises, as he said the words of forgiveness and new life. I was washed of my sins. He never thought they were my sins, but his words of absolution helped heal my dark soul in a way that no therapist could. I don't recall what I wore that afternoon, but I envision a white dress that is worn during Baptism. If this sounds dramatic, then I have described this life changing experience well. It certainly did not take my history from me, but my prayers finally felt heard.

There was still one more thing on our agenda that afternoon, but first we both needed a break and some fresh air. So, as we replenished our bodies with cold water, we stepped outside, where for the first time I noticed one of my favorite smells; fall air. Breathable air that does not suffocate. Unlike summer air, it does not have the feel of a heavy wet blanket holding your chest motionless. To me, fall air feels like freedom. In one effortless breath, I felt like permission to breathe, granted...

Feeling rejuvenated, it was time for part two of today's plans. When and where would we bury Sara? Just the thought of her being buried anywhere on these grounds brought such joy to Rose's heart. As impossible as it seemed, this was finally going to happen. Fr. Terry and I walked the grounds at the Monastery, and came to this place that he thought would be a nice spot. It was a quiet and private spot surrounded by tall beautiful fir trees. This scene made you want to lower your voice to a whisper. These trees had a gentle but strong look to them. And then I saw her. There stood a beautiful white statue of the Blessed Mother. I did not think I had any left, but my tears fell once again. All my years of life, good or bad, I have always prayed to the Blessed Mother. Now my Sara could possibly be buried right next to her in the most holy ground. This was perfect. A sense of hope came over me. I said, "Fr. Terry could this be the place ?" He nodded before the words even came out of my mouth. He smiled, and said yes. A very old dream come true.

Over the next couple weeks I tried to hang on to that peaceful feeling the Blessed Mother instilled in me, as we planned Sara's service. We were preparing an overdue, very private, Catholic funeral Mass for my Sara. As I type, I cry thinking of how healing this was for us.

During these couple weeks preceding the service, not everything was as focused as it may sound here. My head began to fill with a cyclone of Daryl's words. All his noise disturbed every move I made. It was like he was really back. If my fear wasn't so all consuming, I would have been very angry. I just wanted to bury my baby. Could he really stand in my way from six feet under ground? I required frequent emergency assistance from Virginia to keep moving past his voice. I was frozen with fear once again. A dead man was invading my days and nights. I could not escape. Nightmares ravaged my sleep. One dream in particular, I had written in my journal, described my state of mind vividly…

"Last night, I dreamt we had open heart surgery without the benefit of anesthesia. This man cut me open, and above his mask I could see he had no eyes. (I never could see Daryl's eyes) This doctor with no eyes, then sent me home right off the operating room table. No one took care of me. When I got home. I had diarrhea all night until I passed out…"

The aftereffects of this dream were very disturbing to me. I started to doubt I could actually go through with this funeral service. I knew I was actively breaking all of Daryl's rules, and as promised he would surely kill me and cut out my heart. Virginia reminded me that Daryl may be pitching a fit in my head, but he is dead, and this dead man could no longer hurt me. She also reminded me that in therapy I had been breaking the rules for a very long time, and this was no different. Deep down I believed that with the help of Fr. Terry, my family, and my steadfast therapist, I would get through this part of my survival. It was a fight each day prior to the burial date, but I decided I was going to plow though all of this fear and do the right thing.

As a team we came up with a date and time for this outside sacred ceremony. On Tuesday, October 7th 1997 we would finally put Sara in a safe resting place. Everyone joining me at this service would have a part in making this the most special day.

Virginia and I created a list assigning everyone involved a job. I found this exact list written on yellow paper just the other day inside a journal written from that time. Sharing this will give you an idea of the preparation for that day in October.

1. Carry the box- my father
2. Fr. Terry say ceremonial words.
3. Flowers for Ceremony- Felicia (sister-in-law)
4. Marker for the grave- Kathy
5. Flower bulbs to plant. (wait-Kathy)
6. Bible verses read about children- my brother Jeffrey
7. Take letter from the box and read it at the service.- Kathy
8. Bookmarks from the family-Mom
9. A special cloth for the ground-Kathy

10. Short communion mass-Fr. Terry

11. Music-Tommy (young priest)

12. Ending prayer and final blessing-Fr. Terry

13. Bury the box-my dad

14. To mom's to eat after-mom

15. Dad to take picture of the box.

The day before the ceremony my dad called me and asked me to stop by for a quick visit. I drove over to my parents house and walked in thru the front door, which brought me into the dining room. On the dining room table was a wooden box, painted the most beautiful, safe, color of blue I have ever seen...

Blue has always been my safe color. So many things that I have loved are blue. My fathers eyes were the most crystal clear blue. I have always thought they looked liked cracked glass. The one thing about me that I love, are my matching blue eyes. Also the sky is blue, which was a place I found solace through the trees. And of course, the Blessed Mother's dress is blue.

This box was now going to be Sara's coffin, and my dad made it for her. This is one moment in time I will never forget. I was so touched by his humble efforts. Speechless, I walked over to the table, opened the top of the blue box. Inside, was the small shoe box I had been using to hold Sara for so long. My dad had also lined the box with a beautiful cloth. Still unable to speak, I just cried while hugging my dad. Standing in his embrace I felt all his love, strength, and understanding. This box was an incredible demonstration of my father's love that I will never forget. At that moment I felt ready to bury Sara. My fears seemed melted away. I was ready now, all because of this blue wooden box made with love by my father.

And so the sun rose on October 7th and this long Tuesday began. I was nervous and shaky as I dressed for the day. I wore a dress. I wish I could picture it now, but I have no memory of that.

My plan was to travel with my parents to the monastery for the service. When I arrived at my parents house again, entering into the dining room, I saw the blue box sitting right where I left it. On this day, a dozen beautiful pink long-stemmed roses were laid on top of it. Instantly, I thought of the pink roses that grew wild on the wall in the back yard of my childhood home. I am sure my parents chose the color pink for Sara, but in my heart I was remembering the safe roses of my past. Tears fell, but I was comforted by that memory.

Together we silently drove to the monastery. I sat in the back seat with the blue box sitting next me. My left hand on top of the box and my right held the pink roses in my lap. When we arrived every-thing was ready. Waiting for me in this special spot was Fr. Terry, the rest of my family, and a girlfriend that I had bravely shared my secret with. Virginia and John were there with me in spirit. My dad carried the blue box which held Sara, to her new resting ground. My thought as I walked towards everyone was,"This looks like a real funeral." They were dressed reverently for the day. Fr. Terry had his funeral priest attire on. I saw that special purple scarf draped around his neck onto his chest. He was holding the funeral mass book I had seen in church at other funerals. A small table was set for us to receive communion before the burial. I was overcome with the reality that this holy man, my loved ones, and God were all here for me and my baby no one ever knew about. In one big breath I felt be-lieved, and that I was not alone anymore. Little Kathy's legs started to shake. I knew everyone inside was present and aware of what was about to happen. My mom had her arm linked through mine, and we slowly approached the white statue of the Blessed Mother. It did not seem like just a statue on that day. I truly felt her presence embrace me. It was hard, but I let her love in too.

Behind Fr. Terry I could see the covering over the hole where Sara would be lowered. There were gentle greetings and hugs from everyone, and then we began. The entire ceremony was more beautiful than I had imagined. Fr. Terry just seemed to know exactly what I needed. I did not have to do anything but stay in the moment and bury my little girl in this holy place, just as we had wished so many years ago.

One by one everyone in the circle stepped forward doing their part to make this the most incredible day. Each precious word from their mouths validated their acknowledgement and honor of Sara. This was something I never dreamed possible. We were joined by a young priest that brought his guitar and sang for us. His music somehow made the ceremony real. His songs touched my heart deeply. I had met this young man only once before and he was singing at my baby's funeral service. I felt so blessed by his offering. These songs I knew from church, and the sound of his voice kept me grounded in this spot in 1997. I was so grateful for this comforting sound, because there was no holy music when Candy buried Sara the first time… We received communion, and my wavering faith at that moment felt revived once again. As I am writing today, I remember being struck by the power of my family's support. My doubts that they believed my childhood history were no longer existent.

The beginning of the funeral mass helped to prepare me for what was about to come. We were now going to bury the blue box. As a family, we moved closer to the covering over the prepared grave. Through my tears, I read the love letter I had written to Sara. I remember Fr. Terry having to assist me with this. The words brought sobs from the deepest part of my soul. So, he held the shaking paper, and read the words I could longer see. I then placed my letter inside the box to be with her forever. As planned, my dad carried the box to this final spot. He respectfully lowered her coffin into the ground. I remember thinking he was the perfect pallbearer. Again, I was in awe of this act of love.

When he stepped back to join the others, I felt everything inside of me starting to crumble. My legs buckled, lowering me to the ground. On my knees the present escaped me and I was no longer in this holy place. This vulnerable moment brought Rose and Candy to the surface and we had travelled back in time to Daryl's outside place. This huge flashback to Candy burying and naming Sara the first time was now my reality… this was not part of the plan, but is how it happened. My next memory was Fr. Terry on his knees, holding my face in his hands, telling me I was safe, and we were finally burying Sara in holy ground. I had no idea how long it took for me to return to the present, but I did. I must have trusted Fr. Terry's eyes and allowed his words to drown out Dead Daryl's. Once back in the present, I lowered the pink roses on top of Sara and dropped handfuls of dirt into her resting place. My thoughts then were, "How do I leave this spot?" Fr. Terry said a final prayer and the young priest sang another song. The service was over, but my feet would not move. I could not leave until she was completely covered. I could still feel the young parts of me wanting Sara to be safely tucked into holy ground, safe from evil, forever… As if part of the plan, the gardener appeared and shoveled the blanket of dirt to cover the blue box completely. I had chosen a small stone as a marker for her grave. I placed it there knowing I would return soon to visit. The stone reads, "Love is like a Rose." I chose it for Sara's real mother.

I want to end this chapter with the unedited love letter I wrote to Sara that now sits inside the Blue Box with her forever. I found the letter in the very last pages of my old journal, dated Sunday, October 5th 1997.

"Today, on Tuesday, October 7th 1997 you are being remembered openly. You are being remembered by the people here and many others in spirit. We inside are no longer keeping your conception and death secret.

You are part of me.

You existed, even if it was just a short time.

You were so tiny with a tiny soul. A soul so strong, it was never forgotten. Your memory lived deep inside us, only to be remembered openly when it was safe enough to do so. We are honored to prepare a safe, holy place for you. We hope you will find Sara Jaclyn someday.

My tears are our loss of you. You saw blackness and we ached for you. I pray the "Hail Mary", that the Blessed Mother takes you in her arms and rocks you to comfort while healing your wounds. This was a bad time when we were little. We had no power to change anything. I would have kept you and cared for you. Now, I am a mother by choice. I love my son and keep him safe.

I wish you were here, but now you do feel a little bit closer. Today we are making a safe space for you. A place of Peace. You are no longer in Evil ground. You are being blessed and put to rest in Holy ground. A safe place.

Sleep my baby, sleep. We will cover you with flowers. Let good air blow past you. I am sending you with good smells of nature. My rosary beads go with you. I protect you in a silver box, a shoe box, and now the blue box.

The broken stick, rocks, herbs, came from different parts of me and very special people in my life. The picture left with you is of all of us inside, joined with hearts to keep you safe. The candle is so you have light. The blue cloth is to keep you warm, safe, and Blue in spirit. These are all good things, from my heart to yours.

You will never be alone again. Prayers come to you from many directions now. Our truth has been told. Today, I believe God holds you gently in his hands. Knowing this helps to heal the pain of losing you. We will tuck you into holy ground now. This is a safe place for me too, so I will come sit by you, paint near you and breathe good air. You will always be in my heart... I love you Sara."

The Making of an Artist

I think we all have an artist somewhere hidden inside. I did not acknowledge the artist in me until I was in my 40's, but I came to believe she existed long before that. My definition of an artist has changed over the years. I use to think an artist was a person who was gifted at a young age, excelled in art during high school, and then moved on to a lifetime of selling expensive paintings to fancy museums. I pictured historical artists whose names became icons of the artistic world forever. Now, my thoughts on being an artist are so different. What I want to talk about is how the artist evolved in me, a person who had not one artistic bone in her body.

Like many other little children, coloring with crayons was something I loved to do. Receiving a new coloring book and box of Crayola crayons always felt like a special occasion. Opening that brand new box of crayons was a moment I remember vividly. I don't know what was more exciting, that incredible smell when you open a new box, or the beauty of all 64 colors so neatly placed according to their color groups. Picking that first crayon somehow felt important. Trying to be creative, I wanted to choose something bright, like

Wild Strawberry or Electric Lime, but I always gravitated towards the Sky Blue and Violet. I did not know then that color would become such a meaningful part of my life.

Before the age of 6, my little girl drawings were typical for a happy little girl with a safe comforting life. I drew stick figures of my family in every room in my house. Each stick figure pictured, both big and small, had smiles on their faces and bunches of flowers in their skinny little hands They were depictions of my innocent little girl life. Coloring was simple, blissful fun. As I think back, my early pictures resembled what an Impressionist might create, using light and soothing color. There was nothing suspect in those early creations.

There was no question that my pictures changed after Daryl interrupted my life. In the beginning, I may not have noticed, but freehand drawings became few and far between. There was no wonder I wanted to switch to the confines of a coloring book. It was definitely safer to stick to coloring inside someone else's lines. Looking back, whether I knew it or not, this is when I started to shut down any possible personal expression through art. This little girl was going into hiding… A coloring book simply did the creating for me. Anybody could color in a coloring book. No decisions had to be made except for which crayons to use. I could think my own thoughts if I wanted to or just get lost in the colors I chose to decorate the pre made images. What a relief. I could still color and enjoy the soothing physical motion involved when I sat down with my crayons. The repetitive over and over hand motion felt calming, but something had shifted inside. Now, I colored inside the lines and gradually started to press harder on my crayons. No more watercolor looking pictures came from these hands. I noticed I was going through my crayons much faster than before, and had to ask for new ones more often.

My favorite place to color, was lying on the floor in the living room. My parents watched TV from their favorite chairs. My mom sat on the rose printed love seat and my dad in his matching chair. There I was surrounded by the safety of my family. I remember clearly, that circular protective image on a typical evening in our small living room. While I was coloring, my parents thought that I wasn't any different than before Daryl started hurting me. They of course didn't know then there was a before and after… Our nightly family gatherings felt safe, but inside my broken heart I was definitely aware of the lies of omission I was telling. On one hand, coloring was a fun thing to do, but it also served as a sneaky way to keep my horrible secret. My job was to look the same as always. My activities had to remain unchanged, which was part of my disguise. Getting lost in the colors of the characters in the coloring book took me away from those disgusting pictures in my head. There was no chance of exposure within the structure of coloring inside the lines of someone else's creation. Immersing myself inside a cartoon coloring book's world became a personal safe haven for me. My only responsibility was to color neatly within the prefabricated lines. The rules of this activity were easy and harmless. Obeying orders was now my specialty. Daryl didn't know about my coloring, but he would have liked this creative secret keeping technique. Damn, I hate the idea of pleasing him in any form.

As Daryl's Mondays continued week after week, it became more difficult to just stay inside the lines. My color schemes were darkening without my knowledge until the picture would suddenly startle me. Eventually, even coloring books started to reveal the change that was taking place inside. A creative outlet felt important for survival, but I had to keep silent. I had to be more and more careful not to disrupt the facade my art provided.

So, I laid down my coloring books and sought out any stray pieces of paper I could find to draw on. The backs of bulletins from church, old school assignments and backs of grocery lists became my new canvas. Finally, with my own allowance money I bought a blank drawing pad. The only problem with buying a whole pad was that this would be more difficult to hide. You see, the pictures I was now drawing, with those same worn down crayons were not so pretty any more. The pictures on these throw away pieces of paper were in colors of blood red, black, and orange. I didn't like those colors, but I felt magnetically pulled to use them anyway. Those three colors felt mean. Black and red stirred up feelings of anger, pain and fear which were new and vaguely recognizable to me. Deep inside, I knew the ugly colors originated from the drawings on Daryl's arms. The orange and black color combination triggered the vision of the tee shirts, heavy work boots and leather vests that Daryl and his friends wore. I didn't really know what to do with this new set of feelings that had been forced into my life.

Praying these huge emotions away was obviously not working, but somehow using these scary colors helped me purge them out through my tightly held fingers. My tiny fingers ached from pressing on my crayons so hard, digging these wretched colors into the paper. After these powerful coloring sessions my right middle finger had a newly created indentation from the crayon's pressure. Even though I was trying to run from those triggering colors, I remember both my hands soaking up the dreaded colors right into my skin. Feeling unclean from this, I would run to the bathroom in search of the scrub brush. The panicky need to wash, drove me to nearly digging into my skin to get clean. The red and black stains made me feel sick inside. Thankfully, the toilet was in the bathroom, since many times I wretched over the bowl, before scrubbing those memories from my hands. After this disturbing process, I was relieved the pictures were gone, for the moment. All this reminded me of Little Kathy washing in the stream after her visits to Daryl's garage. I wanted to magically wash all this away. On those days, forever keeping my secret, I at least wanted to appear clean on the outside. Unfortunately, feeling clean on the inside, never came until decades later.

The strange thing was, after finishing each picture, I didn't want to destroy them, but at the same time, I wanted no one ever to lay eyes on what I drew. So I hunted for a secret hiding place to store them. A place no one would ever look. Before this, I don't think I ever hid anything from my parents. But just as I was hiding what Daryl was doing to me, by not telling, I also was about to hide these revealing pictures. We lived in a small Cape Cod style house which had rafters upstairs that are sometimes used for storage. This became my first hiding place. Once I turned 10, my bedroom was moved upstairs, so I had easy access to these rafters. I started to use these cubby holes to make a private places to play. If you had opened those little cubby doors, which were right next to my bed, you would have found a pillow, my favorite doll, and some of my toys. Like magic I transformed these stuffy rafters into a little inside play house, with a slanted roof. I felt safely hidden in that secluded cozy space. My parents were well aware that I made this a Kathy space to play. Since this was all above board, it did not seem unusual for me to be hanging out in there. Before choosing this as the hiding place for my dark artwork, I had to consider that my parents did use the rafters for their storage as well. So, I put my thinking cap back on, and came up with the perfect plan. One day, I tiptoed down stairs, into the kitchen, snuck the sharp scissors out of the junk drawer, and ran up the stairs back to my room. I found just the right hiding place in my rafters. Holding tightly the scissors in my right hand, I cut an opening into the paper that held the insulation lining the slanted roof. With shaking hands, I carefully stuffed my pictures inside the insulation, being sure not to rip the paper any wider. There was only one downfall with this genius idea. Unknowingly, I found out the hard way, that insulation contained something horrible that made my hands itch like crazy. So again, I had to run downstairs and wash my hands after stuffing those disgusting pictures in their new hiding place. All this hand washing felt kind of ironic as I think back.

I did color some pretty "Kathy" looking pictures in my coloring pad to be sure my secret would be kept. These colorful drawings were for sharing with family and receiving praise. It always felt nice when one of my pictures made it to the refrigerator for showing off my good work. All this effort was part of my mission to keep us all safe, and at the same time displace some of the ugly pictures from my mind.

I became an expert at living two lives, even with my artwork. Out of fear, I obeyed Daryl's rules, and became the best secret keeper, ever. While I was so busy acting as if life was easy, some strange things started to happen that I could not figure out. Pictures started to show up that I could not recall creating. I would find them in unusual places. For example, I found one under my pillow as I laid down to sleep. I slipped my hand under the pillow to get comfortable, and felt an unexpected piece of paper tucked in the pillow case. The only things I had ever put under my pillow were rosary beads and a loose tooth for the Tooth Fairy to take away, leaving me with a prize. Wondering what this could be, I turned on my bedside lamp, and squinted at my discovery. Once my eyes could focus, I saw the worst picture I ever colored. Quietly I gasped, folding it into my chest. I was shocked and could not catch my breath. This was not a refrigerator picture. It was horrifying. The picture was a depiction of everything I was trying to forget.

This scene drawn with only black and red was even too horrible to put in my secret hiding place. I frantically ripped it into the tiniest pieces my fingers could rip, in an effort to totally destroy it. As small as these pieces of evil were, they could not even go in the regular kitchen trash can. I knew in my heart I had to take this pile of confetti and dispose of it into the outside garbage hole, that was underneath the ground in the back yard. That secret maneuver would have to wait until morning, however. I could not sneak past my parents in the living room and go out into the dark to accomplish this. They would have asked questions I couldn't answer. After stuffing the ripped pieces paper into an old used pink envelope, I then hid it in the rafter space until morning. As soon as the sun came up, I snuck outside and put the envelope where it belonged, in the garbage where all disgusting things got dumped. I remember praying there would be hungry little maggots in the garbage that liked to eat paper.

Even worse than the sight of the picture itself, was wondering where it came from. As hard as I searched my memory banks that night, I had no recall of drawing this hideous picture. That thought would haunt me for many years to come. Had the Boogie man crept into my room and placed it in my bed to terrify me? That day remains very clear in my memory. This dreadful night was the moment that fear found it's way into my bedroom, and never left.

At about that same age, another picture was found that confused the innocent, unaware part of me. The Marie part of me found one of these ugly drawings, colored into the underside of the coffee table in the living room. Marie never knew anything of Daryl's reign of terror, so drawings like these never made any sense to her. Marie was the happy young girl part of me that got A's and B's in school. Everybody seemed to like carefree Marie. I think now, how confusing that must have been for her. Looking back at Marie's discovery, I did wonder why she didn't tell our parents. What I think about that is, on some level, even as unaware as she was of what was happening on the other side of the wall, she instinctively knew to be silent. Marie unfortunately did share the same tortured body as the rest of us, but remained dissociated from the body part of her. So, unbeknownst to Marie, that body part of her must have known the rules, and subconsciously she simply knew not to tell.

Now, that I have a cooperative co conscious system of parts to communicate with, the truth has come out about the artist behind the mysterious coffee table drawing. Rachel will tell her story:

"things just piss me off sometimes… one day after being to that outside playground of Daryl's, i had a really hard time getting Little Kathy back to the house. that creep made her bleed again. once i dragged her down to the stream to clean off her legs, she just wouldn't stop crying. i really hate when she cries. she starts, and it almost makes me cry, and that is just not happening. tears don't come from my eyes. ok, maybe once… anyway, i was so mad at Daryl and his new buddy he had hanging around that day in the woods. Little Kathy always got real scared when he brought new boys with him. he is scary enough to her, and then to bring someone else she didn't know, she couldn't handle it, and the waterworks would start up. we all prepared for what came next. which punishment would she earn for her tears?

…and why did they all wear those same orange and black shirts. orange and black, black and orange. didn't their mom's know how to buy any other colors. is there a special orange and black store?? i was never big on flowery pink or yellow, but i really hate orange and black now. how many more colors is he gonna make me wanna rip form our crayon box? On Mondays, rather than looking at his ugly face, i zoomed my eyes in on those crappy shirts and now i can't ever get those colors out of my eyes.

anyway, back to Little Kathy and the coffee table. well, she never could stop crying that day down at the stream, so i had to take over, clean off both legs, put on new under-wear, and get dressed exactly the way she left her house. as i walked though the back yards, to get to the house, i kicked everything i could see near my feet. rocks, sticks, and dirt flew everywhere. my hands made strong fists. i kept thinking, i wanna punch his stupid shirt and then his nose if i can reach it. "bend down just once Daryl!"

as i walked up her driveway, i knew it was time for me to sit back and let Little Kathy walk into the yellow kitchen where her mom would be cooking something good for lunch. i was so mad that day, i thought for a minute, maybe i would just walk in and blow our cover... even Little Kathy, when walking in through that screen door, knows to put on her little crooked smile and be sweet. today though, i am wor-ried she can't do it, so i lay back, but don't leave her side. her dad didn't come home for lunch that afternoon. lunch went a little faster, and her mom got busy cleaning the dishes right away. she was such a good cleaner. anyway, Little Kathy got a coloring book and crayons out of her bedroom and start-ed coloring in this stupid Minnie mouse coloring book. She pulled out this crayon called pink flamingo and i wanted to puke. i couldn't bear to color in that silly book. i decided no more cute little book, and said, "sorry Little Kathy, my turn."

pushing Minnie to the curb, i slid under the coffee table and grabbed two crayons. my first choice was "eerie black". second choice was, "orange soda." where did they come up with these names? even though i hated these two colors that's what i pulled out of the box. colors are important. i start with that already worn down black crayon i have used before. as tight as i can press, i drew daryl holding his stupid stick. he thinks his stick makes him a big deal. he sucks. i hated him. my crayon felt really mad, and it broke when i tried to draw the stone altar. he had just made Little Kathy lay on it and he made her bleed. i had forgotten to pull out that bloody red color. that is not what it said on the crayon's paper wrapping, but that is what i called it. i reached back and grabbed it. then the red crayon broke too. i had pressed down so hard on the crayons that my hands began to shake. i thought, who cares!!! i was willing to break them all if i had to. i remember how good it felt to get this mad as i drew these pictures. the table didn't care. i really felt like yelling instead of coloring, but this had to be good enough for today. that stupid quiet rule always wins. quietly, i colored even harder. finally i wanted to give Daryl his t-shirt, so i grabbed the stupid orange soda color. the crayon's title does not match what this shirt feels like to me, but it does match the orange soda he made Little Kathy drink in the garage... once he was wearing his shirt, i took back that broken black crayon and i dug his evil symbol on top of the orange shirt. i also drew a head on his body, but no face for him. i don't look at his eyes anymore, but i know they are green. no green in this picture. green is for those pretty leaves Little Kathy gets lost in when she looks up to the sky, flying herself away from that cold stone altar. damn him!!!

jolted from my angry drawing, i hear, "Kathy, Kathy, would you come into the kitchen please?" ...i wished i could keep yelling, i mean coloring. but i left Little Kathy laying underneath the table. her mom was calling her. i knew my place. the drawing of the outside place, and my angry thoughts still remained a secret under the coffee table, until now. yep, it was me, i did it."

Before Little Kathy steps into the kitchen, she notices the scary colors on her hands and wonders only for a minute, how did they get there? She remembers only the pink color chosen for Minnie and these were not Minnie's colors all over her hands... Little Kathy asks her mom, "Can I pee first?" Once given permission, she scooted herself into the bathroom, turned the water on, flushed the toilet, and scrubbed the black, red, and orange down the drain. She then found her sweetest smile, and answers her mothers call.

After those young years of drawing and coloring, I don't remember any art at all. Finding myself doodling in margins of my journals was a familiar site, but that was it until I entered the psychiatric hospital, where I was again introduced to how helpful art could be.

~

...Reluctantly, I walked into that art therapy class hoping the teacher was sick and it was cancelled for the day. I had been told this group therapy was about having a voice, and expressing my feelings without using my words. That actually sounded acceptable to me, but when I was done painting, they wanted us to get into a circle and share what feelings this painting brought up for us. I remember thinking to myself, "You said without words!!!"

Once I allowed myself to put my paintbrush to paper, everything else slowed to a halt. I was able to slip into this open and truthful place inside. Internally, I remember blocking out the therapists and all the other patients sitting around me. I put up tall, thick, invisible walls around me and got lost in the space I created. My only job was to put paint to paper. The knowledge that I was in a locked ward, protected from the outside world, was a comforting thought. I knew I was never going to see these people again, which certainly made it easier to paint my darkest feelings on paper. My newly painted world portrayed both sides of the wall, however, I found myself still in hiding, while avoiding full transparency. I painted symbolic images of my dark side, and with every opportunity surrounded my darkness with light. I made outsiders look for my darkness, and dared them to find it. This was different from when Little Kathy and Rachel painted. A scary picture was a scary picture, and a pretty one was just pretty. I really liked this new combined version of my feelings through watercolors. I was still able to paint my pain, but with my growing talent I was able to become more discreet. I believed that my discretion kept our secret, and we were not breaking the old rules of a dead man.

Even though no one else in the class chose watercolors as their medium, I did. I was on a mission. With watercolors I could use as little, or as much water as I needed to paint the depth of my feelings. I felt like watercolors could help me with my disguise, and still sneak my dark feelings into the painting. Another thing I noticed, is that unlike when I was a child, I did not have to press hard on a paintbrush as I did with my crayons to show the depth of my feelings. I am still not sure if this was a good thing, but it was a difference. It was certainly easier to clean watercolors off my hands, than it was those deep stained crayon marks on my fingers. One of my therapists brought to my attention that the good thing about cleaning up watercolors after having painted some dark bloody scenes, I now merely had to wash off red paint... no more blood. I think that was probably the most important thing the art therapist ever said to me.

By the time I was released from the hospital, part of my self care plan was to continue to paint as much as I could as a therapeutic tool. This did give me something to look forward to when I was preparing for my discharge back into the real world. I started a brand new journal just to make lists of the supplies I would need to continue on my painting journey. My plans to shop in a real art supply store felt exciting. Once released, I eventually went shopping for the colors I needed. This store had everything an artist could possibly want. It was interesting that I actually posed a question to myself concerning whether I was a painter or an artist. That didn't seem to matter when I entered watercolor supply store. I spent hours hunting down all the things I needed to follow my discharge plan of care. I loved everything about this preparation to get started painting at home. The art store was a bit dangerous, however. I filled my basket with every color imaginable, including colors I didn't like. I needed an easel, blocks of watercolor paper, brushes, special pencils, tiny sponges, etc. As it turned out, I found myself in that store once a week getting more and more supplies. The staff there called me by name when I would walk in every week, sometimes twice. I was legitimately obsessed with all this, but better using a paintbrush rather than a sharp instrument cutting my skin, or starving myself to death. Painting replaced some of my very unhealthy habits with a whole new world of healing with color, and I began painting my way right out of Hell.

My son Tim and I lived in an old three family house. Our apartment was a very spacious eight room apartment. It sat on the corner of the street, at the very top of a huge hill. I remember thinking we lived on top of the world. The view was actually pretty nice, especially in the winter when the snow fell. We were on the first floor and had the most wonderful sunroom. This room surrounded me with eight long windows which I adored. These windows allowed me to let in fresh air when I wanted it, (or not). Old fashioned venetian blinds sat at the top each window. These blinds gave me a choice to hide from the world, or on good days, open everything wide, and let in that good natural light. Old french doors with windows separated the sunroom from our living room. Those windows allowed me the opportunity to paint even when Timmy was awake. I had a direct view of my son watching TV in the next room. If I left the doors open just a crack, the TV noise was muffled, but I could still hear Tim's voice and movements.

Even though we had a stereo system in the living room, I set up a smaller version in the sun room just for me. Most of my preferred music at that time was without words. This music resembled my act of painting… No words. So behind those french doors, George Winston's piano music could often be heard. I would surprise my neighbors with something a little more upbeat from time to time.

Piece by piece I built a beautiful space decorated with candles, flowers, and healthy plants. I surrounded myself with books I loved. My blue shawl was always over my chair, and there was always an audience of my favorite stuffed animals. The addition of the stuffed animals was a great idea, because they loved everything I painted and kept it my secret. And last but not least, I purchased a french easel that fit perfectly in the corner of the room, positioned for the best natural light and clear view of my surroundings. The easel made me feel like a real artist, or at the very least made me look like one.

With all these things in place, this new artistic part of me felt encouraged and set free. I mostly painted in the evening and sometimes late into the night once Timmy was tucked into bed. I sat in my well cushioned wicker chair, wrapped in my blue shawl and privately painted from a feeling spot deep inside. There was no title to my technique, because I had none. It was simple, my colorful feelings just flowed onto my special watercolor paper, and time melted away with each stroke of the brush. All of a sudden, I'd look up and the clock would say 2:35. I wondered if that was AM or PM? Looking away from my easel into the darkness through my long windows, I realized it was the middle of the night. Here I was with my light on in this open sunroom, at the top of this hill for anyone to see. Feeling exposed and a bit uncomfortable in my skin, I discovered a completed painting sitting on my easel. It was shocking to look at, because I could not remember creating it. Franticly, I would shut off the light next to me. Those were the times that I was surprisingly faced with the most terrifying pictures resembling my past. These visuals reminded me of the ones Little Kathy found under her pillow so very long ago. Still I felt that my dead perpetrator would know I had done this and broke the rules yet again. I waited for my punishment…There I sat shaking, with tears falling into my lap, wondering what do I do with this painting? Initially I could hear Little Kathy telling me to rip it up as fast as I could and throw it in the outside garbage. Being a little braver than when I was 10, I thought twice about that idea. On those nights I would temporarily hide the revealing painting under a pretty lap blanket I sometimes covered my easel with, closed the french doors of the sunroom, and went to bed. My plan was to purchase a storage bin to keep these pictures safely hidden away. My main concern was to keep them from the eyes of my son and secondly, to somehow hide them from a dead man.

To this day, I still have this bin of those particular pictures tucked away in the back of our big bedroom closet. These paintings are probably the most important ones I ever painted. They were the voice of a secret unspeakable past. I regard them as life saving paintings. By purging these images on to the paper, I relieved the pressure of my memories playing out in my head. Painting it out, seemed to work better than some of the numbing medication I was prescribed. This artistic expression also kept us safe. It became a tool that replaced acts of self injury that continued since I was a young girl. When I was holding my paintbrush I experienced my feelings in a safer way. Sharing my paintings with my therapist helped me to get my words out into the open. Having a voice seemed like a never ending battle. Silence was truly my most dangerous enemy. Daryl knew what he was doing when he forced me into my silent hell. While I was keeping my promise to him, his assault lived on years after he was six feet under ground.

When the seed was planted in the hospital to "paint it out," the young parts of me jumped all over the idea. Permission was given to tell our story without saying a word. I struggle now with the words "I" and "We" as I tell this part of "our" story. The reason I was surprised by my artwork in the middle of the night is because "I" did not paint those pictures. The Rachel, Little Kathy, Caryl, Emma, Daryl part, Andria, Kevni, and Rose parts of me held the paintbrush. Many times they even owned their pictures by making sure to sign them. Talking about those different parts of me has always been difficult until recent years. Therapy gave me the chance to talk about my inside parts and allowed them their very own voice. They were my survival then, and I honor them now. That old bin in the closet may not look revered from the outside, but when I open the cover that faint smell of the paper and old paint triggers a memory of those late night therapy sessions in the sunroom. I will be forever grateful for the hard work of my young ones deep inside. This was their truth in living color…

Gradually, I felt a shift in my whole painting experience. Not really noticing the changes, my paintings morphed into pictures I could actually show my family. I was no longer so surprised or terrified by what I found sitting on my easel. My colors lightened and the content was a little different. The finished product did not appear so literal or dark. I could feel a change inside as well, and I became more curious about the technique of painting with watercolors. I started to study books on the subject and experimented with what I was learning. What seemed to be a common denominator in my process and possibly developing as a style, was I always started with sky. I immersed myself into creating this perfect natural backdrop. This was my favorite part of the painting, which made me love facing that empty brand new piece of paper every time. Blending the fresh new colors felt so comforting. Creating open sky felt safe, and like it belonged to me. This sky did belong to me. It was mine…

The sky that I painted came from that safe place we floated to when being assaulted in the woods. Rose shared in her chapter the need to get away from Daryl while being pinned onto that stone altar. She was looking up, past her unimaginable physical pain. Through her welled up, stifled tears, she saw some escape in the light of the sky surrounded by a natural frame of the trees… With her eyes covered, her climb into the woods had terrified her. And just when she wanted her eyes to be covered, he would the remove the blindfold. She remembered his words in her right ear, "Keep those eyes open!" And so she did. Then came Rose's sky. Whether it was clouded or filled with sunshine, the sky was hers and no one else's. She could fly up above her poor little raped body. In her sky nothing hurt. She was only touched by rays of sunshine and soft puffy clouds. Light as a feather, she danced, and glided back and forth, protecting herself from what was happening down below. She wished she could stay there forever. While that was not possible, she returned to her sky every time Daryl forced her to lay in that cold dark spot. Rose did not know it then, but she was a smart, creative little girl. She helped us survive with her brave escape to this beautiful, endless place. We honored her in each painting as we started with sky, what a great beginning. We painted ourselves right off that altar. Our painting began to reveal the whole truth, the good and the bad. I know now when I look at these creations I see both. It may be discreet, but I know it is there. There are always two sides to our paintings. This was tricky sometimes, but I naturally became good at this style and loved it.

At the time, I didn't see it, but I was getting healthier with every stoke of the brush. As time went on, putting one foot in front of the other, I started to come out of my shell. Painting as part of my everyday life was something I never anticipated. Suddenly, and to my surprise, I objectively saw some of my paintings as good. I started to use the word beautiful when thinking about them. I wondered, "Did I paint that?" Finally, I asked my therapist if she thought they were good enough to show in a small gallery. I brought this up because through her window, across the street I could see this small, unique art gallery. Of course Virginia, turned that question into an entire therapy session, as she should. Being very brave and out of curiosity, I stopped into this very intriguing gallery. Looking in every corner, I wondered two things. One, would my kind of paintings fit into this space? And more importantly, was this a safe place to actually show my paintings? I never said a word about my work that day. I walked in just like any other buyer and walked out buying a pair of handcrafted earings. I also took a sense of safety with me when I walked out the door.

I thought about showing my paintings for a few months, and one day in the fall of 1998, I picked up my small unprofessional portfolio of 6 paintings, pushed the gallery door open, and walked in. I had no appointment, but walked strait over to the owner's desk. The gallery was called, "Living Traditions Gallery." This time when I entered the gallery the atmosphere enveloped me. The owner Ruth Ann had a calm persona with a welcoming smile. The room smelled of incense. I immediately got lost in all the unique creations she had on display. This time I felt more present and open to the possibility of a new artistic adventure. Ruth Ann offered me some tea. Nodding, I accepted her offering. Holding the teacup and plate in my hands, I clearly noticed my legs were shaking as I lowered myself on to the couch. I felt Little Kathy's need to run for the door. I tried to ground myself with some deep breaths. That day the breathing did keep me on that couch. Suddenly I however felt so exposed. I had not yet said one word about myself, or shared a single item from my portfolio. While thinking this was not going well, Ruth Ann warmly moved from her desk to sit next to me on the couch. I think, noticing my nervousness, she began by asking simple questions to ease my anxiety. I carefully recited my prepared answers. Telling her where I was from and what I did for a real job made me relax just a bit. I reflected immediately on my answers and I thought I sounded normal, you see, that was the problem, I did not really feel normal. What Daryl had done to me made me feel different and definitely damaged. Presenting myself to a new person outside of my self made world was always awkward and frightening to me.

The more time I spent talking with Ruth Ann the more comfortable I felt. My words flowed from my mouth easier, and my legs quieted down. Then the big question came. "So what brought you here today?" Then she looked down and inquired, "I see you brought a portfolio with you. I would love to see what you have brought me." At that moment I felt like someone hit pause in my brain. I just stared back at her with my prefabricated smile. Again, I needed to breathe and try to be in the present. Those few breaths however, just made tears fall from my eyes. I may have grounded myself. But grounding on that day apparently meant being real. I thought, Oh no, my cover was blown...

I think, I was with Ruth Ann for a couple hours. The time totally escaped us both. During our first meeting, I thought I shared way too much, but it all made sense to her when I revealed the title I had secretly chosen for my presentation, (If given the chance). This title was, "The Other Side of the Painting." Her response was, "Perfect."

And so it began, I stepped out of my tightly wrapped box, and released my voice through painting. No words were necessary. I let my paintings do my talking. Onlookers could think what they wanted. I actually felt relieved by this. I gave each piece of art, (to use Ruth Ann's words), a title that was placed on a white business card, beneath each painting. Naming each piece felt creative and revealing at the same time.

Ruth Ann apparently liked what she saw because by the following month everything was all set, and I was having my first art show, me, the little girl who could only draw stick figures, colored on stray pieces of paper, and then hid them in an attic... I was now about to hang my 24 matted and framed paintings on the walls of a beautiful gallery, in my home town, for family, friends, and strangers to view. All I could think was, "Holy Shit!"

The idea of going through with this event was actually quite terrifying. Now that I could visualize my artwork covering the walls of the Living Traditions Gallery, I started to panic. Every, "What If?" I could think of came spewing out. What if no one likes my painting's? What if no wants to buy one after all this hard work? What if I can't let the buyer take the painting away, when they hand me the ridiculous amount of money they were willing to pay me? What if I cry when they carry my favorite paintings away? What if Daryl's family sees my name and comes into the gallery? What if my co workers coming to the opening hate my work? That was a lot of "What ifs?" Thankfully, I had the what if meltdown when no one was in the Gallery.

What I haven't shared about this space in time, was that Virginia moved away to another state. I had started with my third therapist, which I thought was again impossible to survive. I clearly remember the last session with Virginia. We talked about where we have been and how far we had come... Right at that very moment there was a huge crack of lightening that made both of us jump. A huge storm rolled in for this last session. Virginia laughed and asked me if I ordered the thunderstorm for today's goodbye. I did feel like weather matched my strong broken hearted feelings. She had been a great therapist for me, and I depended on her so much. Virginia was always there for me. I remember saying there was not enough paper to write all the feelings I had to say a proper goodbye. We had a hug goodbye. I promised to keep working hard to heal from my traumatic childhood. She said while holding my hands, something I will never forget. She said, "I will see you in Heaven." She hoped we would both end up there, and assured me we deserved that special place when it was time. One of the last things Virginia said was, "I hope one day to see your paintings spotlighted in a gallery. You have grown so much. Your paintings are meaningful and so beautiful." She continued to share how she would miss watching each painting grow to completion. I remembered bringing each painting into our sessions at different levels of completion. We took time to reveal the importance of each stage of the story the painting was telling. Well,

Virginia moved far away and never did get to walk into my art show, but she was so very proud to hear about it when wrote her telling my exciting story of becoming an artist.

Once again, I did survive the transition to another therapist. A couple months after Marci and I started working together, the art show became a reality. My new therapist was very excited about this huge venture I was taking on. The day my show was to open, Marci made herself available for a field trip session, and I gave her a private showing of my work at the gallery. With this hour so graciously offered by Ruth Ann, Marci and I stood before each picture, and talked about both sides of the painting. Ruth Ann gave us complete privacy and provided us with many boxes of Kleenex. She already knew me so well. As draining as this session was, it helped me to understand all that I was feeling about opening those doors to the public and sharing something so personal. During the gallery tour that day, we put three, "Not for sale " signs up. There were 3 paintings I truly couldn't part with, but did want to present. Marci said, "You are the artist, and you get to choose what to sell and what to keep for yourself." That was always a hard lesson to learn. I do have a choice now. I did not as a child. After my field trip with Marci, that night as nervous as I was, we opened the doors to the Gallery, happily welcomed people in to see my work.

I did have to write a Bio for this showing. Preparation for opening night seemed almost impossible. Again, that exposed feeling rose up in me… I did after many crinkled pieces of paper, come up with something I could live with, and that Ruth Ann surprisingly really loved. I am sharing it with you today because I am amazed at how clearly I explained, "The Other Side of the Painting".

"The Other Side of the Painting"

My name is Kathleen. I've lived in Bristol all my life. I have been a Registered Nurse for 22 years and am currently working at Bristol Hospital. I am a mother of a nine-year old son.

I started painting four and a half years ago in the Spring. The studio in which I work is a sunroom with lots of natural light and fresh air, coming in through eight large windows. My technique has truly been my own. At the start, I painted lollypop trees and stick figures. To further develop my technique, I read books. I discovered I really enjoyed the experience of painting with watercolor. With study and practice, I improved. I realized that I had things to learn and something special to offer. My paintings became gifts from my heart.

I sit down to a white paper and start painting sky. The colors blue and purple are very important to me. They signify safety, truth, and freedom. This feels like the creative opening for each painting.

I created paths in the picture, as I continually look to the other side of the painting. There is much symbolism in my work. Each sky, each rock, each tree, bird and each body of water, all have special and significant meaning.

Gathering my pieces together to prepare for this show helped me to see the healing thread that connects them. This connection unifies my past and present, and gives me promise for tomorrow. This brings me a sense of great Peace. My painting takes my truth from within and now I share it with you.

November 1998
Living Traditions Gallery

My paintings were shown from November 5th-28th. The exhibit was very successful. I made a fine salary for my efforts. I remember my son saying, "Mommy can you just be an artist and not a nurse." He liked the idea of me working at home and painting, it seemed like more fun to him. I tried to explain to Timmy that I was just not that good, and I needed to keep my day job.

The titles of my paintings were very important back then, and still remain special to me today. My favorite one is displayed on the wall directly to my left, as I type. This picture is called, "Protecting Sara Bear." I know that it is "Rachel" in that picture holding Sara Bear protectively from the big high flying bird in the sky, and the dark looming tree over her. We can only see the back of Rachel, as she cautiously looks into the distance. She is also surrounded by beautiful wild flowers. In this painting I see fear, love of her stuffed animal, some anger, and the very protective part of me.

Coming up with titles for each painting was never a challenge. When I painted the very last stroke onto the paper the title just came to my lips. Either a smile or tears would follow this moment. Until then, the feeling of success was something I never allowed myself. To actually put a name to my work was like my seal of approval. There was a little more to this process, however. The few words in each title was like giving a little piece of my secret away. Putting the title next to the picture for others to see felt like very risky business for me. Titles were a hint into my side of the painting. Still hiding somewhat, I could not completely give away what was going on in the scene as I painted my truth. So, I left that up to those who truly looked into the meaning of each piece of my art.

Here are few examples of the titles:

Trees Have Flowers Too
Seeing through the Trees
Hiding Fear
Simple Support
Above The Edge

Path To Home
Three Children
Stairs of Stone

I have not painted in years. I think the main reason for that is the tides changed in my life. I didn't need to paint anymore. My creative outlet had truly served its purpose and my healing went in different directions. I still have my easel and supplies to pick up that creative part of me again any time I feel inspired to do so. I cherish all that watercolors brought to me. I sincerely thank the psychiatric hospital for making me go to their therapeutic art class. People that knew of my artwork from years back sometimes ask me to paint for them. I only did that on one occasion for someone very special to me. And unless the others read what I have just written they will probably never know why I said I couldn't do them that favor. The artist in me is not gone. She will paint again when she feels that urge. Her colors remain safely wrapped in my heart, just as those trauma paintings are safe in their bin in the closet. My house does look like a small art gallery if you were to take a tour. As I walk by each painting, I recall why it was created and feel comforted by it's presence.

My Marci

Marci came into my life just before I had my one and only art show. On the outside it appeared that my life was going fine. My family saw the art show as a turning point for me and it was, but just not the way they perceived it. Yes, I gained confidence in my self, and in some ways became less isolated. In my eyes, publicly showing my paintings was an excellent cover for what was really going on inside.

I have gone back to my journals from that time in my life and was struck by the discord of my insides and my outside appearance. The kid parts of me were the experts of disguise and I had just followed their lead as my body grew older. The exposure of displaying my paintings was a big step, but so much of my history was still deeply hidden away. Making these discoveries, written in black and white, as I put this book together just stopped me in my tracks. For those that knew me as a nurse or Timmy's mom, never knew what a mess I was inside. My journal entries make me wonder how I ever made it out of my 40's let alone into my teen years. Every single day, I frantically tried to find my way out of this tornado that some would call survival. This healing journey had already been long and complicated. I was so tired. The end of this path was nowhere in sight.

So, I entered the Marci chapter of my life. I had just been overwhelmed by another loss. Another person I loved and trusted to be there for me was leaving, and I felt that familiar feeling of abandonment. When Virginia left, fatigue slapped me in the face. How could I search for another therapist, another lifeline, and in the end, just another person that would leave me? I wanted to give up this whole healing journey thing. For me, those two pretty words meant walking through Hell, barefoot... How many more Virginia's were out there? How would I find someone who was going to "get me," understand us, and believe We exist? And above all, how will I survive Dead Daryl's threats against telling one more person the darkest details of our story? But, I still had so much work to do, and I knew it. Every morning I crawled out of bed after a sleepless night, wondering where will my strength come from today?

After interviewing prospective victims (I mean therapists), to work with me, I walked into Marci's office in the summer of 1998. She absolutely was my last stop on my therapist hunt. I promised myself that if she was not the one, then nobody was. I was not traveling light that day. My right shoulder ached from carrying an overstuffed tote bag with all the things I needed to feel safe trudging through this interview. I imagined a soldier stepping off the helicopter, lugging his tightly secured backpack off to war. My bag was prettier than a soldier's, but felt just as heavy. I walked tall so I would not appear defenseless. What was hidden in my bag was Sara Bear and a few of her friends. I brought my current journal, a "New Therapist Quiz," my blue shawl, and a magic wand. I prayed this magic wand would be all powerful, I wanted Glinda's from the

Wizard of OZ, but I only had this glitter filled blue one. I hoped with one quick pass of a sparkly wand over this candidate's head, Marci would instantly become the one to support me as I walked deeper into the darkness of my past.

What weighed my tote bag down the most was anxiety, fear, and the battles of my past I had not yet fought. With my legs shaking under my colorful gauze skirt, I imagined myself wearing combat boots, carrying hand grenades and wearing camouflage while dragging myself into this new office. I did not know what to expect, but I would be armed for battle. When Marci opened the door to the waiting room, I put on my most innocent smile, lifted my heavy bag, and slipped by her, to walk that walk, down the hall to her office. What I did not know then was that this scary place would one day transform into my lifelong safe haven… I picked the small couch to sit on, so I could have room to lay down my heavy load of secrets, held tightly next to me. I remember looking down at myself and thinking, "What a sight!"

After enduring all the personal drama going on inside of me, I looked over at the other chair in the room. There sat this pretty young woman, with this face that almost immediately, I thought I could possibly trust. She had a sincere smile and beautiful blue eyes. I thought, "Hmmmm, be careful, don't judge a book by its cover." Right away I could feel the kids inside gathering in groups. They seemed a bit excited, even delighted by the color of her eyes. The young ones wanted so much to have another Virginia to be safe with, and to them, those blue eyes were a big plus. Marci may have only seen one adult woman with curly hair, blue eyes, and a fake smile, sitting on the couch clinging to a bag of God knows what. In reality there was a small crowd of kids all squished together, eyes wide open checking her out. We never did need our therapist checklist that day. The instant connection did not require checkmarks on a piece of paper. To us she just felt safe, smart, and strong. (and her eyes were blue) It struck me funny that Marci didn't have a notebook in her lap. I thought, is she going to remember all this chaos that has filled her office with my first entrance? And the answer to that question was yes.

Thankfully one more time we decided, with minimal internal discussion, that Marci would be our therapist. I remember hearing these words inside,"Ready or not, here we come!" Marci could tell from that first hour that we would need more than one session a week. She got out her appointment book and we planned to meet on Mondays and Thursdays. That sounded perfect to me. By now, you know I hate Monday's, and it was safer for me to be in her office rather than my apartment. The idea of Thursday made sense as well. This felt like a whole week of support. The next appointment was never too far away.

After all that planning, Marci decided that the first week, I needed three sessions. I was saying Goodbye to Virginia at the beginning of the week. The thought of that was weighing heavy on me, and Marci was concerned with my safety. She was right of course, that week was exceptionally difficult. So with safety contracts written and signed, the torch was passed from Virginia to Marci.

Two ironic things happened on Monday, 07/20/98. The first I already shared with you. At the strike of ten o'clock, the beginning of my good bye session with Virginia, a huge thunder storm burst from the sky. Deafening thunder, lightening that lit up the office, and hail, all came from the heavens. We survived that intimate, heart wrenching hour, complete with what I thought was mother nature's opinion on goodbyes. Afterwards, I sat silent in my car to calm myself, and then drove like an old woman directly to my session with Marci at 12:30pm.

I had done my homework in preparation for that session. I, and my tear stained face, walked into Marci's office, got settled onto my couch, surrounded on both sides of me with even more comfort items than the first visit. My level of fear that day could be estimated by the number of stuffed animals I was carrying into the room.

I knew on the drive to see Marci that today's hour would be for Black Flower. This would be a hard session. Our Sweet Black Flower had been struggling with shameful body issues that day. With our head down and blue shawl wrapped tightly around her, she spoke so softly that Marci had to move in closer to hear her scared, weak voice. Tears fell, as she continually tried to cover every inch of her body, curling up into a ball. She tightened the shawl so no one could see her skin. The few words Black Flower muttered were revealing why she felt the need to cut her skin. Just as these secrets started to pour from her broken body, she looked up so Marci could hear her, and out of nowhere this big bird flew strait at us, smashing into her window. Nothing broke, and the bird was probably fine, but Black Flower dove to the floor in fear, covering her head like she was in a foxhole.

Black flower cowered next to the couch, and cried, "no! no! i'm sorry, i'm sorry, i shouldn't say things like that. Daryl can still hear me... oh, my body hurts down there. oh, make it stop. i promise to stop talking. don't yell at me. make the bird go away! i will stop. we won't, come back here. i promise... Marci you better go hide. he will hurt you too. it is all my fault. i'm so so sorry!" She continued to cry until she couldn't breathe enough to get her words out. Marci got right down on the floor and told Black Flower there were only two people in the room and that was just the two of them. It took some time, but she assured her that she could open her eyes, that they were safe. Black Flower managed to untangle herself and climbed slowly back onto the couch. Marci wisely closed the blinds and explained that this bird just lost it's way and couldn't see the glass. The idea that this bird was Daryl's punishment against her for having a voice was not true, but trying to explain that to this little abused girl was a very tall order. The fight to assure us that Dead Daryl was really dead became Marci's mission in life. How do you convince children who were faced with this evil man over and over again that he was really suffering in the fires of Hell.

The adult part of me knew he was dead (sorta), but still that magnetic pull to visit Daryl's tombstone frequently drew me back there in the spring. I was drawn robotically to the cemetery where he was said to be buried. Yes, there was a stone with his full name engraved on it. The grey stone also had inscribed the date of his death, and still I had my doubts. I disguised these private graveside rendezvouses by incorporating the hilly paths that weaved straight through the middle of his cemetery as part of my running route. I looked back over my shoulder every time I passed through those metal gates. Each time I ran these familiar rolling hills I watched for him half expecting to see him sitting there on his motorcycle laughing at me. There were times, I could almost feel this deadman's breath on my neck. To be perfectly honest, I had one goal when I got to his gravesite. I was looking to see if the inconspicuous pile of stones I had placed on his gravesite remained exactly the way I had left them. As I neared his plot I could feel my whole body weaken, draining my runner's high, and replacing it with unrealistic fear. Slowing my pace, I casually glanced to my left, and felt a slow quivering exhale. I acted as if I needed a rest to catch my breath and paused in front to the stone, to acknowledge my perfectly placed V shaped pebble markers, untouched. I remember thinking, "Is this for the kids piece of mind or mine?" That was a very good question…

Anyway, Marci earned her first badge of honor that day in her office. Somehow her gentle kindness and honesty combined with great strength, got through to Black Flower. She thought Marci must be one of the good guys. And the pet name for Marci began. Black Flower began to call her "My Marci."

It brings a smile to my face thinking back to those first days with Marci… One by one each of my young parts wanted to peak out and meet this woman that Black Flower now called her Marci. I could hear rumblings of jealousy inside, "What do you mean, 'your' Marci?" Maybe, in this case, that green eyed monster was a good thing. Curiosity mixed with their great need for Marci's type of support brought them each cautiously to the forefront. I could see how very brave they were making their first appearance's into yet another office, sitting face to face with this nice lady with the blue eyes. She seemed safe enough, but what they feared was breaking that damn promise of silence again, God bless them. They survived what Daryl did to them, but they were still holding so much pain and fear inside. I could not have known then that the real work had just begun. Now, a few years into therapy, the adult part of me realized I carried this uncomfortable fear of the unknown everywhere I went. When I think back, this unspoken feeling was a realistic fear considering the depth of trauma that I had gone through. I repeatedly stuffed all this evil shit deep inside just to live any kind of normal life. Just like when I was little, I continued to live two separate lives. It took all my energy to keep separate what went on in therapy from our everyday life.

Week after week, as I sat in Marci's waiting room I had no idea what that upcoming hour would be like. I longed for the days I could casually stroll into my session and talk about a problem I had a work, or discuss a discipline problem with Timmy. Instead, when I walked through the door I imagined a diving board right smack in the middle of her cozy office. As I looked at the diving board, I would pause and wonder, will I climb that ladder today, walk my shaky legs to the end of the board, peer over the edge and dare to jump?… Instead of coming up with any answers, a rapid stream of questions would flood my head. "Can Marci save us? Is she a good swimmer? Does she have life preservers on her book shelf? Is she strong enough to catch us or pull us to the safe edge of the pool?" The biggest question was, "Is there any water under this slippery diving board, and how deep is it? Will I splat onto cement and break into a million pieces? Who will put Humpty Dumpty back together again? Will I drown in the water? Can I save myself if Marci can't? Am I brave enough to do this? Do I just want to stay under the water and gently fall off to sleep?" With all those questions rushing through my head, I went and took a seat on her couch, scared to death.

Little Kathy was the one that kept trying to step forward next. She liked those blue eyes, and hoped to make this nice lady, her Marci. She felt so lonely when Virginia left, and desperately wanted to have another Virginia in her life, so she nudged her way to the front of the line. I wonder now, how did she get so bold? You could not miss Little Kathy. The incessant shaking of her left leg made her entrance a dead giveaway. Unfortunately for her, she makes herself known even when she is trying to hide. Poor thing cannot make that leg stop unless she leaves completely or gets some help to calm herself. When I first recognized what was going on, I wanted to help her leg relax. I gently rubbed her knee to try to sooth her anxiety. Sometimes that helped, but if she was really on a mission to be noticed, even holding that leg down would just make things worse and her right leg began to mirror the left. She had been silenced long enough, so I stopped trying to disguise the Little Kathy part of me. Sometimes in Marci's presence, I thought, "What you see is what you get." But, that tale telling leg would shake so much, it made noise, and was strong enough to move the furniture she was sitting on. I promised myself, the next session I was going to wear a long skirt to hide the intensity of all this. We had hardly been seeing Marci a month and I was positive she was wondering, "What did I get myself into? This woman is totally nuts." Laughing at myself, I thought, "Who am I kidding? I have nuts tattooed on my forehead." But no, it did not seem to phase Marci, especially once she knew what that seizure like shaking was all about. It was very simple, Little Kathy had entered the room, and her relationship with this sweet, terrified, six year old had begun.

With all this elbowing to push her way to Marci's couch, sometimes she would simply go silent when given a chance. Her tears would squeak out and she shook like a scared little puppy.

Little Kathy

yikes, why did i have to be so nosey? this marci lady is not gonna like me. she is gonna get mad that i keep moving around like this. keep your feet flat on the floor. i wish i could make this stop. i'll close my eyes really hard and hold my breath. maybe that will work. Daryl would know how to make it stop. then i thought he was in the room because in my ears i hear, "STOP YOUR FUCKING SHAKING!" my legs freeze. looking around i don't see him. only Marci is there sitting in her chair. i sure hope Marci didn't yell at me like that. she doesn't have a mean face. she is pretty, and i like all the little toys she has on the table next to us. i wonder if she will let me play with them. i'll try not to get them dirty. she has lots of books in her room too. she must be a real good reader. i bet she was in the top reading group, not like me. thank god we brought Sara Bear. i will just hold her tighter and maybe i can say hi. maybe if i share Sara Bear, she will share those little tiny stuffed animals with me.

why do those tears keep falling out of my eyes. i feel so bad. what if i throw up on her nice couch? do ya think it's ok to take tissues from the box? oh maybe i better go away... Oh no, i think she just asked me a question... "Hello. My name is Marci. Can you tell me yours?" Virginia always says to take a deep breath and just say at least one word. with my head down i whispered, "Little Kathy." ok, i did it Virginia. i wish i didn't say a word. saying my words just make more tears. why does that happen? will she say to go home if i don't talk anymore? my heart hurts so bad. i wish i could talk but my throat has a big lump sitting in it. oh no my legs are shaking again. i just want to go in a corner and color. she has other things for kids maybe she has crayons and paper. i wish i could ask her. no words will come out. i must look so stupid sitting in this big chair, everything shaking all over the place...

uh oh, she is getting up. i guess it is time to go. i want a Kleenex to wipe my nose before we have to go. when i lean over to reach for a tissue, Marci handed me the whole box. i peak up and nod my head a little. i don't want to be rude, but i really can't talk right now. i probably will need the whole tissue box to clean off all these tears. this feels embarrassing, so i put my head down, wipe the tears off and blow my nose. yuck. I start to pack Sara bear back into my bag. can i please stop my crazy legs long enough to get me the heck out of here? it must be time to go by now. where is her clock? the filthy clock in daryl's garage would tell me how much more time before i could go home. i really just want to go home... but marci didn't walk to the door to let me out. she starts to pull something out from under her chair. yep, time to go!!! I don't care what time it is. i scramble to get my stuff, but this couch just gobbles me up and my feet aren't helping one bit. my body is trying to move towards the only way out of here, but my eyes really want to know what marci is hiding under her chair. in my head, i hear my mom say, "remember curiosity killed the cat." hmmm, but i want to know what surprise she has under there. once i see it, then i'll run away, really fast. what could it be? oh god, what if it is like daryl's surprises?... slowly she pulls out this really big pad of paper. boy i wish i had one like that. it's almost as big as what my teacher had at school in second grade. she slides the pad right in front of my couch. wow, it is so big and not a mark on it. all blank. you think she will let me be the first one to color on this? boy, i wish i had some crayons. just seeing this pad makes me feel a little better all ready. i look up for just a minute and see the clock tucked into the book case. it doesn't look like Daryl's clock. it's a black little box with red numbers that lit up saying 10:25. i have only been here for 25 minutes? seems longer...

"Little Kathy, would you like to color for a while?" oops, i must have been daydreaming again. she is reaching over to me with a small box of crayons. WOW! how did she know i liked to color? i can see my hand take the yellow crayon box.

i am thinking, thank you so much, and nod my head a few times. the box feels small though. i really like my 64 colors, but 8 will be ok. i slide off the couch to sit on the floor, being sure to stay on my side of the room. part of my legs are right on the big pad. this body seems so big sometimes. i keep looking at her to see if this is ok. she nods her head. i put Sara bear down for just a few minutes while i color. hmmm, what should i make for Marci. i know!! she has blue eyes, and so do i. i can make a picture of both of us sitting on our chairs. and i like all the colors on that bookcase. i can put that next to us. it has so many colors though. I wish i had my 64 crayons.

i am glad to find a blue crayon in the little box. i want to do eyes first. make two for me and two for her. do i have to draw my glasses? no they are funny looking. drawing bodies is hard to do, but i get that black crayon to draw my body first... drawing my arms makes my hands tighten and they turn into curled up fists. i jump when i feel the black crayon crack in the palm of my hand. all at once, the paper rips too. oh no, this can't happen here. i can't break Marci's crayons. i am all crunched on my knees, sitting right on top of the pad. i hate this big stupid body. i really want to go home now. i can hardly see anymore. my glasses are all clouded up and wet. i hear a lady saying, "Little Kathy take a big deep breath. come on, I know you can do it." I pick up my head, and Marci is sitting on the floor too. why do i do this? i don't remember Marci getting off her chair. i look around because i can smell oil and cigarette smoke. oh my god, did i go back to that garage? did i take Marci to that awful place? is it Monday? i need to see a calendar. what time is it? is it after 10 o'clock? they all say I don't ever have to go back there...

my left hand is holding Sara bear's leg real tight, and my right hand is holding a tiny piece of black crayon pushing right through the brand new paper. i feel my body rocking a little. how did i get here? Marci must be so mad. this is not a picture that goes on at the refrigerator. my head hurts like it is gonna crack open. can i just lay my heavy head down. i am so tired. i am sure Marci can't even see my eyes anymore. i just want to sleep. i need some help. somebody please help me..."

Without even looking up I knew that Little Kathy had come and gone. She goes nowhere without Sara Bear, and her furry friend lay right beside me. The piece of paper in front of me was definitely her signature. The crayon colored drawing was still terrifying to me and filled me with sadness as I studied it. My chest felt heavy as I looked down at my hands which were holding my body up. I recognized that familiar picture from my past and from Little Kathy's recent efforts to talk to me using her crayons. Mesmerized by her drawing, I felt unsure of my surroundings and picked my head up to investigate as I tried to ground myself. And crack, my head was met with the bottom of a table apparently we were hiding under. How did I get here? I couldn't put together when I saw Marci last. I wondered, where had she gone? and where'd she put us? Rubbing my burning eyes under my glasses, I tried to clear the cobwebs I was lost in. On all fours under a wooden coffee table, I thought to myself I really need three Tylenol for my pounding headache. Safely ducking my head lower, I managed to get out from under this not so clever hiding place. I desperately tried to refocus. Looking around for my pocketbook, I was startled to find myself in a room I had never seen before. The space was relatively small, clean and orderly. It certainly looked like a therapist's office, just not mine. My questions were many, but mostly I wanted to know where Marci was and how did I get here?

A few minutes of confusion passed and then I heard a gentle tap on the door I was plotting to escape from. Remaining silent, I thought, "Do I answer the door or stay in hiding?" I heard myself bravely say, "Yes?" I held my breath in anticipation, hoping it would be Marci's face peaking around that door. I exhaled slowly when I realized, for once, I got my wish. Scrambling to untangle myself and get off the floor, I thought once again, "What a sight I must be."

Marci paused for a moment trying to see which part of me was now present. I respected her for finding each one of us important enough to know exactly who she was addressing. With that, she simply asked how I was feeling. I had more questions than answers for sure, but seeing her face gave me comfort. Trying to appear calm, I told her I was a little confused about what I was doing in this room. I remember thinking maybe I had done something wrong that I was unaware of. My face must have given away the fear I was hiding, and right away she assured me that everything was ok. She shared with me that little Kathy had taken over the majority of our session, our hour was up, and the adult part of me could not find my way back into the room. She could not let me leave or drive in the state I was in.

We had run past our time and she had another client in the waiting room. To keep me safe, she found an empty office for me to decompress and regroup, so to speak. She later told me she made sure the room was totally safe for my kids inside to rest, play or color. The sharpest thing in the room I actually managed to find was on the floor in the corner under that table, was a paperclip. Strangely, I remember taking that with me when it was finally safe for me to leave. She helped me reorient, and answered the many questions I had. She explained to me she had a very full day, but that office would be free all day if I needed it to stay safe. In her hand she was holding a yellow Do Not Disturb sticky note she had placed on the door, so no one would come in while I was there. She brought me some cold water and said when I felt up to leaving to take the sticky note with me, to indicate that I was gone. I did just as she said that day and many other days in those beginning years with Marci. To this day, I remember thinking that offering me a safe place after a really tough session was probably the nicest thing anyone had ever done for me. To this day, not only have I felt she is the rockstar of all therapists, but her kindness is exceeded by no one. Marci totally won the love of my very distrustful and tired young parts pretty much from week one. While this relationship might seem very complicated, it really was quite simple. She listened to our every word and somehow made us feel heard. She is always honest with me which allows me to be honest with her and myself. Sometimes even after all these years I enter that room and think there is a little magic inside those four walls. She has heard the roughest part of my trauma years. She is the keeper of my darkest secrets that I shared with no one else on the planet. She allows me the space to work things out and be safe doing it. Because of the safe room, and the do not disturb signs, I felt free to go to the scariest places inside without the fear of being sent home before I could safely care for myself. Who would have thought that one extra step could make such a big difference.

I kept ongoing journals throughout these two decades with Marci. When I reopened these journals as I started to write this book, I found my little yellow sticky notes wallpapering the inside covers. I remember taking the little yellow papers home for two reasons. One because it was in Marci's handwriting, and it felt like I was taking her home with me. And two, because it reminded me of the respect she had for my kids inside. Rose was right. She is my Marci…

Full Circle

Marie:

   "my mother really wants me to sleep better at night. i think she feels sad that i have such bad dreams every night. i probably keep everybody awake too, because sometimes i make noise walking in my sleep. i never knew anybody that walked around when they were asleep. i don't remember getting out of my bed, walking all the way downstairs, and sitting in the dry bathtub. who wants to lay down in a bathtub in their clothes? that looks kinda dumb and is really embarrassing. i know that is hard to believe, but that is where they find me sometimes. there i am, right in the tub, all curled up in a ball wearing my pajamas. my parents probably think i am a baby and i am not. i am 12.

   what i do know is that i bet my nightmares are worse than anybody else in the whole world. before i wake up from my nightmare the terror takes my breath away, like somebody punched me in the chest and knocked the wind out of me... i remember once when my friend was walking with me in the snow, he pushed me down and i fell into a snow bank. i couldn't breathe for a few seconds. he was sorry, but i really couldn't breathe at all. when i fell, it was like my body forgot what it was suppose to do. what i remember about that was that my eyes were bugging out and i was trying to scream. i was so scared i might die if my body didn't breathe again right away. that bug eyed screaming is how this night terror makes me feel just before i wake up. my skin is always covered with sweat sticking to my pajamas. the disgusting sweat makes me shiver like i am standing in the snow naked. what I don't understand is why are my eyes open when this happens. shouldn't my eyes be closed when i am dreaming? i don't know why this happens every single night. i try to think really hard if it reminds me of anything when i am awake, but this dream has more feelings in it than people or places. so when i try to figure it out, i come up with nothing... and frankly, i rather not think about it at all.

anyway, my mom talked to my doctor about me and my nightmares. he said something about me needing more attention, but i think that's really dumb. my parents always pay attention to me. sometimes, i think i get more attention than i want. i like to have privacy too, you know. i am 12 now and keep a diary so i can have extra privacy. no one can read my pink diary. it says that right on the cover. "Kathy ONLY," but does that mean me too? it has a golden lock with only one key in a secret hiding place and I know where it is. the diary arrived one Christmas morning. I know there is no Santa cuz i'm 12, but it still feels nice to get something special you asked him for. my parents must have known i wanted a diary when they wrapped it in pretty Santa paper and put it in my stocking. I thought it was the best gift ever as soon as i unwrapped it, but wondered what do i have to write about? school, boys, friends, cheerleading? one time, someone wrote little Kathy's whole name on the school bathroom wall and said she was a hoar. i don't think i really even knew what that word meant, but it made me feel real bad... maybe i could write about that yucky feeling i sometimes feel at night before i got to sleep. even if the dream doesn't visit me on one night, i still feel awful inside waiting for it. since i was a little girl this awful feeling crept into my bedroom and wrecked my sleep night after night. i am surprised i ever got enough sleep to even get good marks in school. i guess i must be kinda smart, because i am so tired all the time...

my doctor got this genius idea, that i should go to see a guidance counselor. what can a counselor do for me when i don't even know what happens in the stupid dream. it makes me nervous just thinking about going to our guidance counselor. he will probably think i am crazy, and what if i am?

so, my mother must have called the school to make arrangements for me to talk to Mr. Howley. he is new at our school, but some kids say he is nice. my friend Patti, who i have been friends with since first grade, goes to some group he has for kids in 7th and 8th grade. she thinks he's ok, and she would tell me if he was creepy.

i'm still not thrilled with my doctors idea, but here i am with this green corridor pass, that gives me permission to go to Mr. Howley's office during study hall today. it says where i am allowed to go, and what time i can leave the study hall. the pass says i am supposed to go to room 108. where the heck is that? Patti says it is in the new building in my school. i'm trying to decide whether to walk fast to get there on time, walk slow so i won't be there so long, or take a left out that door i just passed, and go home. well, at least the pass says i have to be back for my next class.

this room has got to be around here somewhere. i walked past all the little kid's rooms to get to the new building. six year olds are so cute sitting at their desks coloring. they look so happy. coloring is definitely more fun than science class or history, or even worse math class. i am not good in math.

then it seems i have reached the end of my path in search of this office, because i see room 108 at the end of the hall. it looks kinda private. is that good or bad? everything looks new and clean. i like that. the number is above the door, and the door is half open. my stomach doesn't feel so good all of a sudden. i wonder if there is a bathroom around here. i'd like to know in case of emergency. sometimes my stomach acts up on me and takes me by surprise. oh, just go in Marie...

i tap on the door and Mr Howley stands up and motions with his hand to come in. with a smile on his face he says, "hi Kathy, please come in and have a seat." oh my, everybody calls me Kathy and i never tell them i am Marie. what chair do i want to sit on? i choose the one facing to door to get out quick when it is time. ya know, maybe i should leave. now my head is really hurting and i am feeling a little shaky while i scout out this room. maybe i can ask for a green pass to the nurse's office and just skip this all together. but what will i say to my mom. she knows today is the day i am supposed to see the guidance counselor. and I sure would like him to make my nightmares go away. right now i just feel like i have reported to the principal's office. "take a deep breath" i keep repeating to myself, but the air just sits there...

did he just ask me if he could close the door? i can see his mouth moving, so he must be talking. he still has a little smile on his face, so i guess it is ok so far... he did close the door, so i guess i said yes. i feel like my feet are not really on the ground. i also don't think i could speak if i tried. my mouth is so dry. i would love a glass of cold water. did i pass by a water fountain on the way here. note to myself. if i ever come back here, i am gonna make sure i know where a bathroom and water fountain are. i do see a clock on the wall. i have only been here a few minutes, but am i ever gonna speak? he knows i can, because he has seen me talking in the hallways before.

"So Kathy what brings you to my office?" i heard those words... he said that name again. he does not mean me. i am out of here.

Little Kathy

" whoa, what is this room. who is this man? why am i here? this doesn't look like a regular classroom. there are just a couple chairs and a desk and few boxes of Kleenex. maybe this man has a cold. he has a nice shirt on, and a tie.

he must be a teacher. he doesn't look mean and his hair is combed nice. he smells good. maybe he wears some nice cologne for men. he doesn't look like 'you know who'. i don't see any tattoos on his arms. i look around quick to see if he has any ropes or knives on the shelves over there. nope, and no cameras around. there is a big window behind me. the window looks high enough so no one can see me in here. oh know, he is talking to me... i think he asked me why i came to his office or something? i don't know. i heard him say something about having bad dreams. well no kidding. you would have bad dreams too, if you knew daryl. if you had to go in his garage you wouldn't even need nightmares, cuz you were already having daymares! i shouldn't even be thinking about this here. daryl might find out. maybe i should just leave. but my curiosity always gets to me, so i wanna keep looking around. this office kinda feels a little bit safer than some places. these walls look really thick and made of heavy cinder blocks. they are clean with nice new paint. they look like walls that even superman would have trouble breaking into. i think they are lined with steel so no one could see through them. this room is on the corner of the building. no doors to get in from the outside Daryl world. maybe this is not such a scary place... i finally know what his name is. i see his name plate sitting on the desk. Mr. Howley. ok, i will stay, for a little while anyway.

he came to sit a little closer to me. i am thinking, "ok, close enough!" he stops and sits on the chair right at that spot. what? can he hear my thoughts? is this a trick? no, i think it is sorta ok. he doesn't touch me or make me drink anything. he quietly sits there and then asks me another short question, but i just can't hear him. it is like my ears are turned off. i wish i could hear him.

all of a sudden Daryl's voice is in my right ear. it is so loud, i am sure that Mr. Howley can hear it. i hope not, because if he could, he would throw me out for sure. Daryl's words are never nice... "REMEMBER WHAT I WILL DO TO YOU IF YOU TELL!!! KEEP YOUR FUCKING MOUTH SHUT!! I WILL KNOW IF YOU TELL!!! I CAN SEE EVERYTHING YOU DO. YOU CANNOT HIDE FROM ME. SO KEEP YOUR MOUTH SHUT!HE WON'T BELIEVE YOU ANYWAY!!! HE WILL SEND YOU TO A HOSPITAL FOR CRAZY LITTLE GIRLS AND YOU WILL NEVER GET HOME AGAIN TO YOUR MOMMY!!. WHAT A FUCKING CRYBABY!!!

i am so dizzy, i hang on to the seat of my chair. i start to gag like i am in the garage. please don't throw up here. am i in the garage? i best open my eyes. it's a rule. oh my god, what time is it? is it Monday? is daryl here?... i look up, and i still just see this Mr. Howley guy. now i feel uneasy, because my legs won't stop shaking. why does that happen all the time? my face feels hot and wet. oh no, i'm crying. what is he gonna do to me? i put my head down quick, hold my breath, and wait for my punishment... instead, this nice man hands me some tissues. i take a few and hide my face with them. i don't want him to see my face soaked with my stupid tears. i notice he has leaned his body a bit closer to me. i back up in my chair just a little. what can he be thinking of me, crying, shaking, and now hiding my face? i have this feeling like i want to tell him what i am so afraid of... what would it be like if i told him? i kinda think he is like a policeman who i could tell, then he could save me from going back to facing Daryl ever again. Daryl doesn't know him. i don't think so anyway. this room feels hidden from everybody, but Daryl is pretty smart, and what if he did follow me here?

but really, i know the truth. nobody can save me from him. and i know the rules. my body is marked in blood with Daryl's rules. i learned my lessons well. but i don't want to go back there anymore. it hurts so much. i hate that i am so weak. i want to just spit out the words that could set me free, or get me killed. instead i say no words at all. i just watch my tears drip onto my lap. maybe i can catch them with my Kleenex, so i don't get my skirt wet.

Rachel

ok little Kathy, that is enough. you have to be stronger. you know what Daryl says he'll do if we tell. we will all be in big trouble. now just calm down, and think about swinging on your swings or roller skating, and get the heck out of this room. please don't make me come there. you can do this.

Little Kathy

still looking in my lap, i see my Kleenex is doing me no good at all. my hands are shredding it into confetti... to bad it wasn't all different colors. this pile would look so pretty. i hope Mr. Howley isn't mad i tore up his Kleenex, oops some fell on the floor. i'll cover it with my foot. why are my hands tearing this all up? i need this Kleenex. i would never rip it to smithereens. i know the rules. no crying, no noise, no mess, and rule number one: DON'T TELL ANYBODY!!! oh my, where is the clock? can it be time for me to go now? Mr. Howley is not laughing, but i feel so ashamed and embarrassed. one thing though, i do think he is nice. he doesn't really scare me. he doesn't move to fast, or make me stay still like a statue. he didn't even say any rules. maybe he didn't get to that yet. maybe i will come back sometime if he lets me. but i gotta go now. bye bye Mr. Howley.

Marie

yikes! did i make this mess? i sit up strait, and throw away the confetti pile from my lap. brushing off my skirt, i look at my watch. 40 minutes have passed. it is definitely time for my next class. i read the name on his desk. i want to say thank you Mr. Howley without messing it up. i'm trying to be polite, because i have no idea what has happened in the last 40 minutes. he doesn't look mad, and i don't feel scared, so it must be ok. i pull one more Kleenex from the box just to wipe the last of these silly tears. i guess i didn't say anything to dumb because i hear him say, "So would you like to come back next week at this same time?" i don't want to be rude, so I say, "yes, thank you. do you make me a new pass now, for next week?" and he hands me the green pass, he had already written out.

I don't remember all the details of those visits to Mr Howley's office. What I do know for sure is that room 108 became this safe fortress for me to run to. I was allowed to sit in the confines of those strong stone walls, in the hidden corner of my school. Even though Daryl was always present in my head, in room 108 I almost felt safe enough to tell my deepest secret. Marie probably kept me from telling because she didn't know it happened at the time. She was however very close to knowing because she did survive those night terrors that stemmed from the years of assault. I guess my very creative brain kept her safely in the dark for a reason. Hmmm, maybe I said that wrong. Marie may have been kept on the light side of the wall, to keep us safe from the penalties of telling...

Telling or not telling, I still had Mr. Howley making space for me to sit and have my feelings, cry my tears, and wreck his room with piles of ripped Kleenex. I spent many safe sessions in that room, just inches from blurting my secret out to this patient man, and I am so grateful for that. I can't imagine holding all those young tears in until the day I did finally explode with my truth, almost three decades later. I know my time with Mr. Howley was very important to me, because beyond those visits to room 108, I remember little else of those years, other than the Daryl part of my life. I was so busy trying to forget about the trauma, that I deleted so much of the goodness that went on at the same time. Clearly, Mr. Howley was part of that goodness.

I would love to be able to make one last visit to that room, just to see if it was how I remembered it… My safe little fortress with a man ready to hear my truth. The cinderblock walls helped, but Mr. Howley truly made room 108 my safe place to be.

Telling this next part of my story is like picking up a half read dusty old book, being filled with curiosity and sliding a tattered bookmark from between the pages, to find out how the story ends…

… 45 Years Later

Ever wonder how things happen in your life? Is God or the universe interceding to bring a piece of wonderful, a challenge, or a dark moment into your life without notice? I have totally wondered after more than a few decades, how do I end up sitting in a coffee shop about to have lunch with two very important people from my childhood. In this case, the reunion was an absolute blessing. They were pieces of light from my young, very dark days.

Patti, I had known since I was in grade school. We were supposed to be fast friends forever, but we ended up at two different high schools and life just marched us on in different directions. Our friendship rekindled when as an adult I became friends with her older sister, Jan. Once all the connections between the three of us were figured out, I remember Jan always saying, "You and Patti should become friends again." She even fixed us up to go out as a threesome to attend a Janis Ian concert. Not too long after that great night of renewing friendship, remembering beloved music, some laughter and tears, Jan suddenly became catastrophically ill. An undiagnosed aneurysm in her brain began to bleed. Patti and I worked together to get her to the hospital. We prayed and cried together in the hopes that her sister by blood and my sister of the heart would survive this devastating event. Nine days later Jan died. We were both at her bedside, ever present to her in her last moments. During those very painful nine days, Patti and I drove back and forth for an hour everyday to Yale New Haven Hospital. The first few days we tried to keep Jan alive with hope and prayer. However, after that first day she was never conscious again. As days passed and no extreme medical treatment was working, we quietly planned her memorial service during our long rides to and from our daily visits. Jan loved music, so we picked all her favorite tunes to be part of the service. With each selection we blared thru the stereo in Patti's car, we wept with the memories of our sister... You can learn a lot about a person while grieving together. In my heart I believe Jan stayed with us until she knew Patti and I had sealed tight a forever friendship. And so it began...

My friendship with Patti grew. Wouldn't you know we lived within walking distance from one another which made things easy and comfortable. Having lost my "Squito," which was my pet name for Jan, was a really dark time for me. With both our hearts broken, reaching out and welcoming in this new rekindled friendship was not as easy as you may think, but we had Jan's spirit nudging us closer, every grief stricken step of the way. This was a huge blessing I acknowledge every day.

A couple years after Jan's passing, Patti asked me if I would like to come to a meditation group she was a part of. And you will never guess who ran this group? Yep, Mr. Howley…

She had described this group by saying part of the group was silent meditation, but that it almost seemed a little like group therapy as well. By that time, I had shared my sexual assault history with Patti. This was hard to do because both she and Jan had known who Daryl was. That knowledge made it riskier to tell them my story. But I did it anyway.

After talking about the idea of becoming part of this group over with my therapist, I cautiously accepted the invite to meet with Mr Howley (Pat) before going to the first meeting at his house. I knew I had to see his face again, and maybe say a few words before I made the commitment to join this already closely knit meditation group.

So, there I was nervously sitting at a little table in a Panera bread coffee shop about to meet Mr. Howley again. Patti was at my side. She knew I was both anxious and happy to see Mr. Howley. My insides were clashing so much I felt like I had two pounding hearts in my chest. I wanted to look down at my body to see if this intense feeling was visible. I remember thinking I wish I had worn a shawl to cover all this inner conflict. I had no idea what I would say to this man. Would it be a lot of small talk, or would I dare to tell him pieces of what I was trying not to say so many years ago, back in that room with the impenetrable cinder block walls. And how do you start that conversation? Would I tell him I had Dissociative Identity Disorder? Would he believe any of this? If I told him my story, maybe he would not want me in this group…

Looking down at the paper napkins on the table, I thought, "Do not rip the napkins please." I wanted to demonstrate a little growth in 45 years. And with that, my thoughts just spiraled. If I reveal my secret, while I thought it will put a few pieces of my puzzle together, I still harbored that fear of being looked at as crazy or a damaged person. Then my next big question was how was I going to call him Pat, now that we are all adults. (Mostly adults anyway). I guess all of that is why my legs were shaking almost uncontrollably under the table. I remember thinking at that moment, Little Kathy must be really scared and I was definitely not much help to her. I gently placed my hands on my quivering legs so she would know I heard her. There was, however not much time to dwell on all this, because then there he was in front of me. That same kind gentle face was looking right at me. His hair had greyed, but to me he looked just as I remembered. His safe hazel eyes and that welcoming smile hadn't changed at all. With that first glance at his face, my tightly held shoulders slowly dropped from up around my ears. I felt a big exhale come from the scared little girl part of me. My shaking hands melted into my lap. The fear of shredding the dinner napkin under my fork was gone. At that moment, I trusted I could sit safely next to this kind man I had known so long ago. The forty five years that had gone by no longer seemed unimportant. They no longer existed. Nothing to fear here except that diving board I was about to jump off of. Deep inside my gut, I could feel a few of my inner kids stepping their foot on that ladder to climb up to the high dive. I thought, "Whoa, not so fast!" But surprisingly there was this weird calm coming from inside. I felt a strange role reversal from within. They remembered, maybe better than I, the kind person we had just sat down to eat lunch with…

I took a deep breath, paused, thanked my inside kids for the smile on my face, and started to get reacquainted with Mr. Howley,

I mean Pat. While it has only been 5 years since this meeting, my memory of that hour of reconnection feels foggy and a bit surreal. I don't remember it with total clarity. I believe that was because so many parts of me were having their individual moments in his company, whether they really came out to meet him or not. What I do know for sure, is that I did start to tell him the reason I wept and ripped Kleenex in his office all those years before. Old familiar emotions rose into my already pounding chest… I struggled to remain in one piece and poof, my mind went to another place back in time very far from this coffee shop…

I found myself in the middle of a cherished memory… I took a giant step into the air, with eyes closed, holding my nose, and jumped into the deep end of a cement pool. I could see my little red bathing suit decorated with three little white buttons, a white swimming cap strapped onto my head, and no life jacket… My dad had just taught me to swim that summer of 1964, but a diving board was another story. I was terrified of that high dive. Before I took that brave leap into mid air, I peaked to see if my dad was watching. There he was smiling, on his hands and knees at the edge of the pool. In my head I heard a very loud, "Here goes nothing!" and splashed into the water cannon ball style. I could hear my name as my dad cheered me on to rise to the top and take a big breath. I remembered his instructions, to use my strong arms, kick my legs, turn my head to the left for more air, and repeat. I had learned my lessons well, and free styled it to his welcoming hands reaching into that now, very safe water. The long list of instructions had worked, but the words that brought me to the safety of the pool's edge were, "Don't stop. A few more strokes! Swim to daddy. You can make it!" And I did. The split second my fingers touched the cement edge of the pool, I felt his strong wet hands wrap around my wrists as he guided me to the ladder a foot away. My eyes were still closed for fear of the chlorine stinging them. I could feel his hands on my arms as I climbed out of the water. Even with all that support, my legs were still shaking when my feet reached the warmth of the pool's edge. My favorite part of this memory was the towel he wrapped round my little body. He wiped my face and said, "You can open your eyes now. What a brave girl, You did it!" I remember thinking everything is ok, and I don't ever want to leave this warm towel…

With that confident image in my head, I told Pat Howley my secret, because I was safe, strong, and free to do so now. Out came the words I could not say so long ago. As a young girl, I used Kleenex to prevent a flood of tears from drenching my skirt, and held tight to my words. In this coffee shop I did not have to rip the tissues anymore, because now I could use my words. As I started to speak my truth, a light switched on inside. I realized the tissue confetti in room 108 was my very best effort of releasing my buried feelings. Each piece of the confetti storm was every word I longed to tell. At age 12 my words had only made it from my heart to my hands, and not to my fear filled silenced voice.

One of my goals at Panera that day was to tell Pat about my diagnosis of DID. That scared me almost more than telling what Daryl had done to me. Many people don't believe DID exists. But if I was going to be involved in the group where feelings are shared, I wanted to be real. Real for me means there are many parts of me. (thank God). At the risk of not being believed, I was going to try this confession out in that coffee shop with a familiar group of two before I walked not so bravely into a group of people I didn't know. I still carried around those fears of appearing to be a freak, or worse a liar, if I ever really told anyone my whole story. My bravery paid off again that day. I told, and was met at the edge of the pool with caring support and strong open arms.

Wednesdays

After the reunion with Pat, my Wednesdays were no longer just hump day. In my life, Wednesdays became meditation day. Every week our group gathered at Pat's home from 6-7:30pm. Since I work a forty hour week as a nurse, the commitment I made to show up in the middle of the week was way out of the box for me. But after the first few Wednesday's I knew I was all in. No matter how tired I was at the end of my day, I hustled to get out of work in time to make it to Pat's by six. If it meant I had to leave straight from work in my scrubs with my name tag still hanging around my neck, I was there. Most Wednesdays however, not only did I look forward to the group, but also loved driving to group with Patti. We would get in fifteen minutes of much needed girl talk after escaping work, brushed off the stress of the day, and in a sense prepared ourselves for the next ninety minutes. Still feeling like young BFF's, we always sat right next to each other sharing a blanket. Everyone knew not to sit in our seats, and those two chairs were always open when we walked in the door.

I am writing this after six years of Wednesdays and remain in awe of the transition my soul makes as I walk through the doors of Pat's house. No matter how many people gather on any Wednesday, when I entered that yellow living room I felt myself exhale from the day. The little girl part of me thinks this room had some magic powers. How can simply walking through a door to enter this sacred space make such an internal transformation? Maybe it's navigating my way from one hello hug to the next that had the power. Maybe it is the open space of the room itself. The ceilings are high and the windows are big, giving me a beautiful view of the outside natural beauty. I never feel closed in there, but of course, I never feel much like leaving either. We sit in a circle of couches and chairs. It has always amazed me over the years how four grown adults like to squish themselves onto one couch, but they do. I need a bit more space while feeling connected. The lighting is just the way I like it. Dim and relaxed, with scattered candle light. My eyes always need a rest after hospital light. Sometimes the only noise in the room is made by the sounds of nature outside the room and whatever is clanging around in my head. That quiet in itself is worth the drive to get there.

As I think back to the early days of meditation Wednesdays, the little girl part of me did not always think that the yellow room had magic powers. She and I had to do a lot of listening, watching, and finally testing of waters, before anything resembling trust allowed white magic to fill that space. While we did the sharing part of our ninety minutes, strangely enough, there was a lot of talk about everybody in the circle having different parts inside of them. They may have had an angry part of them or a sad part of them, etc. Each taking some time to name a part of them with a feeling word and then expressed that emotion in the present. This idea made me feel two things. One, was maybe I am not so different after all, and the other was some angry part of me saying, "I'll tell you about parts!" What I struggled to learn was that everyone in the room had different parts that together made up who they are. Those parts arose from different experiences, as did mine. I also learned that my parts just had separate lives, names, and OK maybe outfits, but they too, made up who I am. Finally, I thought I don't have to be in a room of Multiples to feel like part of the group. Without question, I accepted all the parts of this safe circle of people I now consider dear friends. That felt easy. In fact I felt my young ones inside really identified with the different parts of them. Something changed inside of me. What I found after opening myself to this group of people with all those parts, is that no one passed judgement on anyone. This group was like no other. By example, they actually taught my group inside not to judge one another. We all seemed to be hardest on ourselves. With that, I felt acceptance and not so different after all. Magic...

The sharing part of our time together seemed to clear out the cobwebs and empty the noise in our heads. This is when I really began the journey to meditate. This journey appears to be a never ending path, but I am good with that. This path gets pretty confusing at times. My path seems to run out of arrows showing me the way and I get lost. Maybe I should stop looking for so much direction... Pat reminded us to breathe and focus on our breath when we strayed. He even put a sign on the center table that reminded us to be in the present. Both very important things, but not easy to accomplish. Being a breath holder since the age of six, I found this most challenging. I have attempted breathing many times in my life and obviously have accomplished that, but this observation of breathing both in and out was hard stuff. When first attempting to follow the breathing instructions sitting comfortably in my meditation position, tears started to fall... those tears reminded me of a particular moment a long ago with my son Tim. He was just a little boy. I had picked him up after school and not a peep came out of his mouth the whole drive home. Once in the house I asked him what was wrong. He didn't want to talk about it and was doing a very good job of that. His face was beet red. He did not seem to be breathing much. He was holding tight to whatever this horrible feeling was. I gave him a hug and asked him to just take some deep breaths. He never did tell me what was wrong, but what he did say was, "Mom, breathing is gonna make me cry." He needed a couple breaths to get those words out, and then out poured the tears as well. He was right. Once he released those feelings, he also let go of what ever happened at school that day. Tim then went off eating a snack, and playing with Pokemon cards he was obsessed with. Issue resolved. This little story then took me back further, to holding my own breath to survive when I was Tim's age... Suddenly, I heard Pat remind us to observe our breath, both in and out. I wondered, wow will I ever get an "A" in breathing? And will that help me find my way to the meditative state I was striving for?

One Tuesday that April, I was struck with some deep emotions which were triggered by a couple things. One was that the warm damp feel of spring had once again snuck into my world. While I enjoyed taking off my winter jacket, that undeniable smell of the earth and spring air prematurely kept creeping it's way through the open window in the bathroom. Every spring I am amazed by the feeling that sweeps over me and seems to dig its way to my gut and pounding chest. I can't take deep breaths without my tears falling, and I begin to notice I can barely hold my coffee cup for fear of spilling. On that morning, with all that going on, I tried to get ready for work. I struggled to find Kathleen. She is adult and strong. She is caring, smart and the nurse that in an hour needed to walk through the sliding doors of the hospital. According to my watch there really was not much time to care of myself. With one foot in front of the other, I tried to finish each little task ahead of me. I showered, hoping to wash this feeling away with no luck. I brushed my teeth, pulled on my scrubs, and put on a fun colorful pair of socks the kids inside might like. That in itself was a tough decision. In the end, I chose yellow striped socks. My hands were shaking out of control. I did go take my prescribed Ativan to calm my nerves and made an attempt to blow dry my hair. Two minutes into that, I somehow burned my left arm. I ran some cold water over the burn. Examining my forearm I decided it was not too bad, but that was definitely the end of any hairdo. I went curly that day. I really didn't give a shit. The clock seemed to be on fast forward and I was in slow motion. I looked in the full length mirror to make sure all important body parts were covered. I appeared presentable enough to make my way through the halls of the hospital, to reach the solace of my corner office. I kept thinking, once I got to my familiar environment, I would be swept into the world I knew best, and could shake these PTSD symptoms.

I entered my office and closed the door. I sat in my chair which is covered with a beautiful, sheer, butterfly shawl symbolizing my dear friend Jan. My chair also holds a lumbar supporting pillow with a cherished picture of me and my dear friend Julie embossed on it. She was someone who always had my back in so many ways. She had recently died and yet, still she had my back. Feeling her support I positioned both my feet on the floor. I looked around and breathed in all the pictures of my family and friends surrounding me. I rested my hands just above my lap, holding them in the meditative position I was taught. Closing my eyes, I started to focus on my breathing as I had learned in the magical yellow room of my meditation group. I wondered, could I carry all this practice with me into a different room not sitting with the security of my group. What I discovered was, the answer was yes. I sat alone in my own newly created safe zone. I knew no one would disturb me if my door was closed. I felt safe to close my eyes and I slowly breathed in and out. I repeated this until I felt my anxiety of the triggering morning melt away. I veered off my meditative path a bit, to the duties of my day about to begin, but found my way back to my breath. That being my only job at that moment, I felt like I was in the present. I realized that the now was the only place I needed to be. I had grounded myself, all on my own. I felt a tiny smile form on my face. I slowly opened my eyes and reoriented myself to my safe spot. I gifted myself with a few more deep breaths and said a familiar Hail Mary. I prayed in gratitude for what I had just accomplished. Reflecting back for a moment, I paused to acknowledge that I had been blessed to be reacquainted with the kindest of men, my friend Pat, again, not a coincidence. I believe this full circle story was a divine plan I was blessed with. Another prayer answered.

Never Say Never

In the year 2000, I was 45 years old and had been in therapy for seven long years. At that time, my activities of daily living list was written in stone. I rarely veered from my preplanned stabilizing routine. My week went something like this…

- Wake up every morning, take psych medication that I now know kept me putting one foot in front of the other, but hated because they made me gain 30 pounds instantly, putting yet another negative slant on my body image.
- Go to therapy without fail every Monday and Thursday mornings at 10:00. Attend my out of town Tuesday night Survivor group.
- Work; a grueling 36 hours/week as a registered nurse in a hospital setting. I cannot lie though, I loved being a nurse. I found it so much easier to help others, than myself. I did feel pride in that aspect of my life, regardless of how tiring it was.
- Raise an 11 year old son, as a single mom, with all that it entails. Tim was my top priority. My world revolved around the safe care of the precious gift I was given.

In my free time which was generally in the evenings, I spent at home with my son Tim, which was the best part of my day. We had a great relationship and I enjoyed his company more than anyone else's. All throughout my journals, I find precious pieces of light which were my stories of Tim. Those journal pages are marked by dog ears so I can find them quickly.

I read a lot, journaled a couple times a day, and before bed. I escaped to my easel to paint in the sanctity of my sunroom studio. Through those french doors, I exhaled releasing myself to go to a different place. I listened to relaxing music and allowed the creative part of me to fill the room.

On occasion I would have a friend over for supper, or go out to a movie. I did have a few close friends that I talked to daily on the phone, sometimes late into the night. At this time in my life I did tend to isolate somewhat other than therapy, work and spending time with my immediate family. I had carved out a safe world with as little stress involved as possible. My world did not include having a man in my life. I had no desire to complicate things. I did not even try to imagine a love relationship. Been there, done that, and had not succeeded, period. In a weak moment that my mind might wander to this terrifying topic, I would remember that pain that came at the end of all my efforts in the past. This reminder made my next thought, "No Thank You!" I still had the notion in my head that I was not strong enough, good enough, pretty enough or sane enough for a man to want to welcome this boring, but exceedingly complicated woman into his life. That was quite an evaluation of my self-worth and would certainly ward off any possibility of a solid relationship. Besides, I did not need a man in my life… so I thought.

While that mind set felt like an open and shut case, I had a dear friend Julie that thought differently. We worked together side by side on our nursing unit. I enjoyed this friendship more than I can say. We kept each other showing up at work everyday. Her energy always sparked mine into full throttle. We laughed a lot, even at things only we could find humorous. She supplied a break from the heavy heart I carried around as we took care of our patients. She was my confidant. She held my survival story close to her vest, and unless I wanted anyone in my workplace to know this personal story of mine, it was kept secret. We were different in many ways, but alike in so many more. An example of this was, she swore like a truck driver, and me, not a foul word, even though I thought them often. With that, she gave me the nick name, "Mother Mary." All I could do was laugh at this irony…

Julie saw first hand one of my darker moments when I got triggered by an attempted sexual assault I experienced in the work place. After I locked this creep in a bathroom and told somebody where he was, I was totally running for the nearest exit, not knowing how else to get safe. And there Julie was standing in the hallway watching the terrified look on my face. Just seeing her face, somewhat helped defuse the panic state I was in. She gently guided me into an empty room where we talked through what had happened. My voice had changed to the voice of a child, and even with her safe arms wrapped snuggly around me, I shook like a leaf. Julie came up with a plan to help me reign my scared parts back together. She had someone go to my locker to get my pocketbook. She knew I carried as needed medication to help at times of panic, and knew that Marci's emergency contact number also lived in my purse. With all that, still no one knew the mess I was in. She made sure I took my meds, wrapped me in those incredible blankets from the hospital warmer, dialed Marci's number, and waited with me until she called back. Slowly and thankfully, my present world came back into focus. Julie pulled me out of the flashback of the 1960's and got me safely away from that man in room 7. She waited until I was calm enough to drive home. Yep, she was making that happen as well. In her eyes, I had done enough for one day. Her next thought was to go scream at the bastard I had locked in the bathroom. Instead Julie held back a bit, even though he deserved it, and officially wrote up the incident. She also made sure I would never see this man in the safe world of my workplace again. The most important part of what she did for me that day was of course just being my true friend. She helped me maintain my dignity, while keeping my horrible past as private as I needed it to be.

I tell you this story of Julie, because even with all that she knew about me, my past and the difficulties with my present, she still said, "Kathleen, you are the sanest person I know." And I would respond, "And you are blind, deaf and dumb, but I love you anyway."

Julie truly was my faithful friend. What I didn't tell you yet, is that she was a like a dog with a bone. When she knew something was right and needed to be done, she did not stop until she followed it through to completion. Without Julie and her husband Gary, the next part of my story would not have taken place. A smile comes to my face, and my head shakes just slightly, as I joyfully begin to share this unexpected part of my journey.

Little did I know that Julie and Gary had this masterful plan to get his best friend together with her best friend, me. For maybe two months Julie worked on me, and Gary worked on his buddy, Mike. To tempt us, they were manned with pictures and stories of how wonderful we both were. This was in the days before online dating. It was back in the day when matchmakers were matchmakers, and we had a world series winning, tag team of matchmakers obsessed with this challenge. They truly had their work cut out for them.

From my side of the boxing ring, Julie had a woman with DID who was NEVER, NEVER, EVER, going to go out with another man, EVER, period. End of discussion. Julie just shook her head and laughed at that... Gary, on the other hand had a long time, never married, bachelor, living 2 hours away in New York City to contend with, who incidentally had tattoos, and rode a Harley. Truly the odds were against them or were they? I have always thought the two of them must have had some connections with the Almighty, to be able to align the planets and stars to power their efforts. With those connections and their intense nagging, we did eventually cave, but only to just shut them up and finally be done with this craziness. Surely they could not make us fall in love, and get married...

We should have suspected that once we gave them a reluctant yes, they would then go into a full court press. They secretly set up a surprise meeting at work, with me looking like an exhausted, end of a 12 hour work day nurse disaster. This uncomfortable surprise visit turned into post work drinks, and a quick get together at our matchmakers' house. Very tricky... I felt like I was being swept up in a wave I could not paddle against. However, while swimming against the tide, I had to admit (Mike) my soon to be date was cute. Apparently, he felt the same about me. "Ok, good trick you guys."

During this first meeting at their house, Julie did her very best to steer the discussion away from tattoos and motorcycles, thinking that might be a deal breaker. Darn her, she wanted me to be in over my head, before I knew those two minor details. I am sure this hopeful omission on her part was done out of love. But really, did she not think I saw the Harley when we pulled into her driveway? Good try…

And so, this relationship began. We set a date for the following weekend. The four of us would go out to a beautiful quaint restaurant along a river, a couple towns away. I remember thinking this restaurant was a little pricey for a first date, but that is what they chose. The week of preparation was a whirlwind. Julie and I went on a shopping spree (her favorite thing to do) to find the perfect dress for me to wear. She insisted I get a manicure and pedicure before that Saturday. She flat out could not believe I was 45 years old and this would be my very first trip to a nail salon. I went all out and got a French manicure, mostly because I couldn't decide on a color. I have to say receiving some attention to my nurses hands felt pretty nice. All this fuss felt a little silly, but it was fun, because Julie made it that way. We called each other all week to make sure everything was just right, according to her.

I enjoyed the anticipation leading up to date-night, but the most amazing part of that week was Mike. We had exchanged email addresses during our first surprise encounter. I never expected that every day that week I would feel like the leading lady in the 1998 movie, "You've Got Mail."

As I prepared to write this chapter, I pulled out the twenty year old folder I had tucked away containing the emails we wrote during our courtship. Mike and I went to our favorite winery, sat on a couch in a private area with goal of reading every word. We drank a very tasty bottle of wine, lunched on a cheese and cracker platter and read our old letters. Years ago, I had decorated the folder that held our words with a picture of a little boy and girl, dressed in adult clothes. The young boy was down on one knee offering the little girl a red rose. This was a black and white photo except for the beautiful rose he was offering. Today, these letters do feel like a gift or offering as well as a wonderful memory.

Because Mike lived in New York City and I lived two hours away in Connecticut, our emails and phone calls were everything. Almost every morning and evening we both got mail. Both our lives were very busy, but we made time to build this relationship with the written word. Some people say a long distance relationship is too difficult, but not for me. In the beginning, the two hour separation actually felt safe and comfortable. It gave me a bit more space to say the things I needed to share without looking him straight in the eye. There definitely was a fearful part of me that made me want to take the easy way out. So, what was I afraid of?…

I was not really scared of Mike. My first impression of him was that he was kind and a gentleman, despite the Harley he rode, and the tattoos I knew existed on his skin. Logically, I felt I had to give this guy a chance, and disregard those two details, for the time being. Meeting him through my best friend gave me some comfort knowing she had known Mike for many years. I felt pretty sure Julie would not steer me wrong. What really frightened me was what I knew I had to tell him about myself, and my traumatic history. The crazy thing was, that as scared as I was to tell him the nightmare of Daryl and what he did to me, I wanted to tell him everything during this week before our first real date. Deep down, I knew I certainly had no obligation to tell him my whole story on that strict timeline, but I was on a mission to do just that…

In all honesty, my plan was to scare him away, well before I had any strong feelings for him. I had to admit the fear of being hurt again was still looming in my not so distant memory. Those old doubts of any man ever wanting me and my baggage were still present. Without wasting any time, every day that week, between the phone and computer, I told him a very clear story of what happened to me as a child and exactly what that meant for me as an adult. I did not go into gory details, but supplied him with enough information to give Mike a pretty good idea of what he was getting himself into. I told him I went to therapy twice a week and was involved in a weekly survivor's group. I listed every psych medication I was on and why. I told him about my dissociative disorder and still he did not run for the hills. With every email he seemed to be honestly enamored with me. How was that possible? I painted him a fairly grim picture. It was not all we talked about however, and there was laughter and interesting adult conversation which we both enjoyed. I liked him. As gun shy as I was, I admitted to feeling safe with him, two hours away on the other end of a phone. What I loved the most however were the emails I received twice a day. Phone calls can sometimes be effortless, but to sit down after a long day and write a letter seemed more like a sweet gift. He had a full time job and was in college taking a couple courses each semester. He kept late hours trying to juggle all that, so I was amazed that he took the time to write two emails a day. I found myself checking my email way too many times a day in anticipation of his name popping up in my inbox. When his name appeared, I felt a surprising warmth in my chest. I secretly felt the excitement of a blushing 16 year old. This youthful feeling brought me back to a scene where I was staring at a phone, begging it to ring while waiting for my high school crush to call, and then it actually rang… All this fuss made me feel a little silly, but I recognized I didn't want it to stop. So, with the hopes of keeping this good thing going, no matter what time Mike's email arrived, I never left my chair until I replied. As it turned out, that week in September did not go the way I thought it would. My scare tactics were not working so well. Mike did not scare so easy.

The sharing of my ugly past and what seemed like a really complicated present, was met with gentle listening and compassion. He seemed to see something beyond the story I was laying out before him. His letters were sincere and caring. I never once heard any judgement coming from his end of the phone or saw a hint of it in his written word. He then started to share with me the gift of his own baggage. It was my turn to listen, just as intently and respectfully as he did. We did not share the same issues, but certainly understood the same types of feelings expressed. We found we were a lot alike in more ways than we thought. We even shared the same birthday.

There is one email I would like to share with you, because it was pivotal for me opening my heart to him. This letter also reminded me how I must have trusted him enough to share some of my silly rituals with him. Mike was generous enough to let me share it with you.

Dear Kathleen,

Hi! I hope you had a good time at moms. I'm really used to Mike, although Michael is nice. I love the magic wand. I can see how you get lost in it. I picked a pretty confetti piece inside it, and made a wish. Can't tell you what I wished for. (maybe someday, a long time from now) Your park and farm sounds wonderful. It isn't crazy at all. I hope you had a good talk with your therapist, and the animals. I'm starting to think our meeting was meant to be. Where it will lead, I don't know. I have hopes. We were destined to meet. Not just because of our birthdays, and because we like the same things. Maybe you were supposed to meet a guy with a Harley. Someone who will be kind and gentle and loving to you. Someone to help you face those fears and show you that not everyone with a bike is a monster. Maybe that distinctive sound won't be a source of pain, but a reminder of someone who loves you. Wouldn't that be wonderful?

I will try to call you tomorrow night. Be happy.

Michael

This email gave me hope that he might be up to the challenge of building a relationship with me and my flaws…

Our date night felt like it arrived in the blink an eye, even though so much had happened in just a weeks time. I admit I shared many of our emails and delight with Julie, but I think even she was surprised by the connection that Mike and I had on our supervised, double date. I remember Julie joking with me the following day, wondering if we even noticed she and Gary were across the dinner table from us the night before. We of course enjoyed our friends company, but we definitely did not need their matchmaking skills any longer. We were ready to move forward and navigate this new relationship on our own.

That following Monday at work, right around lunch time, I was paged to the nurses station. I admit, I thought to myself, "What now?" I put down the first bite of food I had put in my mouth all day and walked down the hall to answer the page. At the desk, there stood Julie and three other smiling nurses staring at this long slender white flower box. You know the kind that contains long stem roses. Well, this box was tied up with a beautiful purple bow and had my name on the attached card. It didn't take long to figure out who they were from, but I was stunned that this was a gift for me. My hands started to shake and tears fell before I even touched this perfect white box. My friends surrounded me like bridesmaids and pleaded with me to open the damn box. To my surprise, when I finally opened the box and separated the tissue paper to reveal my gift, the site of the twelve long stem purple irises took my breath away. Mike knew I loved the color purple, and we had talked about our common love for Vincent Van Gogh's Irises. I would never forget this thoughtful gift after our first real date, and neither would my friends. From that day on, everyone was all about Mike. He grabbed my heart and the approval of a very tough crowd. To this day the purple iris has always been our signature flower.

The story goes, "We met in September, he got down on one knee that December, and we were married the following October 6, 2001." Julie and Gary stood up for us at our wedding. Mission accomplished.

For the months after Mike's beautiful proposal, I planned our wedding here in my home town in Connecticut. We knew it would be small, with only our closest friends and family invited to our joyous and may I say miraculous event. With Mike in NYC, I pretty much had carte blanche to choose what I thought would be best for our celebration, within financial reason. This was fun, but stressful at times, and Mike was there supporting me all the way. On the days that I was not working, Mike would call me about 08:30 every morning before he started his work day at Standard and Poors on Water Street, NYC. I of course, looked forward to those early morning phone calls. I loved hearing the phone ring, knowing we would connect, chat about wedding plans and be reminded how much I was loved. Sometimes this was the best part of my day. It set the tone, before I began the duties or escapades of my day off.

On this one particular Tuesday, September 11, 2001, I had the windows wide open with that hint of fall air pouring into my apartment. It was a quiet morning for me. Tim was in school, and I sat in my sunroom, music playing with my phone in my hand, waiting for it to ring any minute. No TV this morning, only music and breathing, sitting in my wicker chair. I was thinking he is 10 minutes late.

At approximately 08:46, I jumped a little as I picked up my ringing phone. This conversation started a little differently than usual. Mike said he was looking out his big window, facing lower

Manhattan. We commented that there was not a cloud in the sky in either of our views, but he was seeing something strange. There were papers falling from above him on the 49th floor. We brainstormed for a brief moment wondering if there was a parade or something going on…Who would ever imagine what had just happened? I grabbed a remote and turned on the TV to CNN to see if I could find out what the story was. The picture on the TV was of a plane smashing right into the side of the North Tower of the World Trade Center. I gasped as my shaky voice told Mike what I saw. And at the exact moment Mike was telling me that he was now seeing smoke and fire pouring from the North Tower. I think we were both a little shocked at this visual and thought that this was such a horrible accident. I remember wondering, how does that happen? He said he was going to hang up for a minute to get more information and call me right back. I did not want to hang up, but it seemed important, so I not so patiently waited for the phone to ring again. Each minute was so long… I stood in front of the TV clutching my phone pleading for it to ring again, when I saw another plane crash into the other tower. My legs seemed to turn to jello. As I descended to the floor where I stood, thankfully my phone rang. Picking it up on the first half ring, I heard Mike's voice, and it was much different from the earlier call. He sounded stunned or shocked, with urgency in his tone. He had just seen the second plane hit the South tower from his work window, and I on my TV screen I was glued to. I could not even imagine what that was like for him. This call was so brief, because it had to be. I heard panic activity in the background. He said,"Kath, I have to hang up. They are telling us we need to evacuate the building now." He still sounded somewhat calm, but by now with the TV coverage in front of me, I was not calm. He said again, "I have to hang up, but I will call you as soon as I can. I love you. Talk to you later." Holding back my tears, softly I replied, "I love you. Please, be careful." And he hung up.

That entire day as I watched all the other terrorist's acts play out one after another, I never felt so far away from Mike or closer to him, all at the same time. For that day, he was in the midst of a horrific traumatic experience, while I was watching and imagining it from a distance. Thankfully, my parents came to sit with me and Tim as we waited. I remember never shedding a tear for Mike, which seemed unnatural to me at that point in my life. Letting my feelings out of my shut down heart would have made this terror real, and I wasn't having that, not for a minute. I wanted to be strong for Mike when he called me at any minute. The TV felt like a strange connection to my soon to be husband. My world seemed to stop as I waited until 6:15 that night for Mike to finally get service with his phone, and make that call he had promised me some nine hours before.

While I waited, I chose to imagine him perfectly safe and ok. I prayed harder than ever before, just in case I was wrong. The enormity of that life altering day was not sinking in either. While I knew so many were already dead and it was presumed many, many more people were about to have their very worst day ever... I could cry for them, but I would not cry one tear for me and Mike, because we were going to be ok.

What I didn't know, until that phone call came was that Mike was one of those people in the crowds evacuating the city streets, just trying to get home to safety, helping each other along the way. Like all those other very brave people, he was covered from head to toe in soot, watching the first tower collapse. He saw devastating things, no one should ever see. He walked approximately seven miles from his office building to his apartment in Long Island City.

I don't remember everything about that precious phone call. I needed only to know one thing, and my prayers were answered the moment I heard his voice. What I also heard was his physical exhaustion and emotional fatigue. Regardless of that, he felt pulled to go back into the city to help in some way. The news was telling people not to go into the city. We had to let first responders do their unimaginable job. So, I remember actively controlling my emotions and talking to him in my strongest, yet most compassionate nurse voice. I thought he first needed to rest his body, eat something and when he was strong enough, come home to Connecticut. Trying to get him not to return to the city that night was almost impossible, but he finally agreed to this plan. When we hung up, I finally allowed myself to fall apart, releasing all the emotions of this heart wrenching day. Thankfully, my parents were still there. This exhale of emotion was huge. My tears held all my personal fears and the deep sadness for what had just happened in our country. I felt relief that Mike was ok, but feared what he would have to work through in the aftermath...

After preparing soup, hot coffee, and laid out warm blankets in anticipation for Mike's arrival, at 04:30 I heard the sometimes unnerving, low pipe motorcycle sound coming closer in the silence of the early morning hour. I took some deep breaths, gathering myself as the door opened. This had been a reluctant, long cold ride in from the city. I wrapped him in a blanket and he slid to the floor of my kitchen. Shaking and crying, we sat close in sadness and much gratitude for our personal blessing. Healing started in those few moments on my kitchen floor. I flashed only for a second to another moment of healing that had come to me at that very same spot. In a few hours my parents arrived again to take us to breakfast and go for a walk, simply to be there for us. That expression of love and care felt so good to both of us.

In the immediate days that followed we had some serious decisions to make. Mike had already given his notice at work, since he was leaving his job to move here to get married in about 3 weeks. He did not have to return back to work after this happened, but he did. He needed to be with his team who had just walked through this trauma with him. I know this was a very tough good bye for him and such a brave expression of his love for them.

With all the final arrangements being made for our wedding on October sixth, we started to question if we should postpone our special day. Somehow all that joy of preparation lost it's luster in the aftermath of 9/11. We actually felt a sense of guilt about rejoicing in our love, so close to the enormous grief that had just descended on our country. We thought long and hard about this. We prayed about it, searching for the right answer. What we came up with, right or wrong was, yes we would get married on the day we planned. We decided those terrorists would not take one more thing away from good loving people, us. We knew things might possibly be a little more somber than planned as we celebrated our love, but we wanted to move forward. I remember the enormous gratitude we felt on that day. We also remembered in prayer, those that did not survive and those that grieved them. Our day was most memorable as we were surrounded by our most special friends and family. The beautiful closeness and intimacy that enveloped us on that day made me a strong believer in the power of love.

Part of our wedding celebration was to leave on our honeymoon in St. Lucia the following morning. This was gifted to us by Mike's grandmother. Getting to and from there in itself was quite an adventure in the aftermath of the weeks preceding. Airport security was at an extremely high level. I had much anxiety about being frisked to pass through security to get to our gate. I did pre medicate for this experience, but that day my medicine acted about as well as sugar pill. Fortunately, they did not frisk me and Mike was glued to me every step I made. This may sound childish to some, but I was bringing Sara bear in my carry on luggage to our honeymoon. I hadn't slept without her in about ten years. Mike was already used to that and realized Sara was part of a package deal. Bringing her was never even a question. We were not going to experiment with weaning outside of the country now. When the security guard decided to open my carry on, the panic began. Mike gently put his arms around my waist, simply appearing to be a loving new husband. Then this man simply doing his job, laid his hands on Sara bear and pulled her from her secure spot. Mike held me closer. The guard started to massage and manipulate Sara's soft body, making sure the only thing inside her was stuffing. I started to freak out just a bit, fearing he would cut her body to search further. I started to pull away from Mike to make him stop. Mike kept whispering in my ear that she would be ok and he would not let him hurt her. I have no idea what would have happened if my worst fear had happened, but thankfully we never had to find out. Maybe the guard saw the tears on my face or just felt Sara was not packing anything dangerous. Frankly, at that point I just wanted to go home where it was safe, but we moved forward in the line and went on our vacation. Disaster averted.

Our next challenge was to try to isolate ourselves somewhat from world affairs, simply decompress and enjoy each other in such a beautiful setting. We had to make one stop in San Juan before reaching our final destination. When we landed there and walked into the airport, there was complete silence. Other than the news coming from the TVs, not a word was spoken. The US had just bombed Afghanistan… this took our breath away. During our short flight to our destination island, we made a pact that we would only watch the news once a day. We would choose morning or evening as those times. We felt we needed to be responsible adults and be aware of what was going on in the world. At the same time we desperately needed private time to free ourselves from the lingering anxieties we tried to leave behind.

Following the plan did allow us the time we needed to relax and it was wonderful in every way. We laughed a lot, which we had not done in the last month. This was so healing. We joined in on a few adventures while on the Island. One afternoon, Mike and a very nice instructor helped me get over the claustrophobia of snorkeling. We practiced first in a small training pool. I was so afraid to put the snorkel mouthpiece in my mouth. I was positive that device would not supply me with enough air to survive. This activity was a triggering one for me, but after an hour of encouragement, training and cheerleading by Mike, I was successful. We got on a boat and into the sea we went. Again, Mike close by my side; even holding my hand at first as we swam. I immediately fell in love with the unexpected amazing colors of the coral and schools of diverse fish. With all the wonderment I felt, I released Mike from his guard duty and I swam off alone. Of course I never left his sight, but felt proud that I pushed myself through my fears to find one of my most beautiful views ever. The funny thing was, when the boat whistle blew calling us back, they had to wait for me. I didn't want to leave. I was the last person to climb back on. Many laughed, because by then they knew about my tedious preparation. Who knew there would be therapy on St. Lucia?

The week in paradise was more beautiful than we could have wished for. We did finally unwind and begin to just focus on us and that was so refreshing. In our dreams, we thought we should just move there, but of course felt pulled to return home. I was really missing Tim and wanted to get started on our new life as a family of three. Once we got back home and settled in with the newness of married life, I did pinch myself time and again to remind myself this was real. I had found love and allowed it into my heart. I was incredibly grateful for that. I recognized my inner strength to bypass my historic obstacles and not let them keep me from this joy.

As I reflected back on how Mike and I began, I was overwhelmed with the thought that God was answering my old prayers over and over again in the present. He gave me choices, sending good people into my life and they connected me to other good people. I believe none of these stories in my life were coincidences. Through this chapter in my life, I learned that good things could happen to me if I walked through my fears, and opened my well protected heart. I also clearly learned to never say never...

Gifts Found in Giving

There came a day, about fifteen years into therapy that I could see enough light in my life to imagine the possibility of reaching out to help others touched by sexual assault. As this tiny thought or desire tiptoed into my head, I have to admit I was terrified; and therefore I said not a word to anyone. I feared if I turned the thought into spoken words it would become a promise I wasn't sure I could keep. Privately, I began an online search into this topic. I had not yet imagined what this volunteer work might look like or if I could even find the strength to follow through with it. What I did know is that this desire to help other sexual assault victims/survivors was growing inside of me. Two things were very apparent to me. First, I was grateful for all the help I was receiving during my ongoing recovery. I gradually realized my gratitude was fueling my desire to give back to the survivor that was starting their most difficult journey. Second, I wondered if there was a way that I could help children who silently endured, like Little Kathy did. As a child, I remembered feeling like there was no where to turn for help. I wondered if forty something years later, there was such a place of refuge. If there was a safe haven, I wanted to be part of that. Deep in my heart, I felt compelled to do something…

I came across Sexual Assault Crisis Services (SACS) early on in my search. I went back to their website many times without thoroughly delving into the information offered. That old familiar fear and doubt bubbled up inside me every time I opened the site in my search history. Each time, while doing my research, if my husband came into the room, I wanted to shut the computer down or flip quickly to my Facebook page. I trusted Mike so much, but still felt the need to keep the idea of volunteering with SACS to myself. These secretive feelings were what prompted me to break my silence and tell my therapist, Marci what I was mulling over in my head for weeks. I believe, deep in my heart I had already made the decision to reach out to SACS. The obstacle I kept running up against was the thought that I was incapable of or not strong enough to actually help a survivor in a crisis.

At my next therapy appointment, I promised myself to bring up this undefined and muddy topic. I think I was looking for validation or possibly for her to talk me out of this crazy idea. I remember one big challenge was not to leave this topic for the last ten minutes of the session... In anticipation of this upcoming session I thoroughly read all the opportunities to serve survivors at SACS. I discovered that they offered a ten week survivor advocate class scheduled that winter. I instantly liked the words survivor advocate. This class was ten weeks long including 48 classroom hours. The idea of taking a class gave me just the confidence I needed to fight my doubt driven personal obstacles. As I read on, I discovered that each candidate for this class needed to fill out a long personal application, be interviewed by their staff and then possibly was invited to take the course. As a survivor, that vetting process helped resolve the safety worries I didn't even know I had. Nodding my head as I read, I thought, you can't just let anybody man this type of crisis hotline. I knew that job came with the possibility of accompanying a rape victim to a hospital ER. The survivor in me thought this person needed to be kind, compassionate and strong enough. I learned later, while taking this course, that we had to leave our judgements and prejudices behind to become a supportive advocate. Also I thought, if I passed the course and got certified to do this sensitive type of volunteering, it had to be about the victim. I believed that I did have one thing not everyone had, and that was the experience of being a survivor. Hmmm, I never looked at that characteristic as any kind of positive. As I came to that all important last ten minutes of my anticipated session with Marci, I realized that I had an opportunity to turn around my childhood trauma and use both my pain and healing to hold space for another survivor.

It didn't take long before I realized the education process to obtain my certification was going to be hard work and triggering at times. The class didn't feel like any of my nursing school courses. We were not simply learning protocols and treatment plans. So much time was spent learning the techniques of active listening, compassion and empathy. We were learning how to hold space for someone who has just experienced the worst day of their life.

There were a few chapters during this course that felt most profound. There was one section that I was not sure I could survive. I thought I had prepared myself well to listen to anything they could lay before me. In the end I did plough through the course and proudly obtained my certificate. However, during one particular class we had to acknowledge the elephant in the room. We had to talk about different types of perpetrators, complete with their grooming processes to hunt a child victim. I had read all the homework in preparation for this class. I didn't like it when I read it, and I hated the topic even more during the class. I knew this discussion would be hard on everyone in the room, but just below the surface, I could hear a distracting chatter in my head as the teacher spoke. There were times when I noticed I was exhibiting my great super power of deafness. Apparently, there were some topics that brought strong conflicting feelings to the surface...

Sitting in my chair near the back of the room, I remember a wave of rage rising up inside of me as this lecture continued on and on. Somehow, I put a protective halt to what I judged to be an ugly feeling from coming to the surface We were now two weeks into the course. I knew there were a couple other survivors in the class. I did not want my self described, destructive feeling to enter their space and possibly trigger them. Even with all this going on inside, I still felt compelled to keep listening. Throughout the remainder of the class, I recognized that I was waiting to hear the teacher describe Daryl. I wanted him to be called out, named and hated by all those in the chairs around me. I was no longer learning. I had drifted to a place of remembering my perpetrator. I remember moments when I allowed small pieces of this curriculum into my already crowded mind. I did hear the teacher say, "Child rapists acted out of anger and power." But then I heard her say, "Fortunately, child rapists constitute a small minority of all sex offenders." I thought, "How did I get so lucky?" She spoke about how a rapist grooms a child to be their victim. I understood the grooming concept like the back of my hand. Didn't need to take notes on this part... Trying to disregard this part of the curriculum, I heard myself silently screaming. For my young self, everything good changed to evil in one day. There was the lure of being included and asked to try out for the neighborhood play. I believe Daryl's sister, Debra did his grooming for him. She befriended me and brought me the try out invitation for the play. The little girl in me felt like she had just won a prize, which was being friends with the big kids... Hmmm, my grooming.

This unnerving topic morphed into a discussion describing the secrecy involved during the grooming process. I swear the word secrecy triggered the "Jaws" music to creep into my space. As she listed the reasons secrecy was kept by the victim, my shoulders discretely rounded down into my chest. I became angry with myself for letting this trigger me. I could here my heart booming in my ears and felt my breath shorten as I silently pleaded for a short break. My eyes darted as I found myself creating an escape plan to invisibly sneak away, and abort ship. Who did I think I was, even considering I might be ready to give back? How could I help others, when I still can't take care of myself? Suddenly I felt a burning in my throat and knew I would vomit any second. By the grace of God, the teacher said, "Why don't we break here for 15 minutes and pick up on page three."

I left everything on my desk and sprinted from the room. I was in search of a secluded place to cry these tears that had a choke hold on my throat. When I exited the room, I made sure not to make eye contact with anyone. I just kept moving. I felt lightheaded and disoriented. I made my way to some dim stairwell I did not recognize. My body shook like I had entered a meat freezer and I finally released my overflowing collection of tears. I had not heard the footsteps following me to my isolated respite. The only sound was my own sobbing. Always hyper vigilant, I sensed someones presence behind me. I turned to see who it was. She cautiously sat down one step up behind me. She was the young woman that sat next to me in class. She must have picked up on my anxiety and followed me to the stairwell. Still not wanting to make eye contact, I looked back down and saw her hand reaching out to me. I grabbed onto it as if I was drowning, reaching from the water to safety. She just sat and listened as I poured out my anger and disgust for everything I just heard in class, and why. My feelings were really meant for the dead man that raped me for so many years. This kind woman said that she too was a survivor and recognized in me how she was feeling as well. So, together we just sat in silence and both returned to class a bit late. Our teacher smiled and welcomed us back.

What I learned that day, was to acknowledge my feelings, name them in a safe place and continue to work towards my goal. Meeting another survivor in this circumstance assured me that I was not alone. I eventually could clearly see I was in the presence of a kind, safe and passionate world of soon to be volunteers. We were all learning to advocate for victims of sexual assault. I was humbled and honored to have somehow been brought into a group of people so full of compassion. We all had opened our hearts to hold space for others that had been traumatized. In that room I met some of the best listeners I have ever known. Together, we learned how to do this challenging work, supporting each other on this journey we were about to embark on.

There is one special class towards the end of our course that former advocates who were also survivors come to tell their story. The goal was to listen, and learn from the survivors experiences and what they need from an advocate. This was an extended class to provide time to ask questions and process the experience before leaving for the night. As the survivors shared their truths, I imagined myself holding them up, letting them lean against my shoulder as I listened to their every word. Handing them tissues when they were in need. You could hear a pin drop in the room. For those couple hours nothing else mattered... Only their blend of fear and courage mattered, as they most graciously shared their most difficult days. Occasionally, you could hear each of us taking slow deep breaths, as we respected and supported these women. You could see that even though they had been through therapy and healed over the years, this trauma never really left them. I was astounded by their bravery. In a way, they were passing the torch as they honored their journey, and now generously shared the deepest part of themselves. There were no dry eyes during these couple hours of harsh reality. I heard them say they did not need us to fix anything. What they needed was to be heard and believed. Oh my, I knew that yearning so well. During that session, I decided that along with working the hotline and accompanying victims to the hospital, I would also like to share my story, with the hopes of doing for others what these survivors did for me.

After I completed and passed the advocate course, I felt proud, but a little nervous to begin volunteering. On one hand, I felt I had stepped way out of my box, and onto unsteady round. On the other hand I felt I had opened a door to a place that felt like home. I found a family I didn't know existed at SACS. I realized I had been using my voice as I neared graduation. Listening to my voice shifted something inside. I felt a confidence I had not felt before. I felt like I had something to offer others as I ventured out of the classroom and onto the on call calendar in June. Because of my day job, I could only be on call a few times a month, always needing the day off after call. It seemed the crisis calls came to me frequently after midnight. Each call for help was different from the next. I literally would pray before I dialed the phone to return the call, not knowing what distress it would bring. I prayed for their healing, that I might hold space in the way that they needed and then dialed the phone.

For my own sanity, I admit without using any identifiable information, I journaled about my experiences after a call or accompaniment to the ER. It was my way of honoring the assaulted victim and examining what I learned about myself from this experience. I found a couple of these journal entries and would like to share one of them. Her name has never left my heart, and that is where it will remain. This survivor's name is fictional but her story is as I recall.

This experience was, in fact, my very first call. It was 3:45am when that special ring tone went off and jarred me from my unsettled sleep. With my heart pounding, I sat bolt upright pulling the phone from under my pillow. The answering service said the caller told her she had been raped a couple hours before she placed her call. They gave me her name and number. I scribbled it on the pad sitting on my nightstand. I asked the woman on the other end to repeat the number and then dove out of bed. I quickly washed my face and emptied my bladder. I poured myself some cold water. I knew I needed to be present to (Sue) so I made myself comfortable in my favorite chair and opened the window next to me. I needed some fresh air as much as I needed that water.

When I dialed the phone, I admit my hands shook as I tried to settle myself. This is what I had trained for, and I felt the full weight of my new responsibilities to this caller. I took some deep breaths and said another quick prayer as I waited for her to pick up. On the third ring a very soft voice answered. With the sound of her shaky voice, something unexpected happened. I felt this very welcome calm wash over me. The shaking on my end of the phone ceased and my breathing slowed. I heard my calm voice become very present, just for her. She told me what had happened to her and those details I will withhold. She indeed had been raped and was injured both physically and emotionally. I listened for a long time as she sobbed quietly. I pressed my ear tight to the phone to be sure to hear every soft word she muttered through her tears. I told her I was here to listen and then assured her that I believed her every word. Silently, I remembered that intense need to be both heard and believed. As she critiqued every move she made before and during the assault, my heart sank. I repeated many times, "This was not your fault." I knew it would take a very long time for her to believe that…

We did have to discuss her choice to go to have a rape kit done at the hospital. This is always a very difficult part of the process. During this conversation I had to ask her not to brush her teeth, take a shower, change her cloths or even drink water. It pained me to say those important words, because I knew that those are some things she longed to do, so she might possibly feel more clean. I literally could hear Little Kathy's voice arguing, **"she must go to the stream to clean herself. please don't try to stop her!"** I gave myself a little hug and focused only on Sue. As an advocate I had to offer her options concerning her protection. I reminded her that she did not have to go alone. I offered to meet her at the hospital and assured her she could go through each step with me by her side. She went back and forth making that decision to tell yet another person, and to proceed with what seems like another violation to go through the examination and collection of evidence. I reminded her that this was her choice. That if she chose, she could simply be seen by a doctor to treat her physical injuries. Sue did eventually decide that she wanted to go to the hospital to have the rape kit done. She expressed to me that she did not want this person to do this to anyone else, even though she remained doubtful she had the strength to press charges against her perpetrator. I told her I would stand by her with any decision she made. By taking on the difficult challenge to have the rape kit done, she could prosecute later and the evidence would be secured and waiting for her. Sue had so much to think about, and I sat with her, respecting how difficult this choice was. I knew in my heart that even after getting through this part of the journey, SACS would help her. I thought, God bless them…

I noticed the clock on the wall said 5am. Sue said she could not go to the hospital until she got her three precious small children off to school. I remember holding back tears when she shared her loving priority and concern for her little ones, before herself. I asked her if there was anyone she trusted that she could call to help her with that, but she declined. She did not want anyone else to know what had happened to her. She promised to go to the hospital at 9am. I remember my heart sinking when I heard her say 9am. That meant I was off duty and the day staff was supposed to then take over for me. I was open with Sue about this because it was her right to know. This was upsetting to her and me as well. I felt we had started to build some trust over the preceding hours and I was certain that trust could benefit her when she went through the difficult process of evidence collection.

I could hear her children rustling around in the background and noticed the mother sound of her voice enter our space. I calmly laid out the plan I had running through my head, feeling certain it would work out. She agreed to drive herself to the hospital at 9. Now, I had to talk with the day staff at SACS to continue my support of Sue.

Compassionately my advocate supervisor listened to my morning report concerning a care plan for Sue. She checked in with me to be sure I was ok to continue through the morning, which I appreciated. She allowed me to continue my work and accompany Sue to the hospital. It was comforting as a survivor to know that this organization's main concern was the client and what she needed. Without hesitation the SACS supervisor called the hospital to let them know "Kathleen" would be the advocate meeting Sue, and to notify me when she arrived.

I hung up the phone with SACS around 7am. I had some time to kill before I had to leave for the hospital. I promised my supervisor I would make an effort at self care before I went on this call. I did drink a cup of coffee, took my morning meds and tried to eat some breakfast. I did all that while flipping through my procedure manual to be sure not to forget anything. All that did was make me anxious, so I stopped and remembered what Sue probably needed most is to be supported, heard and gently cared for. The empathy I was feeling was strong and I would use that to simply listen and focus on her needs. I checked my on call bag for the items she may want during the next few hours. This reminded me just how basic some of those needs would be...

I never got the call from the hospital ER until 10am. I remember thinking maybe Sue decided not to put herself through this scary and triggering process. I reached the ER lobby in record time. I didn't want her to wait any longer than necessary. Security escorted me to the outside of Sue's room. I gently knocked, took a deep breath and a nurse let me in. I clearly remember the nurse saying, "Are you Kathleen?" I nodded. The nurse stepped aside and there she was. Sue was sitting on a chair in last night's cloths with a warm blanket wrapped around her. My first thoughts were, how beautiful and tiny she was. She simply looked like any young mother I knew, except she wore a look of sheer terror. She had dried mascara on her face from crying, and her little body was shaking as if it was sitting outside in the middle of winter. I approached slowly and instinctively knelt down next to her. We looked directly into each others eyes and simultaneously said each others name. I exhaled when I recognized our connection remained. My motherly instinct was to sweep her up into my arms, but instead I asked if I could put my hand on her shoulder, she nodded and her tears began to fall again. She grabbed my hand tight and there were only a few moments in the next four hours that she released it. We were now four women in the room which included both a nurse and the MD. Because of why we were brought together, I got the sense that none of us wanted to be in this room, and yet three of us knew from that moment forward, there was no other place we wanted to be. We were honestly here for Sue and whatever she needed.

And so it began… Step by step, we let Sue be our lead. The nurse and doctor began the very detailed evidence collection process by explaining that each step would only take place with her permission. They respected Sue by listening to her voice and letting her make each intimate choice. I knew in my heart that those were two things taken from her just hours ago as she was being victimized. Once Sue gave the clinicians permission to begin, I remember feeling her hand grasp tighten. I looked straight into her eyes, and we took another big deep breath in unison. With our exhalation, I felt all my anxiety being lifted from me, feeling another calm wash over me. Now, as I think back on this moment, I absolutely believe that the calm feeling was the gift of grace. I felt strong and knew in my heart that this situation was not going to trigger me. I was certain I would stay present at least until my work here was completed.

I remember asking the nurse that if it was ok with Sue, to please receive her mouth swabs early in the order of samples. I was remembering that I had asked Sue not to brush her teeth, rinse her mouth, or drink before the test. I imagined her not eating breakfast with her children before school that morning. Sue had understood the reason why, but still I felt sorry about that request. I strongly suspected that one of the things she wanted to do most was clean her body and mouth after what had happened to her. That feeling of being unclean had always been overwhelming to Little Kathy and I thought it might be the same for Sue. Little Kathy always wanted to run to the stream to scrub all evidence of Daryl from her body… Sue was glad for the suggestion and the nurse was happy to oblige. Finally, she could drink some cold water. She drank the whole cup and asked for more. I offered her some minty gum from my purse. We both took a piece.

Every step for Sue was another invasion to her body, even though this time she gave permission to be touched. I remember her reaction when they had to pull a strand of hair from her scalp, including the root. Her mouth clamped down, her eyes closed and tears fell. I just wiped her tears with soft tissues I had brought with me. I wanted her tissue to be as soft as possible and not that scratchy hospital brand. She deserved at least that.

So many steps brought us to the one that can be the most difficult. The doctor had to do a pelvic exam including vaginal and anal swabs. The doctor so gently explained everything she was about to do. It took a few moments, but once Sue agreed and the doctor proceeded. Sue silently wept, and hung on to my hand for dear life. Her only word was "Yes" when the doctor asked if she could move forward to the next step. When the doctor covered her up and came to the head of the examining table, Sue asked, "Are we done?" She answered with a silent nod.

The doctor then requested a urine sample. Next, Sue was offered antibiotics to prevent infection and The Plan B pill to prevent pregnancy, which she took. None of this was simple in any way. I brought my backpack with me as I walked Sue to the bathroom. I was carrying a set of clean comfortable clothes for her to put on since her's were now packed away as evidence. After she was dressed in the purple sweat suit and had washed up best she could, I gave her some wonderful smelling body lotion to use if she wished. She rolled up her sleeves and pant legs to slather the lotion everywhere. I will never forget this moment in the ladies room. After rubbing the lotion into her hands, she brought her hands to her face and breathed in the fragrance of the lotion. When her hands revealed her face again, I saw a faint smile for the first time in four hours. I put some lotion on my hands, and then gave her the bottle to take home.

This very brave survivor chose not to have the police come that day. She simply wasn't ready. She was exhausted and just wanted to go home. Her children were soon going to return from school. Sue wanted to keep their routine the same and meet the school bus, just like any other day. We talked about safety, phone numbers to call, counseling, HIV testing and I walked her out to her car. As we stepped into the fresh air, we stood there for a moment to breathe it in. I think we were both glad for the warmth of the sunshine on our faces. It had been a long, painful process behind a hospital curtain in a small room. I asked her how she might take care of herself that night. I knew that wouldn't be until after her children were tucked snuggly into their beds. She said she might like to take a long hot bath. Her tears fell again. I asked her what kind of music she enjoyed that might be soothing to her. Without hesitation she said, "Gospel music." I still want to cry when I think about this part of the story. I asked her if while she bathed she could play her favorite gospel music. She said she could. This wasn't really advice, but I asked her if she could try as she soaked in the clean water, to let the music and words wash over her to possibly give her rest. She lowered her head, thought about it and then said she would try. In my heart I wanted the music and water to wash away what had happened to her the night before, but knew that is not the way healing from sexual assault works.

Self care is a piece of it, but she would need some level of counseling after such trauma, to say the least. We got to our cars which coincidentally were right next to each other. I knew I would never see Sue again. My part in helping this survivor was over, with the exception of prayer. I knew I would never forget our time together, from the beginning of her crisis call to our farewell in the ER parking lot. She had found a forever place in my heart. We had a hug good bye and I let her leave first. As she pulled out of my sight, I reached into my pocket for my rosary beads I had carried with me in prayer for Sue's strength, and mine. I truly believe the beads worked that day.

Exhausted and most grateful, I cautiously drove back home. In that 20 minutes, it became obvious to me that in the midst of Sue's trauma something very special happened. While I started this volunteer work to give back and serve others needing support, I found that I received more healing in my own journey. I could see myself in each survivor I sat beside or listened to on the phone. Every story very unique, but so similar all at the same time. I found myself healing the alone part of me. When I was little, I believed there was nowhere to turn without someone getting hurt, so I remained silent. The young, alone part of me eagerly watched while someone like Sue was being helped, heard and supported. As I sat with each person in crisis, the young assaulted child in me felt comforted somehow. This intermingling was not part of the plan, but it is exactly what happened and I am grateful.

After a few months of being on call with SACS, I was approached by the staff inquiring if I would like to share my survivor story at the next survivor advocate class. The question initially took my breath away. Simultaneously, I was filled with excitement and a somewhat paralyzing fear. Exposing my story to a group made me feel like the emperor with no clothes. All the reasons why this was not a good idea circled around in my head in tornado fashion. A small piece of me however, felt validated. I felt believed. I cautiously accepted their request regardless of my negative internal conversation. As I stood face to face with this adult advocate, I only heard part of what she was actually asking me to do. I was remembering how it felt sitting in advocate class when my teaching survivor shared her most personal story. I remembered never doubting anything she said. I empathized with her. My body shook, feeling what I thought was her anxiety... My mouth formed her words to help extricate them from that silent place within. I heard what she needed after sharing such personal traumatic experiences. She used the word "choices"over and over, because in her past she had none. Now she had choices and a very brave voice. When I sat in her class holding tight to my secret, I realized that by telling my story, I too could help our novice advocates support survivors. This could be a new way to serve others while giving a voice to the many parts of me inside. The thought of serving in this fashion made me wonder, maybe all that happened during my childhood was not in vain. I could share my painful past and possibly bring comfort to someone else, through the support of advocates I helped to train. With that thought, I said yes.

The very next week, I walked into the same classroom I had my advocate training and told my story. In my case, I do believe the anticipation and preparation was much more terrifying than the actual speaking engagement. I needlessly wrote my entire story down as if it had not been imbedded into my brain many years ago. I walked to the front of the class, sat on the chair behind a desk, took a deep breath, opened my notebook and realized I could not read one single word. Yep, in one glance down at my handwritten words, I suddenly was at a first grade reading level. My hands and legs trembled, my heart raced and I recognized my symptoms of shear panic. Thankfully, I had the sense to look up and out of myself. When I did, I could see the face of my teacher, April. She was just a few steps away. She looked right into my eyes and breathed a big breath in and out, so I might follow her lead. I did exactly as she demonstrated and somehow found my voice. I slowly began to say the words I never imagined speaking in a public forum. To my amazement, my story just flowed like clear, free rolling, healing water. When I finished, it was respectfully quiet except for the simple sounds of emotion in the room. The Kleenex box was being passed from one person to the next, and then one by one there was a flood of questions directed to me. I liked the questions, because the answers would give clarity to how it feels to be a survivor of such trauma. The answers would help the advocate in training gain a new sensitive insight into what a survivor might feel and need. Some questions were tougher than others, but I knew I only had to answer what I was capable of. In this forum, I was given the right to choose what I wanted to share and what I needed to keep private.

Once I spoke in a few of these classes, it felt easier even though the story never came out the same twice. Sometimes, there were things I knew I could not reveal and other times I was extremely open and my words formed easily. Both scenarios seemed to be ok, because I did the best I could, and the feedback was always positive. My shaking legs no longer seemed to matter, even though I was always pleased when I stood behind a podium that hid my incessant shaking. Little Kathy's trembling legs actually reminded me why I was in the room of an ever growing crowd of people telling our story. In the end, the shaking reminded me that I was spokesperson of Our story and that together We could possibly help other little children as well as adults.

Towards the end of my volunteer work with SACS, I found myself on a few occasions standing before a large group of professionals, including social workers, psychologists, child advocates, police officers, lawyers and medical personnel. These were all amazing people who had dedicated their lives to helping sexual assault victims. For many in the room, their focus was solely on young children. I remember thinking, "These are my people." I knew as I scanned the engaged faces in the room, that they had the expertise and desire to make a difference in this challenging sensitive profession. I admit, I was a bit intimidated to speak in front them. Quickly, I realized my self doubt stemmed from Daryl's old words still lingering in my head. What I imagined was that in his dead eyes, I was telling our secret to the scariest of people including police officers and prosecutors... With that thought, I promised myself and the kids within, I would not screw this up. I would speak of my past trauma, and help my audience somehow gain useful information to help others like me. Maybe, just maybe, this group could stand with each survivor, help heal them, and prosecute the Daryl's of the world. I would have stayed there all day answering every intimidating question asked, if it meant there would somehow be justice for survivors.

During one of these speaking engagements, which took place at a large local hospital, I was invited by the child advocate team to tour their therapeutic and diagnostic wing specifically developed for the child victim/survivor. I was so honored to take this tour. When we entered this special place I could feel a flashmob of emotions journeying to the surface of my soul. What made the biggest impression on me, beyond the generosity of those walking beside me, was the fact that there were several rooms fashioned specifically for each young age group. The comfort items such as toys and soft blankets in each room were thoughtfully placed to fit the age of the victim. At one point I asked if I could sit in the 6 year old room and the 10 year old room. I let those parts of me feel the care that these rooms provided. I remember thinking, "Rooms made just for me." Each step I took as I toured was done as if we were in a sacred place. Quietly and reverently, I walked and paused at each room. The Emergancy looking room where a rape kit might be done nearly broke my heart but at the same time, I felt a sense of healing there. Someone truly cared enough to make a space just for kids... I left that day after lunching with the staff and gratefully carried out a bouquet of flowers, I shed a few tears, but they were definitely the healing kind. I never anticipated the gifts I received that afternoon. I went in with the intention of just speaking my truth, doing some supportive teaching and driving home. I was granted so much more than I can describe. I got a clear view of the incredible changes that have taken place since I was a child. I was so grateful.

That year (2010) I worked with SACS on a couple projects. One was to collect clothing that a rape victim could be provided with after having a rape kit done. The survivor needed to give up their clothing to evidence collection and then needed something soft and comfortable to wear home. Coincidently, the hospital where I was a nurse was changing the scrub color the RN wore to navy blue. Previously, we could wear whatever color we fancied. The hospital wanted the RN to be clearly identified on sight, by color. The change was made much to the chagrin of most involved. So, I got an idea that since we could no longer wear our different colors to work, it might feel good to donate our gently used uniforms to the survivors in need. I wrote a letter explaining the idea, made several copies, shared it with the powers that be, and was given permission to run with this charitable mission. The response was incredibly generous. My husband and I were able to fill his truck with multiple bags of comfortable scrubs in many different colors and sizes to benefit the survivors in our area. This was so exciting to have all my work friends step up and participate in this caring act of kindness. We also, as a team at our hospital, collected backpacks filling them with personal items of need after having a rape kit done. From toothpaste to new socks, we filled backpack after backpack. I was so grateful to my co workers. They always went above and beyond in their profession and they exceeded my expectations with each of these projects.

There came a time when I had to decrease the time I spent volunteering. I loved working with SACS. I respected and was grateful for everything they did and stood for. This organization did so much for the survivor and I will always support them. I did notice however that I was moving into another phase of healing and needed all my energy to work on that. I worked full time as a nurse and my son needed a different type of attention as he entered his teens. So, I stopped doing crisis calls and continued to help with speaking engagements only. Eventually I stepped back all together. I did continue to send good people to possibly become advocates. I always carried my SACS cards with me letting survivors know SACS existed and how they could be of assistance. I will always continue to provide awareness about sexual violence and inform those in need where they can get help if they choose.

During my time with SACS I was given two volunteer awards. I remember being dumbfounded and humbled as they called my name to receive such an honor. One award was called, "The Child First Award." The words on the framed document said, "In recognition of your contribution to our community to increase awareness of child abuse and to enhance services for our children." It took me a while to read those words through my tears. As the award was presented, the first thing I saw was the pictures of seven little children wearing colorful outfits and big smiles. They are all holding hands... What I saw in that picture was my kids inside standing together to help one another and other children in need. The smiles in the picture are still hopeful for me. This award was bestowed upon me by the same people that walked me through that beautiful children's center. (The Hartford Multidisciplinary Team and The Aetna Foundation

Children's Center) This plaque continues to remind me that in this day and age there is help and education offered to fight for and protect our children. I received this accolade in April, which is Sexual Assault Awareness Month and Child Abuse Prevention Month. I was so humbled that day. While I know working under the guidance of SACS and volunteering my time was a very giving thing to do, I was blessed beyond description with incredible healing during this time. These years with SACS changed something deep inside me forever.

Does it Ever Really End?

"It has been said, 'time heals all wounds.' I do not agree. The wounds remain. In time, the mind, protecting its sanity, covers them with scar tissue and the pain lessens. But it is never gone."
~ Rose Kennedy

The first time I heard this quote I cried, knowing that Rose Kennedy had nailed my reality. This week I heard the quote again, and it felt like a gift from the universe. As I sit here, about to turn 65 years old, decades away from the crimes perpetrated against me, and over 20 years of therapy, I still can be triggered into the tailspin of that familiar nightmare of my past. The tears still fall and I am suddenly seven years old, sitting in a place no one should have to return to.

Black Flower and I tell this story together today. She is the body part of me… Body memories seem to be the hardest for me to fight. You can try to climb out of your body and may actually think you have sometimes. In reality however, if you look down or into a mirror, it is what it is, your same old body, inside the same old skin.

Just typing the word skin makes me pull back from the key board as tears fill my eyes. I have to own these tears. They puddle on my lower eyelids and then fall onto my cheeks. The trigger is mine in the present as I reach for a tissue. I know I have to walk through this yet again.

For the past week, I have struggled daily to use all my therapeutic tools to think rationally in the present, forcing myself to avoid returning to my youthful solutions. I started to get what I thought was a skin infections on my hands. Kathleen, the nurse part of me, knew exactly what to do, and how to begin to treat it. I applied the appropriate medicine and thought, "I got this." The next day, I saw that it was spreading slightly, so I saw a doctor. He said to continue the same treatment and he would look at it again in a couple days. Now that all sounds pretty strait forward, and I am sure that is how the doctor saw it. The important piece of the story I neglected to report to the doctor was that this rash made me feel dirty, like I was poison or even worse, contagious. I did not divulge to him that a part of me wanted to cut the evil skin off my sinful hands. I did not tell him that this rash on my hands had travelled deep under my skin into that dark part of my soul. I have treated this darkness inside of me hundreds of times. Each time, I prayed it would never come out of remission again. So, day and night I challenged this ridiculous personal battle to heal my skin infection which seemed to be colliding with my soul… So Doc, this is a big f'ing deal. But how could he know? I was an expert of disguise.

My obsession became greater each morning, resuming the moment the alarm dared to wake me. I armed myself with purple gloves, a few packages of cheap white wash clothes I borrowed from the hospital, along with extra towels. I declared war on my disgusting hands. The plan was to touch no one with my poison skin and to keep this infected skin from my face. What I needed was a vacation, so I could go into hiding. This felt like a full time job.

My goal was to prevent my diseased hands from spreading its infection to any other areas of my body, or God forbid to anyone else. I wore the purple gloves to shower, washing my face, hair, and body. I then removed the gloves and cleaned my hands last and often. I could feel a new ritual developing as I was sure not to forget a step of the cleansing assault. Keeping my self busy helped me from staring at my hands in search of any new sites of infection. My anxiety was stuck on insane for a week. Every move I made circled back to these Daryl stained fingers. I really wanted to get the cheese grader and shave at least the visible layer of infection from my skin.

Thank God, Marci's name was written in blue on the kitchen calendar for that Monday. I thought, there it was, my ten o'clock hour of respite. Only a couple more hours until I could find some safety in her office. She was the third person I would reveal these poison hands to. If I could have avoided telling anyone, that is the way it would have stayed. That old "secret feeling" was back with a vengeance. The change in the present is that I did let the top off my explosive anxiety with Marci. I knew in her office, I was safe to tell again why I hate my hands so much, and what this stubborn infection on my hands had stirred up inside me.

That was the thing. While all my inside parts feel separate, we really do have the same pair of hands. They are a little bigger now, but they are the same hands that turned the door nob to open Daryl's garage door and reached to climb up onto the rough stone altar in the woods. Loosing my battle to stay in the present, these hands felt that same shameful filth of all 19 of my inside kids. The wise, smart, compassionate part of me knows that this shame had not been mine to own for a long time. It was always dead Daryl's. The body part of me sometimes cannot see through to those wise thoughts in my head. It is almost impossible for me, when having an in my face body memory, to stay clear of looking right back into my history. The rash was ugly and it felt itchy and uncomfortable. It wouldn't magically go away simply because I imagined myself floating in the pretty blue sky... Dissociation for me is much more difficult now than it use to be. I have spent decades trying to live in the present, while taking my life back. Despite my daily efforts, all I wanted to do was run away, hide in shame, cut my skin and keep silent. Thankfully, the plan of silence I wanted to hold on to, started to crack open as soon as I saw Marci's face.

During that therapy session she reminded me of an intense but beautiful scene from the movie, "Beloved." A very wise woman in this scene was preaching to a small group with such passion that it made me feel like I was her only audience. What her words asked me to do was to really love my body. She was asking me to love my eyes, my feet and my mouth. She asked me to love all parts of my body. I can remember the first time I watched this scene at the movie theater. The Black Flower part of me thought, "How is this possible?" and she just curled up in a ball hiding all her body parts in shame. This strong woman preached to her congregation hidden safely in the woods far from their persecutors. Black Flower, while trying to muffle Daryl's words her head, listened closely to this brave preacher. When she finally spoke of her hands, Black Flower's ears came to attention. She listened as hard as she could to this passionate woman. She opened her tear filled eyes as wide as possible, hoping that would increase the volume to ensure hearing every word. Remembering this movie, Black Flower's tears fell because she struggled not to hate her poison hands in the year 2019. She wanted to believe this preacher woman's chanting...

"And O my people they do not love your hands. Those they only use, tie, chop off and leave empty. Love your hands! Love them. Raise them up and kiss them. Touch others with them, pat them together, stroke then your face 'cause they don't love that either. You got to love, you!"

Her words coming through the speakers in the theater felt like a personal prayer over me. I could feel myself hidden in the woods, hanging on to every word. She showed me with every movement of her hands, what she hoped I would do. She asked us to love our body the way our creator loves our body. This loving woman knew that only I could do this for myself. In the days of Daryl's assault I just couldn't love my body. I hated it. Now immersed in the turmoil of healing my hands, my triggered soul could not find the strength to love the hands I was trying to disown. With great joy, this empowered woman kissed both of her hands, one at a time. She clapped her hands as if they were a newly found gift. With her hands she gently touched her face in a loving manner. The truth in her words, the motions of her hands and her believable spirit made an imprint on my ailing heart.

I was grateful that a few years ago Black Flower was brave enough to share with Marci her experience of watching the preacher woman at the movies. Our faithful therapist has been the keeper of our most meaningful moments. So, with a gentle smile growing on Marci's face, sitting just a few feet across from me, she kissed her hands one at a time, and reminded me that I can love my hands once again. Black Flower's tears fell and we simply could not kiss our hands. I knew that I would when it was time and I would be sure to bring Black Flower along. I could clearly see this holy woman's image in my head. I held that thought until I was able to love my hands. That day, I planned to meditate on what it would be like to respect my God given hands enough to honor them with a kiss. Maybe, somehow with that kiss, the medical treatment would work faster.

Quietly, I prayed that my mind, body and soul could soon make a connection to help heal my hands.

When the first line of treatment was not working fast enough, I took a big risk. I carried Marci's faith with me like a lucky coin. Dressed in my blue work scrubs with a sparkling white jacket, I sat down in the nurses station next to Matt, our surgical PA. I took a big breath, and let my tears fall, as I put out my hands.

Matt and I had become good friends since my position at work had changed. We worked closely together. I often thought of him as my right hand. Usually at work I am the upbeat, positive person, offering him his favorite chocolate in the morning. Surely, he was not expecting this morning's emotional greeting.

This time when I told the history of the mess on my hands, I revealed what it was triggering in my soul. Matt knew of my sexual assault history in broad terms, but had not ever seen the raw emotion that I was laying before him. He very clearly heard the desperation in my shaky voice. As I presented my hands to him, I whispered how I was afraid to poison anyone else. He patiently listened to every crazed word I blurted out. When he thought I might be done, he talked about what the next treatment step should be. Trying to find that nurse part of me once again, I agreed with this plan and he wrote me a prescription for a topical steroidal cream to fight this fiasco on my hands. He gave me the reassurance that I needed, the medical answers to my questions, and treated my huge anxiety with respect. He may never know how much that 15 minutes of his time meant to me. I, of course thanked him profusely, but there were still those 18 other silent parts of me that were so grateful as well. I could feel them, all in line, wanting to peer out at this kind man, wondering if he was really a safe person.

I started the treatment as soon as I got home and then had the downtime of a long weekend to see if it would work. To my amazement there was almost immediate improvement. The nurse part of me felt confident I would get my hands back, but I still had to contain all the kid parts of me. This medicine had a steroid in it that gave my hands a whole new sensation to contend with. It felt like pins and needles lightly poking my skin. I was ok with that, but it was just one more trigger. Now these hands seemed to demand attention every second of the day.

You may be asking what was this skin problem triggering exactly?… And if you have read the chapters preceding this one, you can probably imagine. But I really started this chapter to say the words out loud. These are the words I have been avoiding during the three weeks it has taken me to write this part of the chapter…

To avoid typing my triggered memories, I created a lengthy laundry list of important things to busy myself with. I randomly followed the list by taking Facebook timeouts, cleaning bathrooms, reading articles, and took ninety minute walks, literally in between paragraphs. (It was a good thing I had not forced a deadline upon myself) Fortunately, I did find strength and some bits of creativity during those long walks. Preparing myself for the walking distraction, I created a new playlist to blast into my ears while I tried to pound these memories out of my head. I titled the playlist "Power." The list got its name because the music seemed to have super powers. Once on my distraction walk and I hit play the selections energized me to walk at a faster pace than the days preceding the skin infection. I climbed hills with a vengeance. Mercifully, this playlist invited me to let out the building emotions I was trying desperately to ignore. While this process was going on internally, my sunglasses became my disguise to protect my vulnerability from the outside world.

At the end of the day, there were lyrics that remained on repeat in my head as if I wore my earbuds to bed at night. I was waking up with these words streaming in my mind over and over again: "Do you think my scream got lost in a paper cup? Are we helpless against the tide? I take my life back, Can you hear my voice? All I can do is keep breathing, It's always darkest before the dawn, Silenced all these years, Keeping my head above water, One foot in front of the other, You are not alone, I pick myself back up." There were a couple powerful lyrics that lingered the longest. Those words actually sent me back to my computer to reveal what the rash on my hands was triggering. These words felt like an inspirational creative gift. The line, "There is an army rising up! Break every chain!" gave me the courage I seemed to be lacking. These words helped me to acknowledge the united internal strength I possessed. And of course, all of the lyrics in Lady Gaga's song, " 'Til it happens to you," that inspired me to write this book, again became my anthem to face the issue I was struggling with.

I now recognize how important this three week pause in my writing process was. I believe I needed to take those long walks, scrub dirt from the floors and feed myself with music to examine what I was avoiding. I needed to reflect and dare I say respect the body memories triggered by the present day rash on my hands. I was in search of the clarity found in my truth. After gifting myself with these three weeks, early one morning before the sun rose, I found myself at my computer effortlessly writing the poignant snippets of my past that triggered the enormous reaction to the rash on my hands. The next couple paragraphs reveal that flow of memories…

"I see Little Kathy's hands cautiously turning that greasy garage door nob. I see her shaky hands lower her pants to pee in a dirty bucket. She feels the scratchy rope restraints in her palms, handing them off to her perpetrator, to then tie her wrists. I see, and try not to feel the body parts Daryl made her touch, each dirtier than the next. With eyes closed, I see Daryl forcing many of our kids to touch or hold dead birds, feeling this lifeless ball of feathers. I can feel the hands of Rose leaning up against the dirt walls of the hole Daryl lowered her into. I see the bugs that crawled on her hands making them franticly wave those crawly things off, gasping for air, while feeling buried. I feel unwanted body fluids on all their little hands… The sticky feeling of blood on Rachel's hands, as she would clean up for Rose or Little Kathy. I see Candy's hands that were so gentle and reverent, slowly burying things she should not have to bury and digging the unholy dirt with her fingernails. I see Daryl's hands on mine forcing me to cut into my own skin. I can feel Daryl Part's hands being forced to hold Daryl's big evil stick, that had once assaulted us all. I feel the burning heat on the palms of our hands that were nearly forced into a blazing fire pit. I feel Rachel's hands grip the grass and gravel as she waited for the motorcycle tires to hit her head. I see our hands praying for mercy each night before attempts at sleep. This goes on and on for each one of my parts inside; different for each."

As I obsessively washed my hands in effort to erase the triggering rash, I felt Little Kathy's hands in the stream after Daryl released her from the garage on Mondays. I use Dove soap now, but I still smell Little Kathy's Ivory soap. As I dried my hands, I tried not to press to hard. There were brief moments I felt like scrubbing palms and fingers raw, but these hands have been through so much. In reality I didn't want to cause them any further pain. I took a moment and realized I was starting to feel compassion for my hands instead of my familiar disgust.

In my more sane moments, while healing my hands that week, I recognized that my hands in the present are used for good things.

While I pull my hands back from the past, I take pride in my choices to use them in helpful ways. I remind myself that I make those choices every day now. There were no real choices when I was six. I thank God every day that I did not follow Daryl's lead. I have read that sometimes violence moves from one generation to the next. Sometimes, sadly a victim can turn into a perpetrator or simply not survive. I was one of the lucky ones. I had the original good side of the wall, the love of my family, an incredible amount of good therapy, and the spirit God gave me. In my case, love won.

As I continued to treat and heal the infection on my hands, I wanted to focus on the wonderful things my hands have experienced. I remind myself and acknowledged that these hands gently held my new born son welcoming him into the world, where my hands would fight everyday to keep him safe. I remember my hands daily clasped in prayer for peace. I visualize these hands planting flowers and vegetables, to then bring to our table. I remember my hands petting and grooming our dogs, to give them love and comfort. I envision and watch my hands work at my chosen profession to help, comfort and heal the sick. I see my creative hand painting our deepest feelings onto a perfectly white canvas. I can see my hands gently reaching to my husband in love.

During a week in May every year nurses all over the country celebrate their profession. It is a week of recognition, smiles and free lunch. The most important part of that week came to me in the last few years. The pastor of our hospital comes to each one of us and asks if we would like our hands blessed. I remember the first time I was asked that question. His words caught me off guard and unexpected tears immediately fell from my eyes, and have every year since. A blessing for My hands? "Yes, please." And so our pastor took my shaking hands in his and said these beautiful words.

"May your hands be an extension of your heart.
    May God's spirit and your compassion be the strength
        of your hands.

    May others see a glimpse
    of God by the touch
        of your hands!"

...and as I accepted this prayer for my two hands, I quietly accepted the healing prayer for my 19 pairs of hands, individually. That would be 38 little hands and 380 precious little fingers. Sounds crazy? Maybe... But not to them or me. These hands survived way more than their share of pain and shame. They have hidden in pockets way too many times. Our hands are now the survivor hands that bravely typed each word of our story.

As I wrote each chapter of this book, I bravely shared it with my best friend, Patti. As you have read, the first part of the book was written in the first person by my kids inside. Patti is probably the one person that knows that they did really write those chapters themselves. As she would read each chapter aloud to me in her wonderful expressive teacher voice, I felt like she met each young part of me first hand. Most of the time, during those private chapter readings, I was very much aware that I did not remember writing the words she read. Even though I knew our story, it was like hearing it for the first time in a new way. Listening to my friend respectfully read this most difficult story, with the Kleenex box close by and a glass of wine in hand, I imagine the little fingers of a child pounding out these words on a keyboard she could have not known how to use. I was in awe at their brave honesty. Sometimes it was difficult for Patti to navigate through the horrible spelling and grammar which we had to struggle to clean up. I did decide from that first chapter that the absence of capital letters was ok with me as they wrote, and I would never edit that out.

After another week passed I still felt some triggers from this skin issue, until a nurse friend of mine, Cathy miraculously stopped in my office. She popped in to ask for supplies she needed in the Skin Clinic. I have known her for 20 years, but was never so happy to see her face. She asked me a question which I certainly did not hear. All I could say was "Thank you Jesus!!!" A light bulb went off inside at the sight of her and I began pleading for her to examine my pathetic hands. In a blink of an eye she said, "You have Psoriasis. It only comes out on hands and feet. Do you have any on your feet?" All of a sudden I was happy to say, "Yes, on my right foot." My only words to her at that point were, "You mean I am not contagious?" she shook her head and I jumped up, hugged her and told her, "I love you." I showed her the medicated cream I had been prescribed and she said that was perfect. Again more tears fell. In the real world, who wants Psoriasis? Answer: Nobody. She said it would go away in a couple weeks. With that sentence, I could feel the "poison feeling" deep inside melting away. I felt myself coming out of hiding, and that desire to carve my skin off was just plain old gone. Of course my friend Cathy had no idea that all this inside stuff was flooding my system, but it didn't seem to matter to either of us. I remember finally saying, "What was it that you needed Cath?" At that point I would have given her the entire storage room if she needed it. Every day after that, she watched my hands heal and told me what steps to take next. When she said it was ok to go get a manicure, I booked an appointment for a couple hours later.

I went from hiding my imagined poison hands to letting a sweet manicurist take gentle care of my hands. I promised myself not to cry all over her station and just sit back and enjoy. The massage with fresh cucumber smelling lotion was the best part. The important thing for me to acknowledge here was that I allowed myself to experience the care given to my hands. I gave myself permission to notice that she was not afraid of my hands. I tried to be in the present, enjoying the cucumber smell replacing the old rancid smells of my memory. Surrounded by other clients sipping on wine, chatting about shopping sprees, and watching the Food Network on the TV screen in front of us, this beautiful woman simply did her job. She had no idea she was comforting the dark, painful memories of the little children inside me. I could feel Black Flower's caution and Rachel saying, "Finally, someone is doing something about this!" I heard the adult part of me praying nothing unusually young sounding would come out of my mouth. It was interesting that during the 90 minutes I sat in that chair, the manicurist and I spoke mostly about the love of our children and the importance of their happiness. I gave her a ridiculously big tip, walked out the door and literally felt free from bondage. I thought to myself, "We made it." And unlike many years ago, we did not cut our skin in search for freedom. We found a new way to heal.

This story brings me back again to Rose Kennedy's quote. Yes, the wounds do remain. Scars do form. Those old dreadful scars did open for a minute in my life again. It would be foolish of me to think they will now remain closed forever. I know better. I am proud to say that this time, when that flash flood of memories nearly pulled me under, I didn't act out on myself. Instead, I made the decision to ask for help. I acknowledge that in the present, with the supports I have built over the years, help did come to me and I survived. I do believe Rose Kennedy's quote. My wound remains and now the scar tissue is once again covering over all that reopened raw tissue until the next time. I have to say, I am strongly in the present most of the time. When the triggers of life start to pick at my scars, I am much quicker to take care of them and move on. So while the title to this final chapter sounds hopeless, it is not. A wound like this one, doesn't ever totally smooth over and become as if it never happened. It could not. It was too deep. There will always be a faint white scar to remind me of the original one, but it will never be as painful. Truthfully, at this stage of my life, I don't want to forget what happened to me. I think to myself, my perpetrator is dead and suffocating in the thick unforgiving mud of hell. He died at a young age, never to hurt another child. I was undoubtably sure I would not see my teenage years, yet I sit here telling my story at age 65. With every revealing tap on this keyboard, I laugh at Daryl's number one rule of silence. I am stronger than I think, even when surrounded almost daily by triggers of my past.

Recently, my husband and I went out to lunch at a favorite bar of ours. I have to say, I go prepared with the awareness that sometimes this bar can turn into a biker bar. Mike has made this bar feel safer for me simply by his presence. We like to go on Sundays to watch sports, have a drink and talk. The food is insanely delicious there and the building itself meets all my safety qualifications. It has many large windows, not too dark and it's very spacious. Most of the time, I do not feel captured or claustrophobic sitting at this bar. This particular Sunday as we approached Crabby Al's it looked unusually crowded. As Mike noticed the many bikes parked in front of the bar, he said, "Maybe we should go somewhere else for lunch." I did hear his voice, but my head was already in a silent foggy place. My ears heard only a whisper from his mouth. I was listening to the deep sound of Harley pipes, but even that sound was muffled. My brain seemed to be shutting down as my stomach lit up with fire. My legs felt like spaghetti as I tried to climb out of Mike's truck which seemed much bigger than when we left the house just two towns away. Strangely, I felt like an audience watching my body place my feet onto the black tar of the driveway. My legs started to quiver when I inhaled that first breath of bike exhaust. Trying to stay adult was a bigger struggle than usual, because the present looked and smelled like an unsafe place I had been to long ago. I felt the familiar feeling of flight or flight rising up inside me and then I felt Mike's hand take a strong hold of mine. In my head, I heard from deep inside the soft words, "Ok we have a lifeline."

I could hear Mike's voice trying to say something, but my ears felt blocked like I was on a plane and needed a stick of chewing gum. I did hear him say, "Kath, we really don't have to stay." I considered his offer, but part of me was determined to fight this building fear. The roar of bikes and abhorrent smell of exhaust was grabbing hold of my arm and dragging me down the dirt road to my place of torture. I could no longer feel my feet, but I could see they were walking toward a place that Mike and I enjoyed. My inner conflict was deafening. I remember checking to see who was really holding my hand. I exhaled when I saw Mike's wedding band on the hand clenching mine. I thought, "Ok, I am still ok." Mike was letting me move at my own cautious pace. With each baby step, the adult part of me tried to focus on our regular and very funny bartender Tina, who would at any moment smile at us, saying, "Hey, how you guys doing?" She will pour us some wine and I will relax...

I tried to take a deep breath as Mike opened the door, but the first visual inside the bar was a endless sea of the two combined colors I hate. Orange and black leather jackets were everywhere. I could smell beer as I move closer to the edge of this wave. With my toes holding tight in my flip flops, I could feel the pull of being sucked down into the undertow. I whispered to myself, "Kathleen, just put one foot in front of the other and hold tight to Mike. Just silently weave thru this crowd of Daryl look alike's. They are not Daryl. He is dead. Really, really, dead." Mike took the lead to guide me to our goal of the only two empty bar stools. This would be my finish line and it was only a couple yards away. I wondered, would my weakened legs drag me there? My hand focused on the strong grip of my husband, while my mind bounced from the present moment of walking into a familiar bar and a wooded biker hangout in 1964... Reaching the bar stool, I almost could not sit on it. I realized I was waiting for permission to sit. The struggle to obey dead Daryl's orders from the inside was really loud. Mike respectfully pulled out my barstool and then helped me sit. He pulled his chair just a little closer that day. Somehow crossing my imaginary finish line allowed me to recognize we made it to our familiar spot, just like the Sunday before.

Tina, our bartender, looked more frazzled than usual. She was busy serving the growing crowd of thirsty bikers. From my perspective, it appeared she had to be the bouncer too. Finally making it over to our spot she said, "Hey, how you guys doing?" just like I knew she would. She laid our lunch menus down in front of us and took our drink orders. Waiting for our drinks, I knew where I was, but that day our Sunday hangout had been invaded by flashbacks, reality checks, and a possible therapy session ahead of me. I remember thinking to myself, Marci (my therapist) would say, "You don't have to stay in this spot. You have a choice now." I knew that thought was true. I remember deliberately making my choice and sticking to it. I chose to stop Daryl from destroying my relaxing Sunday ritual. With that as my firm intention, I just had to survive this challenge I was surrounded by.

Oddly enough, the vicious tide started to shift when one particular Daryl look alike sat down next to me. I could smell both his stale cigarette breath and his freshly poured shot of whisky next to me. I thought, "Gee this just keeps getting better." Next, he leaned over my invisible boundary and starts to strike up a conversation. He's lucky I didn't puke all over his black leather jacket, or reach for his ridiculously long chain hanging from his neck to strangle him on the spot. Mike quickly snuggled in closer, placing his arm around my shoulder, and they began to talk about what this big charity ride was about. As I mentioned before my husband owns a motorcycle, black leather jackets, and ugly orange t-shirts with Harley written on them... Somehow, God in all his profound wisdom, placed this kind loving man who rides a motorcycle into my life. I remember when we met I thought, "Ok God, this is a joke, right?" But the friends that God sent to introduce us supplied me with the assurance he was different. I somehow gave this very patient man a chance to prove to me that God, Julie, and Gary were right. Mike did teach me that not all men that rode motorcycles were evil.

The next few minutes soothed my soul just a little. The conversation that Mike had with this character next to me calmed the fear deep inside. I no longer felt the need to run away in the little red sneakers of my 6 year old inside. This crowd of scary looking bikers had gathered on this Sunday to honor a young girl who was killed one year ago in a fatal car accident. I could not hear clearly the whole conversation my husband was involved in, because I was too busy looking to the very end of the bar. A very tall man in a pure white shirt stood there. He looked a little out of place in this sea of black and orange, but seemed to be the center of attention. He was showing a group of people pictures in his phone. This man's face looked soft and full of love, loss, and pride. He was shaking hands and accepting warm hugs. In the corner of my eye, I saw the Daryl image next to me point his finger to the man in the white shirt.

In this case two plus two did equal four. The man in the white shirt was the father of the 20 year old girl this crowded benefit was honoring. Her name was Liv and this ride was called "Liv for Life." This scary crowd was here to honor her and donate to a scholarship in Liv's name. I felt Mike's squeeze on my shoulder. He said, "Kath, you want to give a donation in honor of Liv? It is a good thing." My answer was of course yes, but I was still glued to my chair. Thoughts swirled in my mind. How do we make a donation? What will we have to do? What if this is a trick?... Those frustrating thoughts raced through my head for just an instant, but I still didn't know how I was going to move my body. Mike thankfully did the navigating for me, and found out how to go about donating. He said all we had to do was go see that man in the white shirt. I remember Mike saying again, "This is a good thing." I smiled with tears in my eyes and took a moment to feel the lower half of my body that had not yet come back into the room. I said to myself, "Just breathe Kathleen. Think about Liv." Mike helped me off the barstool and we walked through the sea of black and orange to the man in the white shirt. My self imposed tunnel vision felt like a blessing as I put one foot in front of the other.

The next thing I knew, I was shaking the hand of Liv's dad. I never did remember his name. Mike spoke for both of us, as I left my voice back on the barstool. He told him that we were not part of the ride, but we heard what this charity ride was about and would be honored to donate to the scholarship fund. The man in the white shirt thanked us and opened his phone to share pictures of the love of his life, Liv. Seeing her face changed everything inside me. She was beautiful. Her face was bright and her smile touched my soul. I remember touching his arm as he shared these precious moments with us. There was one picture of Liv standing shoulder to shoulder with her best friend on a beach enjoying sunset. Their backs were to the camera and they were facing the water with a beautiful shawl wrapped around the two of them. They looked safe and their love was captured perfectly in this picture. Her dad said he was going to blow the picture up because it was his favorite. He had tears on his face as we talked. One year had passed since he lost the light in his life. I could see both the darkness of his pain and the love he held in his heart for his daughter. My words went silent except to say how beautiful Liv was, and I kept repeating, "God bless you." I am not sure if all the God bless you's I heard in my head actually escaped my mouth, but I guess it was ok. I hugged the man in the white shirt, and Mike offered our donation. Somehow the money did not seem like enough. Liv's dad thanked us and we turned to walk back to our spot at the bar. From behind I heard someone yell, "Wait a minute!" I turned around and a woman standing with Liv's dad handed us two of those elastic bracelets people wear to honor a cause. This bracelet was purple (one of our favorite colors) and in white the words, "Liv for Life" were engraved. Still filled with the emotion of seeing Liv's pictures, we reverently put the bracelets on and in an instant we became part of the group. A good group…

My head began to clear and I brushed pass that biker guy sitting next to my spot at the bar. He said, "Look I guarded your wine and steamers. Some big dudes wanted them, but I protected them. I only had two." He laughed, and I smiled thanking him for his kind gesture. I did look to see if there were any empty clam shells, but only for a second. In the midst of this crazy experience I almost slid my bowl of steamers in front of him in gratitude. Since I was now more present in the room, I reoriented myself to the surroundings of my space. I saw my purse and phone sitting next to my food and realized this scary guy guarded my valuables as well. My first thought was the old saying, "You can't judge a book by its cover." I did laugh inside at the irony of all this.

As this dreamlike afternoon was coming to an end, did the terrifying thunder of all thirty motorcycles revving up to exit the parking lot, still shake the earth under me? Yes, but at that moment the sound did not suck me back to 1964. I was able to feel the startling fear, turn to my husband and know I was safe. I had survived another reminder of my horrific past, but this time I eventually understood that I was ok in the present. Walking out to the truck, I was very clear in that moment that the assaults of my childhood were definitely in the past. My job now was to live my life as a grown woman and breathe in my new life. I paused for a moment as I climbed back into Mike's truck and I honored all nineteen selves I was blessed with, and took one deep breath.

When I was young, I came to the conclusion that maybe my grandmother might be wrong. She said, "Kathy, just pray the Hail Mary. She will hear you and always protect you." Totally believing her, I did exactly what she said until Daryl stepped in as the devil himself and tried to break my soul. Very quickly his evil acts smothered my hopes of my prayers protecting me. The treasured memory of my pure white first communion dress changed to a tarnished beige, and eventually faded into black. Little Kathy eventually imagined that filthy garage had impermeable steel walls that must have muffled her praying voice. She wondered, with her inside voice weakening, lying on that horrible altar in the woods, "is nobody up there?" Those were dark lonely times when she was forced to run to the clouds to find freedom and safety. When I was six or seven, I thought when a little girl prayed, magically everything she requested would just become reality. What Little Kathy quickly discovered was that her rosary beads worked better praying for that snow day in January, than Daryl canceling her Monday morning appointments. For six long summers, no matter who she prayed to, Daryl never stop hurting her. Feeling defenseless, she could no longer find the strength to ask for help, for fear of Daryl's violent promises. Who was a little girl to believe? The terrorizing man that kept his threatening promises, or what seemed like a hearing impaired God?

What I could not possibly understand as a child, and did not believe until after about 15 years of therapy as an adult, was that yes, they did hear me. Tears fall as I remember the moment that the fog cleared, and I could see that I had been given the merciful gift of dissociation, as an immediate answer to my prayers. God had provided my young brain with the strength to split away from what was being done to my precious six year old body. Some may think that dissociative splitting sounds like a mind breaking down. I now see that for me it was a necessary, creative escape, which gave me the power to survive the unspeakable.

When I started to write this book I remember that old shame tugging at my heart beginning to resurface. At one time, I thought that dissociation at the high end of the spectrum literally made me a crazy person. How could having 19 people/parts living in one body be a healthy thing, or even a thing at all? Those self judgements almost prevented me from writing my book. I wondered if anyone would believe what deep inside I knew to be true. I remembered my own confusion when I opened my journals to so many distinctive handwritings. Each entry divulging a different emotions, stemming from disgusting acts of violence. Each cryptic handwriting had their own truths to tell. Moving from one page to the next, we all had unanswered questions to wonder about. In some ways however this brought me some clarity. I was aware of many incidents when I lost big blocks of time from my life. These journals helped me understand where that time went. In the end it was my journals and my undeniable memories that helped me push through my fear of being disbelieved. I knew my truth and knew it needed to be told.

The light in all this darkness was simple. This six year old would have suffered more than she could survive, without her creative God given powers. It seemed Daryl had stripped all her other powers away, and God in all his love delivered her the strength of spirit and grace to transcend this evil through dissociation.

And so it began, her fight to live... She learned to disappear from the horror. A new part bloomed inside that had a refreshed strength to escape her broken body, dry her tears, let out her anger she despised or calm her when she was sure she would explode with that scream locked in her chest. Her power became strength from many within.

Totally separate at their birth and later co consciously joined in their growth, each part stood together, to fight the evil that walked into our life. With the mothering part of me, I proudly introduce all the names of my inside kids. I honor them every day of my life.

Little Kathy, Emma, Lilly, Rachel, Rose, Candy, Andria, Black Flower, Invisible, Ellen, Marie, Caryl, Kevni, Iris, Daryl Part, Scarecrow, Prince, Lady, and me, Kathleen/Kathy

One day, as a group project, we painted a simple picture of our rosary beads. Inside the circle of beads were written wishes we hoped to receive. At the time I really didn't believe these wishes or prayers would ever become a reality, but I was mistaken...

"To be clean. Our bad pain gone. To not be scared. To not cut anymore. To eat right. To not act on Daryl's order's. Good for people to love us. To work together more. Daryl Part not to hurt us. To be heard by

God. To understand. To feel happy. To dance without pain. To feel Happy. To get through the pain. To find hope. To not feel scattered. To feel safe inside... For Monday's to be Monday's, Lilacs to be Lilacs, noises to just be noises, and Spring to be Spring."

With gratitude in the year 2021, I am seeing a great big high five and some joyful fist pumping coming from within. With Baseball always being our biggest Spring distraction, the vision of that walk off home run celebration at home plate, inside the sacred walls of Fenway Park comes to mind. One thing we all agreed on is our love of the Red Sox. Being a Red Sox fan in many ways resembled my years of life. The majority of our years were a struggle. I never felt I would succeed in our battle to beat our opponent... Somehow with the support of our fans, years of hard work, in the midst of heart break, we just kept trying. One challenge at a time we got stronger. We never gave up. We acknowledged each small victory until one day we won the big one. For me, finally winning the world series looked a little different from the long time coming trophies won by the Red Sox in 2004, 2007 and 2013. However, the scene where all the players rush the pitcher at the last second of the game just might have mimicked the joy in my heart, when I finally felt free from my perpetrator, when I no longer heard his quiet rants in my right ear, when I could really trust love in my life, when I felt strong enough to take a long walk in the spring air, when I could step out of myself and help other rape victims, when I could drive down my childhood street without freaking out for the rest of the week, when I could let my husband love me and feel safe in his arms, when I could walk my dog on a wooded path, when I could pull into a garage and not flash-back, when I could gather lilacs and place them in a delicate vase on my kitchen table, when I didn't panic when my husband brought in the mail, when I no longer had to cross the street because birds were in my path, when I no longer could see scars on my self injured skin, when I no longer needed a scale to decide the fate of my day, when I could look in the mirror, smile, and think she looks pretty, when I could sit in church and feel worthy, when I realized God did not misplace my prayers, when I felt God's love once again, when I knew I had survived... When I finally felt safe enough to use my voice to tell my story without fear, I realized I was unbreakable...

When my son Tim was a senior in high school he took a psychology course. He was given an assignment to write a paper about a psychiatric diagnosis. He chose to write about my diagnosis, Dissociative Identity Disorder. He asked if I would feel comfortable being case study A. I cautiously agreed. For the next month we worked on this paper. I have a fond memory in my head of Tim sitting on the couch with his laptop, surrounded by all the books from my personal library I had once hidden under that same couch. It tickled me that he had his Red Sox cap on, inside out and backwards, rally cap style. Ironically, on top of his cap Tim was wearing one of those books opened and balancing perfectly on top of his head. On the coffee table between us was his soft drink, some popcorn and my glass of Cabernet. I was laying on the floor wondering if I was doing the right thing sharing this information with my son. I had tried to hide this depth of detail from Tim most of his life, but somehow at the age of 17 we were ready to take this step towards openness and growth.

The finished product was perfect. I had only shared what was asked of me and didn't answer questions I couldn't. Tim's teacher was very supportive to my son as we walked this journey together. The bragging mom part of me would like to tell you he got an A+ on his paper with a comment that he should try to publish the paper in a journal. For me the best part of the paper was his last paragraph. I say this because as I read it through my tears, I felt like Tim really understood me, what I had been through and respected what I did to survive. I'd like to share it with you.

"In closing, this paper was important to both me and Case Study A. She thought it was important to have someone be able to tell her story even if it were a brief explanation in the scheme of things. I found a lot of personal growth in the study of her different parts and their functions. It was also important to see how far she's come from the time she was a little girl going through hell to a middle aged woman beginning therapy, to a Co-Conscious "multiple" who survived just about everything life could throw at her. I would just hope that her story would not only be an informative paper but also one to show courage and ability to survive, that only few people could ever possess."

Epilogue

I took my sandals off and placed them on a wooden shelf. As if in slow motion, I quietly walked up the carpeted stairs approaching the room I would be practicing yoga in for the next couple days. This would be my first ever yoga retreat. I was wearing brand new yoga clothes in the hopes of feeling more confident, but I still felt somewhat self conscious walking around this big retreat house, when I only knew one other person the building. It wasn't like me to venture out to a retreat weekend alone, but I challenged myself to be brave for this event. I opened the heavy door to our yoga room to get a sneak peak before we actually started class. What I saw was a much bigger space than I imagined. My thought as I entered the room was it feels like church… I almost found myself looking to my left for holy water to bless myself with. If I were to speak, it would reverently only be a whisper. The cathedral ceiling was held in place by heavy white beams. Sunlight was shining through big windows up above onto rows of purple yoga mats on the carpeted floor. The sight was welcoming and felt like a sacred space. All this, and I had not even taken my first deep breath.

It was early July and warm in the room. I chose a mat a few rows back and to the left of the small stage near a large oscillating fan. Even though the room was vast and airy, I feared my occasional claustrophobia that has historically been triggered by the temperature of the room. I prayed the fan could avert any unwanted panic. I prepared my spot by laying down my own folded yoga blanket, the props I needed, and placed my journal at the front of my mat. My journal was created by Elena Brower, the presenter of this retreat.

As others trickled in looking for their comfortable spot in the room, I knew it was time for me to start to stretch my back before class. Three weeks earlier I injured my back, literally from too much sitting in a car. I could not believe that because of that, it was possible I might have to cancel the retreat I had been anticipating for months. At first I denied the whole thing and realized very quickly that was not a good treatment plan. I had easy access to medical treatment, so I asked for help and gratefully followed every instruction given to me. The hardest part of this treatment plan was to rest my back. This took an incredible amount of discipline for me to put my practice on hold in order to heal myself. I did not do one yoga pose for 21 days prior to walking in the doors of the retreat house. I was determined not to miss out on this special weekend I had set my sights on. As I began to stretch, I sent up a quick prayer for my back to behave. My prayer was answered. My breathing became easier with each move I made. I looked up from the child's pose that I was breathing into, because I heard that comforting voice I had welcomed five days a week into my personal yoga room over the past year. The retreat was about to begin. Elena had stepped onto the stage in front of us. For the next few moments, the previous 18 months flashed quickly before me as I wondered, how did I get to this place, in this pose, on my purple mat?...

My thoughts immediately brought me to my friend Sarah. We were first colleagues at work and quickly became a forever friendship. Sarah is thirty years my junior, but that did not seem to matter. We connected personally almost instantly. Sarah is kind, honest and very generous of spirit. There was a calmness about her that attracted me to her. I was curious about how grounded she presented even at times of stress. Early on in our relationship, she shared with me the importance of a daily yoga practice in her life. I listened to her talk about what yoga did for her. It sounded interesting to me and even enticing, but I never really thought that would be something I could become dedicated to. Her routine was yoga in the morning before work. I remember one of her Instagram hashtags that said #yogaeverydamnday. All I could think was, I could never make time in my day for that, or could I?

As our relationship grew, we began seek refuge in each other's offices. We discovered a grounding respite from a hectic day in these two spaces. I smile when I think of the abundant gifts we offered to one another on those days. A listening ear, a warm hug, breathing space, Kleenex, clarity, calming words of encouragement, and many times a good laugh. And in specific, Sarah shared her essential oils with me. I didn't have much knowledge about these oils and didn't think much of them, until I inhaled the scent from the tiny bottle called Renew. The name fit it perfectly. The scent calmed my nerves a bit, allowing me to breathe easier and rejuvenate my spirit. That deep breath capturing this new fragrance allowed me to return back to the task at hand. Now, I am sure Sarah's presence also had something to do with my renewal. What I found was that I seemed to form a connection between Sarah's friendship and that beautiful rejuvenating scent. One day, before she went on vacation, she stopped by my office to hand me the little bottle to keep safe while she was gone. As usual I gave her dark chocolate from my candy jar, followed by a big hug. That was our system.

While I was busy writing this book, Sarah was busy becoming a yoga instructor. I thought that was an amazing goal for her since she loved her own daily practice so much. You could see she really wanted to share with others her passion of yoga. So one day, she asked me if I would like to join some co workers in a yoga class she was offering. I wanted to say yes, but I had about 10 really good reasons why I might not. I didn't know one single yoga pose. I didn't have a yoga mat. What would I wear? Yoga clothes felt too revealing. Was I strong enough? How would I get from my office, through the hospital, to the place we would be having class wearing leggings and flip flops? Would all that body movement be too triggering for me? Would I be able to walk the next day? My left shoulder had been bothering me. I'll be too tired after work… I will spare you the remaining excuses, but I think that was a pretty good picture of what I was thinking. Well, Sarah respectfully had an answer for all of it. She of course had a spare mat. She was giving a very basic class. Most of the people coming to class were beginners. I could wear what ever felt comfortable to me. I might even enjoy the class…

I tossed around all the pros and cons and reluctantly committed to attend. We actually decided to have our class in the waiting room of our surgeons office. We gathered there and moved all the chairs against the wall making a space to lay down ten mats. Sarah began the class with her calm voice inviting us to breathe in and out several times. This breathing helped to slow the craziness of the work day, which then allowed me to focus on the present moment. She kept her promise to teach a simple class. Stretching, twisting, bending, and breathing, kept my focus on myself sitting on my rectangular blue mat. I realized half way through class that I not once noticed anyone else in the room but Sarah. I trusted her voice, which made her instructions from one body movement to the next feel more like an invitation rather than an order. I noticed I didn't need to keep my eyes open for much of the class. Sarah spoke clearly and I knew what to do next. I strangely felt free to modify any body movement to what felt safe and comfortable. Again, I didn't have to follow exact orders... She reminded us to breathe many times during that ninety minutes. I figured she must have been talking directly to me because inhaling and exhaling was not my speciality.

Halfway through the class I felt something deep inside I did not expect or plan on. I felt the tears trying to collect in my throat. Where was this emotion coming from? Out of nowhere, I noticed my hands didn't feel like my own. I opened my eyes to check on them. My arms were shaped like ballet arms, right down to the tips of my pretty little fingers...There was this shift deep inside me. I could feel the presence of the Emma part of me. That quiet gentle part of me who taught Little Kathy to finger dance, so she could secretly escape what Daryl was doing to her. Emma had joined me on my yoga mat. My body actually felt smaller as I struggled a bit to focus on Sarah's voice. I was not afraid, but I felt a well of un-defined emotions rising into my belly. I took one big deep breath, trying to contain whatever this feeling was. We must have neared the end of the class, because Sarah asked us to gently sit up on our mats. Once settled in comfortably, Sarah, in her most calm ground-ing voice spoke words that reminded me of my meditation group. The phrases sounded like a prayer, "May you be happy. May you be healthy, May you be filled with loving kindness. May you be at peace...." I could no longer hold back my tears. They poured down my face. I had to surrender to this flood of emotion. It was not going away.

With my eyes closed, this moment felt strangely private in this room of eleven. My body had moved in a new way triggering some old discomfort, but not in a shameful way. It felt good to move freely. I chose to move into positions that in the past may have led to something horrible. On my mat that day, nothing bad happened. Instead I was getting pleasure from stretching openly and was met with kindness. It was then that I realized that my friend and very first yoga teacher had gently placed herself on my mat with her back touching mine to support me. While she was the only person in the room with eyes open, she must have seen my tears and honored my feelings without saying a word. She offered a slight touch of her strong back and allowed me to feel her supportive breathing. Tears of comfort began to mingle with those already washing my face. No one ever held space for me in that way before... I am sure no one was privy to this healing moment I will never forget. Even today, I can actually feel her warm back supporting me. Quietly, she stepped away and I could hear her invite the group to breathe slowly in and out again to come back into the room. We opened our eyes. With hands in prayer position, we bowed our heads. I truly learned the meaning of "Namaste" that day.

This taste of yoga gave me some serious food for thought... One other time, during Nurses week, Sarah made available a space to do another short yoga/meditation class. Again, I experienced emotions that felt like healing to me. This seriously made me consider making yoga part of my everyday life. Something was happening emotionally when I moved my body parts in those different poses. Apprehensively, I wondered if maybe the remainder of my healing journey had something to do with my body, the scene of the past crimes done to me. I admit, I had avoided this area of internal work for decades. As I examined this theory, my feelings migrated to Black Flower, the body part of me. She had received so little of my focus and nobody needed it more. She deserved to feel safe in her skin. The thought of venturing into this body of work felt just a little terrifying, but I made the decision to try. I had gained so much strength over the years and I wasn't getting any younger.

Unfortunately, that sore shoulder I mentioned earlier turned out to be a torn rotator cuff. My surgeon said the complete tear was most likely caused by the labors of 42 years my nursing career provided, and possibly a ridiculously slamming high five I engaged in while cheering for my favorite football team. In case your wondering, it was to benefit the New England Patriots. I also wondered but never dared to ask, if all the yanking and pulling of my left arm while Daryl dragged me up that hill in the woods had anything to do with it? I thought, yes... I hoped this tear could heal with conservative, nonsurgical treatment, but that was not the case. There was more damage than I imagined. Right before my surgery in November that year, I literally had to wear sweatshirts with side pockets that acted like a sling. I walked around with my left hand in my pocket to support my shoulder. My plans for starting a yoga practice were put on hold until I recovered and rehabbed from this surgery. Being an orthopedic nurse navigator, I knew I would be restricted from bearing the kind of weight yoga requires for many months. To say I was disappointed was an understatement. In my job I often ask my patients about their goals after a total joint replacement. They all had hopes and dreams planned for post recovery. For many, these goals are what powered their efforts to work hard at recovering completely. So, my personal long term goal became incorporating a daily yoga practice into my life. I had no idea, when I made that commitment that, A) I would reach my goal, and B) Yoga would change my life.

My recovery was long, arduous and sometimes triggering. I worked religiously and did everything my surgeon and physical therapist, Kevin said to do. The first few months were painful. Ice became my best friend. I went to physical therapy three times a week and only hit my amazing therapist once, full disclosure, maybe twice. I had to tell him the condensed version of my story including my PTSD symptoms so he could create a plan of care for my treatment. By risking my privacy, Kevin was certain to tell me what he was going to do before he had to manipulate my shoulder. He was most respectful when it required certain body positioning such as laying on the physical therapy table, both face up and much worse face down. He took his time, was patient with me, and was supportive of my tears that came out of nowhere, God bless him... Well, I succeeded in my efforts to regain full function of my left shoulder. Not so patiently, I waited until I was cleared to practice yoga. Almost a year later that blessings was bestowed.

First order of business was to go shopping for all things yoga. Yoga cloths, yoga mat, yoga blocks, and pretty yoga blanket. Next, I needed a private space in my house to practice. Transforming the spare bedroom into my private yoga room was exciting. Even the cleaning aspect of creating this spot just for me was fun. The bedroom that once doubled as my dressing room now had white candles and a dark teal colored scarf draping an old bureau. I gathered special personal items creating a simple reverent altar that looked beautiful placed on the scarf. I took up the scatter rug from the center of the room, then shined up the hard wood floor making a spot for my mat. This space was just big enough for me. Perfect.

During my down time while recovering the previous year, I read yoga books and watched more than a couple of yoga videos. Deep down I realized I needed Sarah to give me some private classes. I had so much to learn, but still did not feel comfortable going to public classes. I remembered the emotions brought up when doing my first yoga classes. Nothing had really changed since then. Moving my body in a new way still felt way too personal and intimate to expose myself in a group. So, I found myself in Sarah's yoga room tucked in one corner of her house. Her room was bright with natural sunlight streaming through her two long windows. This room felt sacred, and I felt most reverent entering into her simple personal studio. She so sweetly had prepared a beautiful and most thoughtful sequence of poses, just for me. In her typical generous Sarah fashion, she had written down each step, complete with stick figure demonstrations. She knew me so well… We were both cautious with monitoring my shoulder. Every pose she would ask, "How does this feel?" And to my surprise, my answer was, "Good." We strung those poses together with many reminders to breathe, and came up with a good beginners practice for me to take back home.

Shortly after that class with Sarah, she planned to have her friend and yoga teacher give me a class that focused on protecting my shoulder. And with that guidance, week by week I developed a daily morning yoga practice. I also added a little ballet into the mix and fondly called my new routine, "Baloga". This blended practice gave me the opportunity to enjoy those beautiful flowing movements of ballet. One day, Sara checked in with me to see how I was progressing. I told her I had fallen in love with getting up before dawn, doing my routine and then moving on to work at the hospital. My commitment was sealed. Sarah suggested I might enjoy taking yoga classes online with glo.com. She had taken classes with them in the privacy of her home and was fairly certain I would like to try it out. Sarah even gave me suggestions of who I might connect with as a teacher. I wrote down the name Elena Brower on a sticky note and slipped it into my scrub pocket. Once home from work I searched this yoga website and hunted down the name, Elena Brower. I read about her, watched her short video, and looked to see if she gave beginner classes. What drew me to Elena as opposed to some of the other teachers on the site was her voice. This voice was welcoming, soft, and very calming. I remember thinking she could have been a grammar school teacher. Her instructions were so clear and precise. Because of that, I was amazed I really didn't have to look up at my laptop screen to move from one pose to the next. Her words guided me perfectly. During the first class I took, she asked us to breathe in a way I never tried before which magically grounded me in the present. At that moment all that mattered was right there on my yoga mat. During one particular class she invited me to choose each step I took during that sixty minutes. Her invitation to choose each body position made tears fall. Again, so many of the poses felt exposing and triggering which is why I chose to do this practice in private. Given this necessary choice to move, I was convinced Elena was a perfect match for me. So just like that, Elena became my every day teacher.

We had never met and yet I felt like I knew her so well. She shared much of herself as she taught. Wanting to learn more about my new teacher, I watched You Tube interviews, and podcasts where she was the guest or presenter. Things that seemed to matter were suggestions to look inside myself and listen. My focus of integrating my body and soul became the issue I chose to examine closely. Once I opened the heavy door closing me off from that idea, changes began to take place at a much faster pace than I imagined. One morning after my early morning practice, I recall having a truly pivotal life experience. I rolled up my mat and went to put my rings back on that were in a small dish on my altar. I looked up and saw my face in the mirror. Even with not a stitch of makeup on and incredibly messed up hair, what I saw was a pretty face with blue eyes looking back at me. I didn't judge or criticize her. She looked kind and gentle. Above her head were two pieces of masking tape. One read, Kind World and the other, Reverence. I thought, this is my world now. I felt clear, simple, and reverent. In this moment of clarity, I saw a beautiful light coming from this woman. Something had changed in me. I did not feel so heavy. My baggage had lightened. I remember literally looking down at my physical body to check for some harsh reality. As I stood face to face with myself, I saw with my own eyes the exact body image the mirror reflected. It may have been the very first honest view of myself since before Daryl changed everything. I paused to acknowledge that view and took one deep breath…

One afternoon, Sarah stopped by my office to make a quick visit. I was with a patient, so she waited for me to get back. I had brought my Practice You journal to work to finish up a morning journal entry I was working on. Sarah saw Elena's beautiful journal sitting on my desk. When I returned, I was surprised and elated to see my friend sitting on my desk. Almost before our hug, she said, "I am going to see Elena Brower in New Haven next month. She is giving a doTerra essential oil and yoga workshop. You want to join me?" Well, is the pope Catholic? My thought was, how do I sign up? We sat down to my computer and registered immediately. To say I was excited was an understatement. In a million years, I never thought I would get to meet with the teacher I respected so much. My mind raced… I had always wanted to tell Elena how much she had helped me with my personal growth, and now I might get that chance. I knew I would be happy to just see her from a distance, but I envisioned I might write and hand her a letter of gratitude, if given the chance. The thought of taking a class live, with her physically in the room was a most unexpected gift.

So, on February 23, 2019, Sarah graciously drove us both to New Haven, Connecticut just an hour away, to Elena's workshop.

We sat in the foyer of this amazing yoga center so beautifully called, Breathing Room. I felt again like I should whisper here. I guess yoga studios do that to me. Then Elena gracefully entered the room, wearing a long black coat. Felling like a silly old groupie, I nudged Sarah's waist and not so quietly whispered, "That's her!" For me, it felt like Lady Gaga had just walked in the door. Gaga had inspired me through her music to write this book, and Elena helped me feel whole enough to finish it. Both felt like blessings from above.

Both workshops were perfect and much more than I could have hoped for. As it turned out, I regard this evening as a life altering moment in my life. The most significant encounter of the night was not exactly during the workshops, but rather between them.

The discussion of essential oils was intimate with about 25 people. We all sat on our mats, huddled in half circle. My seat for the next hour was about five feet from her. Elena became a regular person to me in that sixty minutes. She had such passion for the oils and for what they can do for others. As she shared her joyful knowledge with all of us, I thought she has so much grace and light about her. I perceived her as funny and engaging. What struck me most was how deeply she looked people in the eye while in conversation with each of us. Those qualities, I love in a friend. I devoured the information about essential oils that evening which would later become part of my daily life as well. I made note during Elena's presentation, that the fragrance of the oils she shared with us made me feel something unique with each one and I wanted to know more. What I knew for sure was that my sense of smell has always been heightened one. For me, that was a double edge sword. On this night, it was simply delightful.

When the first workshop ended, I could feel a nudge in my side from Sarah. She knew I wanted to give Elena my thank you letter, and saw that the break between workshops as a good opportunity. Sarah of course offered to set up my mat near hers and get me ready for class, giving me a few private moments to express my gratitude to my teacher. I admit my old feelings of doubt and fear came to the surface, but somehow when Elena stood up, so did I. Holding my letter in my ridiculously shaking hands, I took a few steps forward and approached her. I could hear the nerves in my voice as I began to thank her for being my teacher. It felt strange because we had never met, but she understood all that, because I am one of the reasons she and glo.com do what they do. During the few moments of the private time I had with her, I ended up saying so much more than planned. I told her why I needed a private practice which meant sharing briefly my dark childhood past. She reached out to me with a hug, I had not anticipated. She held space for me to use my voice, and I felt heard. She told me how sorry she was that this happened to me. She told me how brave I was. One thing she said stuck with me in particular. She said, " Your healing is a healing for all women." With that, somewhere I found the strength to say out loud that I had written a memoir about what happened to me, and how I survived. I shared that this book gave voice to the long silent child parts of me. She hugged me again and then turned to reach into her purse and pulled out an essential oil touch roller bottle. She rolled a deliciously soft scent onto her arm, then mine, and handed me the bottle keep. I don't remember if she said any words when she did that, but words were not necessary. The words that came to my heart in that moment were, "You are never alone." Next, with our arms locked she spoke softly into my ear. "Send me the title page of your book, along with the first couple chapters. I will read it and send it to my publisher." I took a deep breath inhaling her loving kindness and generosity of spirit. I felt a new energy come into my person. In that moment I committed to continue my challenge to bring my story out of my safe space, and move it fearlessly into the world. I felt a transformation going on inside of me which stemmed from a gift of gratitude and a generous heart.

After some serious contemplating I did exactly what Elena asked. This required some significant hard work editing and polishing what she had asked to read. I was energized by her encouragement and carried her grace as I worked. Sarah helped me with the computer work of making my book look like one as we prepared a PDF of the beginning of my book. While doing all that, I could feel confidence growing inside myself in all aspects of my life. My usual fears and self doubting seemed to melt away. Finally, our work was done and together Sarah and I hit send.

Elena very generously read what I sent that very day. She wrote me, to say that she would now send it off to her publisher with my permission. We spoke on the phone, where she told me my book was filled with a story that needed to be out in the world. I truly believe that now. Even though the publishing company did not feel my book was right for them, they too, felt that my truth should not be left in my laptop. I had been prepared for the no, and surprisingly in response, I felt even stronger that I should move forward to get my book published. I took some time to remember reading other survivors books and how they helped me. I recalled honoring their bravery and courage to heal. Even though I would not wish my past on anyone, I knew how honored I was to be in the presence of another survivor. I had told my story standing before them and then held space for their sharing. Reading their books, I was simply meeting them through their very loud voice in print. I prayed one day to be in their good company on a book shelf or in a lap as they read my truth… A candle had been lit inside my soul and I knew only I could blow that fire out. I did not see that happening. It felt ironic that I reaffirmed my commitment after receiving my first denial.

~

Elena's voice called me back into the room as our first yoga session of the retreat was about to begin. My body felt relaxed and loose from my stretching. I was ready. In those first moments, I had no idea what to expect or what an incredible healing experience this weekend would develop into. I just took it one step at a time, one pose moving to the next and definitely one breath at a time. My working plan was to try to simply stay in the moment and remain open to what was next…

In the two days that followed I could never have imagined the depth of healing I was about to experience. I realize I must have been ready for this to happen, but will forever be grateful for the sacred space of this Yoga room, the safe guidance of my teacher, and the generosity the universe offered me.

At the end of Saturday mornings two hour session, it was finally time for Savasana. That most welcome rest which comes at the end of yoga class. Lying flat on my back with my eyes closed, I felt the stillness of my body. Even though I was in a room of 50, I felt quiet and inside myself on my purple mat. Elena invited us to relax one body part at a time while feeling the supportive ground beneath us. I took long deep breaths in and exhaled completely at a slow com- fortable pace. All that mattered at first was the promise of my next breath. I wish I could remember Elena's words that may have led me to the next place I found myself. What I do remember is how safe I felt in my aloneness. I believe the community I was surrounded by in that very spacious room offered me a sense of protection.

I realized I had left any judgement of myself and others at the door when I entered this room a couple hours earlier. I felt calm and so very still. My body seemed weightless and no longer burdened by old fears. Behind my eyelids, I saw a clear blue empty space. It was bright like a perfect cloudless fall sky. This vividly blue moment is when I first felt tears on my cheeks. I realized I had the smallest of smiles forming on my mouth. I no longer felt the ground under me as I had a minute ago, but that seemed ok. This open inside space oddly felt familiar. My mouth silently prayed the Hail Mary. I however was not praying with fear in my heart. This prayer was not asking for help. I was just feeling the pure grace of my prayer.

And then miraculously, with the blue backdrop, one by one, each part of myself appeared before me. I saw each of them so clearly. I met them with gratitude for the infinite ways they helped us survive what Daryl had done. I told each one privately that I loved them. I held them close as I released them from their duties. I assured them they would be with me always, but that I now had their back. I promised to take care of them and protect them. When it was Black Flower's turn, I could see the body part of me more clearly than ever before. She was not covering herself. She had shed her layers of baggy clothes with no need to hide her shame. Her armor seemed to crumple to the floor under us. I felt a love for my body as I saw Black Flower in a new light. Our body was no longer something to be ashamed of. It didn't tighten or go limp in fear. I felt her relief and possibly a glimmer of self respect coming from her. This was a new concept for her. She only had mere glimpses of respect for any part of her in the recent past, and now was stepping onto a brand new path. This is when I felt my heart crack open. Still, I was not afraid. I felt safe in my vulnerability. I became aware of the tears pouring into my ears. Were these tears hers or mine? At that moment I chose to believe the tears were a blend of both of ours. My Right hand was gently covering my eyes and my left hand laid on the center of my chest. I was holding on to myself, wondering if I might crumble. What was this all encompassing feeling present in my body? How could I be so overwhelmed and so at home all at the same time? I recognized that this feeling resembled a warm hug that was holding all parts of me in one place. This place was my center, my home, and this spot was blue. I recognized that I had cracked open a very heavy door internally. I had feared what was behind the door since I was six. On this day, alone on my purple yoga mat, all of me finally felt ready to look inside. With this spiritual opening, I envisioned a dusty old Hope Chest in the corner of my new space. This old box did not frighten me so I dared to open it. What I found was everything I thought had been stolen from me. I found my true self. I found the little girl who was loved greatly by her family. My happiness and innocence were neatly folded in one corner. I found my little girl crooked smile and her silly laugh. I found once again her strong faith in God with all her Hail Mary's lining the inside of the chest. I found her ability to dance without music. I could smell the once abandoned flowers she loved best. I found all the things Little Kathy had thought were gone forever. Most importantly, I found my voice that predated the evil that had come into my life. I felt lighter and free from the hold of my past trauma. This new found freedom allowed me to exhale and my breathing became effortless...

In the distance I heard Elena's voice inviting us to come back into the room. My tears still poured, but I felt cleansed and blessed by what had just happened to me. It was amazing to me, that as I laid flat on my mat, I no longer could detect the every day body memory of the painful scraping on my back. My back felt soft and comforted by the cushion of the mat. The physical sensation that had been imprinted on my skin from the stone altar in Daryl's woods was gone...

I remember thinking I was brought to Kripalu for just this moment. This long journey felt like God's plan for me. I knew I would continue on this path and welcomed the thought. There was no doubt that the prayers of my childhood were heard and answered, again.

CPSIA information can be obtained
at www.ICGtesting.com
Printed in the USA
BVHW041605160321
602658BV00013B/705